Wireshark Wonders: From Rookie to Protocol Pro

Table of Contents

Chapter 1: Introduction to Wireshark

Welcome to the world of Wireshark, where packets are your breadcrumbs, and protocol analysis is your quest for network knowledge. If you're new to the world of network troubleshooting, the idea of diving deep into the mysterious sea of data packets can seem daunting, like trying to find a single fish in the ocean using nothing but a magnifying glass. But fear not, intrepid network adventurer! Wireshark is your trusty magnifying glass, guiding you to the heart of any networking mystery. It's not just for the experts; anyone can use it to navigate through a sea of binary bits, making sense of the chaos lurking beneath the surface of their network connections.

Now, let's start with the basics: what exactly is Wireshark? In simple terms, Wireshark is a network protocol analyzer, a fancy name for a tool that captures and inspects the data packets that zip through your network. Imagine every website you visit, every email you send, and every file you download as a little packet of data being whisked across the network. Wireshark lets you see these packets in all their raw, unfiltered glory. It's like being able to read someone's text messages but without the awkwardness of them knowing.

But why, you ask, should you care about packets? Well, here's the deal: when something goes wrong on your network—whether it's a slow connection, dropped packets, or just general mayhem—Wireshark is the superhero you never knew you needed. Think of it as your network detective, constantly analyzing the traffic between your computer and others, trying to crack the case of the mysterious "why is the internet so slow?" It's like CSI: Network Edition, minus the dark alleys and too-cool-for-school detectives.

Wireshark isn't just a tool for troubleshooting, though. It's a great way to understand how networks work. By inspecting packets, you can see the magic that happens under the hood, the invisible dance of protocols, and the quiet conversations between computers that make the internet as fast and furious as it is. Sure, it sounds like a niche interest, but the more you know, the more you realize how vital network analysis is to just about everything we do online. From streaming movies to sending cat memes, it all relies on smooth packet flow.

Let's take a brief walk through history. Wireshark was originally called Ethereal (yes, that was its name—sounds like something out of a fantasy novel, right?). It was created in 1998 by Gerald Combs, a man who no doubt saw the potential for decoding the mysteries of network traffic. Ethereal was later renamed Wireshark in 2006, possibly because it sounded cooler, but mostly because it was trademarked by a certain company that made a living off of "ethernet" cables. Either way, the rebranding didn't hurt Wireshark's popularity—if anything, it made the tool more accessible and famous among tech enthusiasts.

Speaking of popularity, Wireshark is the go-to network analyzer for everyone, from the novice home user to the seasoned IT professional. It's open-source, meaning it's free for anyone to use, and it runs on multiple platforms: Windows, macOS, and Linux. So, whether you're a Windows devotee, a Mac aficionado, or a Linux guru, Wireshark has got your back. The best part? You don't need to be a network expert to get started. With just a bit of practice and a whole lot of curiosity, you'll soon be navigating the deep, packet-filled waters like a seasoned pro.

But don't get too cocky just yet. Wireshark isn't a magical "fix-all" tool; it's a tool for those who are ready to dive in and understand what's going on behind the curtain. If you think of the network as a bustling highway, Wireshark is your speed radar, helping you detect speeders, roadblocks, and traffic jams. You can see all the cars (packets) whizzing by, but unless you know what to look for, it's easy to get overwhelmed. Wireshark doesn't solve your problems automatically, but it arms you with the knowledge to pinpoint the root cause, which is half the battle.

Now, let's talk about the user interface (UI). For the uninitiated, Wireshark's UI might seem like the cockpit of a fighter jet. There are buttons, dropdowns, and menus everywhere. But don't worry, with just a bit of navigation, it'll start feeling like second nature. The main window is where the magic happens. Here, you'll find your packet capture window, full of data moving faster than you can say "packet capture." At first, you might be staring at it, wondering if it's some sort of complex alien code. But give it time, and it'll start making sense.

Speaking of packet capture, let's touch on how to actually start capturing packets. It's as easy as clicking on a button. Well, almost. There's a bit of setup involved—after all, you're diving into the deep end of network traffic. But once you've selected your network interface (essentially, the "door" through which your network traffic flows), you're ready to begin. Click the capture button, and suddenly, your screen fills up with packets as if the network has exploded in front of your eyes. It's a glorious, if slightly overwhelming, moment.

The real trick is what to do with all these packets. You can't just stare at them forever, hoping for the answers to appear like magic. No, Wireshark gives you the power to filter and analyze the packets to find exactly what you're looking for. It's like having a giant pile of puzzle pieces and a magnifying glass that helps you pick out the pieces you need. You can filter by protocol, IP address, port number, and a variety of other parameters. Want to see all the HTTP traffic? It's a breeze. Looking for a specific conversation between two devices? Wireshark's got you.

As you get more comfortable with Wireshark, you'll start using advanced features like "Follow TCP Stream" or "Statistics." These are like secret weapons in your Wireshark arsenal, allowing you to trace a single conversation or gather high-level insights about the traffic flowing through your network. Want to see how many packets were sent during a specific period? There's a statistic for that. Curious about the average round-trip time for your network? You guessed it— Wireshark can provide that too.

But let's not get ahead of ourselves. First, let's address the most important question: why should you care about all this packet mumbo jumbo? Because, in the digital age, understanding your network is crucial. Everything we do online relies on data packets traveling back and forth, from loading a website to sending an email. By understanding how packets move, you'll be able to troubleshoot problems like a pro, ensuring that your connection stays smooth and reliable. Plus, once you've mastered Wireshark, you'll have a party trick that'll make you the life of any IT gathering.

One thing to keep in mind, though: Wireshark is powerful, but it's not omnipotent. It can't help you understand the network traffic if your device isn't actually sending or receiving packets. It's not going to magically fix a broken cable or fix an issue with your router. But when it comes to capturing and analyzing the traffic that's already moving through your network, Wireshark is unparalleled. It's the Sherlock Holmes of packet sniffers, helping you put the pieces of the puzzle together.

With all that said, Wireshark is more than just a tool—it's a gateway to a deeper understanding of the world of networking. By using Wireshark, you become part of a community of network enthusiasts, engineers, and professionals who are all on a quest to better understand the digital realm. Whether you're troubleshooting your home Wi-Fi or working on a corporate network, Wireshark gives you the knowledge and confidence to take control.

In the next chapters, we'll dive deeper into how Wireshark works, how to install it, and how to start capturing packets. You'll learn about filtering, analyzing protocols, and diagnosing network problems. But for now, take a moment to appreciate the incredible power at your fingertips. With Wireshark, you're no longer just a user of the network—you're a detective, an investigator, and a network wizard all rolled into one. Buckle up, because your Wireshark journey is just beginning!

And one last thing: If you're wondering whether Wireshark is really as cool as we're making it out to be, just wait until you capture your first packet. Then, you'll see exactly what we mean.

As we wrap up Chapter 1, let's pause and take a deep breath. We've just dipped our toes into the exciting world of Wireshark. If you're still feeling a bit overwhelmed by the idea of packets zipping across your network, don't worry—you're not alone. Everyone starts somewhere, and the good news is that you've already made the first step toward becoming a network detective. Wireshark may seem intimidating at first, but like anything new, it becomes easier with practice. Soon enough, you'll find yourself effortlessly navigating through packets like a seasoned pro.

One of the best parts about learning Wireshark is that it's as much about discovery as it is about problem-solving. Every time you capture and analyze packets, you're uncovering the secrets of your network, one byte at a time. Think of it like decoding an ancient language—each packet you inspect tells a story. Maybe it's a story of your last web browsing session, or perhaps it's the tale of a network slowdown that's been bugging you for days. Whatever the case, Wireshark lets you read between the lines of the digital world, and that's a skill that can't be overstated.

Now, before you get too comfortable with the idea of packet hunting, remember that Wireshark is not just about pointing and clicking. It's about understanding what you're seeing, making sense of the data, and knowing when to act. We've barely scratched the surface of the features Wireshark has to offer, but don't worry. As we dive deeper into future chapters, you'll learn how to filter through data, analyze various protocols, and become more efficient at pinpointing the problem in no time.

Speaking of efficiency, let's talk about what makes Wireshark so powerful in the hands of someone who knows how to use it. The ability to capture packets and analyze the details of a network is invaluable. Let's say you're troubleshooting a slow connection, and your Wi-Fi feels like it's powered by dial-up. Wireshark can tell you exactly what's going wrong. Is your network overwhelmed with traffic? Are there packet losses causing delays? Wireshark doesn't just give you vague answers; it arms you with the data you need to solve the issue.

And if you ever find yourself feeling like an imposter in the world of packet analyzers, rest assured that even the most seasoned network engineers were once beginners. Wireshark is as much about learning as it is about doing. The more you use it, the more intuitive it becomes. You'll start recognizing patterns, noticing trends, and understanding what to look for without even thinking about it. So don't be discouraged if you don't get everything right away—this is a journey, not a race.

As you continue on this journey, you'll realize that Wireshark isn't just about solving problems. It's also about enhancing your understanding of the entire network ecosystem. Whether you're monitoring network performance, debugging network configurations, or just getting a closer look at how data travels, Wireshark offers insights that make you a more informed network user, or even a network superhero, depending on how you look at it. No more throwing your hands up in the air when things go wrong; instead, you'll be able to dissect the issue and address it head-on.

There's also the added bonus that Wireshark is constantly evolving. The development community is always working on improving the tool, adding new features, and updating protocol dissectors. This means that as Wireshark continues to grow, so too will your ability to analyze more and more sophisticated types of network traffic. The digital world is ever-changing, and Wireshark keeps you on the cutting edge, making sure you can handle whatever new challenges emerge.

In fact, one of the things that sets Wireshark apart from other tools is its large community of users and developers. You're not just using a piece of software—you're joining a global network of people who share your passion for network analysis. Whether you're searching for a specific solution in forums or chatting with fellow Wireshark enthusiasts at conferences, there's always someone out there willing to help. And if you run into something that Wireshark can't solve? Well, there's always the option of writing your own dissector, extending Wireshark's capabilities to meet your unique needs. Now that's some serious power!

But let's not get ahead of ourselves. The purpose of this chapter was to introduce you to Wireshark in a way that's approachable and, dare we say, fun. Yes, even packet analysis can be fun when you see it as a treasure hunt—each packet is a clue, and the more you uncover, the clearer the mystery becomes. With Wireshark, you're not just a bystander in the digital world; you're a detective, an explorer, and a network guru all rolled into one.

So, what's next? In the following chapters, we'll explore how to install Wireshark, navigate its user interface, and start capturing packets. We'll take a deeper dive into the world of filters, protocols, and troubleshooting techniques that will elevate your skills to a whole new level. And as we progress, you'll begin to see the patterns, connect the dots, and become the Wireshark wizard you were destined to be.

But for now, take a moment to revel in the excitement of starting something new. You've just learned about a tool that opens up the world of network analysis and gives you the power to solve problems, improve performance, and understand your network like never before. That's a pretty big deal. So give yourself a pat on the back—you're already well on your way to becoming a Wireshark pro.

Remember, the road to network mastery isn't a sprint; it's a marathon. Keep exploring, keep questioning, and, most importantly, keep having fun. Wireshark is here to help you navigate the digital world, and with every packet you capture, you'll unlock a little more of its secrets. Welcome aboard the Wireshark adventure—let the packet sniffing begin!

Chapter 2: Installing and Setting Up Wireshark

Ah, the sweet, sweet moment when you decide to dive into Wireshark—and, naturally, you'll want to get started by installing it. This is where the magic happens, and I promise, it's easier than you think. If you're expecting a complex, 10-step process that involves deciphering cryptic error messages or battling with a myriad of dependencies, don't fret. Wireshark's installation process is smoother than a well-tuned Ethernet cable, and I'll guide you every step of the way.

Let's begin with the basics: downloading Wireshark. The first thing you need to do is head to the official Wireshark website. It's like visiting the bakery of the internet, except instead of pastries, you'll be loading up with the finest network sniffing tool around. Once on the site, you'll find a big, shiny download button waiting for your click. Don't hesitate. Click it, and you'll be redirected to a page where you can select the version that matches your operating system. Windows, macOS, or Linux? Wireshark is versatile, so whatever your preferred platform, there's a version ready and waiting for you.

Now, if you're on a Windows machine, the installer file you download will probably be a `.exe` file. Go ahead and double-click it—yes, this is the moment when your computer will invite Wireshark into your life. A friendly installation wizard will appear, guiding you through the process. It's much like a helpful tour guide showing you the best route through a city. The wizard will walk you through choosing installation options, like whether or not you want to install the additional tools Wireshark offers, such as WinPcap or Npcap (more on those later). But don't worry; you don't need to be an expert to make these decisions. Just follow the default options, and you'll be good to go.

For macOS users, the process is equally simple—just download the `.dmg` file, double-click to open it, and drag Wireshark to your Applications folder. Easy peasy. Linux users, I haven't forgotten about you! Depending on your distro, you'll be able to install Wireshark via the terminal with a simple command. For Ubuntu, the magic command is `sudo apt install wireshark`, and for Fedora, it's `sudo dnf install wireshark`. The terminal is your best friend, so don't be shy! After a few seconds (or minutes, depending on your internet speed), the installation will be complete.

Once Wireshark is installed, it's time to open it up and take it for a spin. But before you dive straight into packet analysis, there's one crucial step that many forget: running Wireshark with administrative privileges. This is because capturing network traffic requires higher-level permissions, which your regular user account may not have. In Windows, you'll need to right-click on the Wireshark icon and select "Run as Administrator." On macOS, you might be prompted to enter your password, and on Linux, you can run Wireshark with `sudo` to grant it the necessary permissions. Don't be alarmed when the software asks for these permissions—this is Wireshark ensuring it can do its job of sniffing out packets.

If you try to launch Wireshark without the proper permissions, you may encounter a "no interfaces found" error. This is like trying to play a video game without plugging in your controller—it's not going to work, and you'll just end up frustrated. Once you grant the appropriate permissions, Wireshark will be able to access your network interfaces, and you'll be ready to begin capturing data.

Speaking of network interfaces, let's quickly talk about the Wireshark interface setup. After opening Wireshark, you'll be greeted by a nice, clean window with a list of available interfaces to capture from. These are the "doors" through which your data travels, and Wireshark will help you peek through those doors to see exactly what's going on. You'll likely see several options listed, such as your wired Ethernet adapter, your Wi-Fi network, or even virtual adapters for VPNs. If you don't see your desired interface listed, it could be that the necessary drivers aren't installed—or worse, that you haven't granted Wireshark the necessary permissions to view it.

Once your network interfaces are showing up, it's time to dive deeper into the configuration. Wireshark is pretty flexible in how it handles various network adapters and capture options. For example, if you're on a Wi-Fi network and want to capture packets, you may need to enable monitor mode on your Wi-Fi card. This allows your network adapter to "listen" to all nearby traffic, not just the traffic destined for your machine. For the more tech-savvy among us, it's like switching from a private conversation to overhearing everyone in the room. It's very powerful, but can also be a little nosy—use it responsibly!

Once you've selected your network interface, you're almost ready to start capturing data. But before you do, I recommend checking the preferences menu. This is where Wireshark lets you tweak various settings to suit your needs. The preferences menu is like a kitchen full of different cooking tools—some may be used daily, others only in special situations. For example, you might want to adjust the packet capture buffer size, which helps prevent data loss during long captures. Or, if you have a fancy graphics card, you might choose to enable hardware acceleration for smoother performance. It's all about making Wireshark work for you.

Now, if you're a power user (or aspiring to be), you'll want to enable packet capture filters. This is where the magic happens. Packet capture filters allow you to limit the traffic Wireshark captures, which is particularly useful if you're looking for something specific. For instance, you can set it to capture only HTTP packets, so you don't get bogged down by a flood of irrelevant data. Filters are incredibly powerful, but they're also the kind of thing you'll want to experiment with over time. Don't worry if you don't get them perfect right away—it's all part of the learning process.

Once everything is set up, it's time to hit that big, green "Start" button and begin capturing packets. It's like turning on a high-tech microscope and staring at the tiniest details of your network traffic. As soon as you click "Start," Wireshark will begin capturing packets and displaying them in real-time. You'll see them whiz by in the main window, each one containing an ocean of information—IP addresses, protocol details, packet lengths, and more. It's both mesmerizing and, at first, a little intimidating. But take a breath, because this is where the magic truly begins.

But don't rush to capture everything just yet. If you're on a shared network or a public Wi-Fi, be mindful of privacy. Wireshark gives you the power to capture all the traffic around you, but that doesn't mean you should. Just like you wouldn't read someone else's diary, respect the privacy of others' data. This is especially important in professional environments where security and confidentiality are paramount. Think of yourself as a network Sherlock Holmes, carefully and ethically investigating the case—no need to get too nosy!

Next, let's take a moment to discuss WinPcap and Npcap, those additional tools that Wireshark occasionally requests during installation. These tools help Wireshark capture packets by hooking into your system's network stack. If you're on Windows, WinPcap was the traditional choice, but in recent years, Npcap has become the preferred option. It's faster, more secure, and supports the latest technologies. Don't worry too much about which one to pick during installation—just follow the defaults, and Wireshark will take care of the rest.

After the installation and setup, you're ready to explore the deeper features of Wireshark. You've got your interface, your filters, and your preferences all lined up, and now it's time to get to the fun part: analyzing packets. The real power of Wireshark comes when you dig into the packet data, decode the protocols, and start finding patterns in the chaos. But first, let's take a step back and appreciate how far you've come. You've just installed one of the most powerful network analysis tools available—and it's now at your fingertips, ready to solve whatever network mysteries come your way.

So, what's next? In the next chapters, we'll start getting into the nitty-gritty of capturing and analyzing packets. You'll learn how to filter traffic, interpret various protocols, and, of course, troubleshoot network issues like a pro. But for now, take a moment to bask in your accomplishment—you've installed Wireshark, and that's no small feat! Welcome to the world of network analysis, where the real fun begins. Now, let's get capturing!

Now that you've got Wireshark installed and running, it's time to roll up your sleeves and dive into the world of packet capturing and analysis. But before you get too carried away, let's take a moment to appreciate the sheer power of what you've just unlocked. You now have access to the kind of insight into network traffic that even seasoned network engineers would envy. With Wireshark, you're no longer just a user of the internet; you're a digital detective, decoding the cryptic communications happening all around you. And all it took was a quick download and some basic setup.

But with great power comes great responsibility, and with Wireshark, you need to be aware of your surroundings. While it's tempting to start capturing packets like a kid in a candy store, you need to remember that packet capture can involve sensitive data, especially on shared networks. So before you go diving into a packet capture frenzy, consider the ethical implications. Be respectful of others' privacy and ensure you're capturing only the data that's relevant to your investigation. It's not just about finding the problem—it's about being responsible with the data you uncover. After all, you're essentially snooping on what's happening under the digital hood, so use your newfound powers wisely.

The good news is that if you do things correctly, Wireshark will help you stay on the right side of privacy and security concerns. One of the most crucial skills to develop is knowing how to filter your captures. That's where the magic happens. Instead of capturing every single packet that comes your way (which could be a lot, and I mean *a lot*), Wireshark allows you to apply filters to limit what it captures. For example, if you're troubleshooting a slow web connection, you can filter for HTTP traffic and skip over the other types of noise that may distract you. This focused approach helps you avoid getting overwhelmed while also ensuring you zero in on the traffic that matters.

The filter system in Wireshark is one of its most powerful features, but don't let it intimidate you. You don't need to be a wizard with regex (regular expressions) just yet. Wireshark provides an intuitive syntax to create filters that help you focus on specific protocols, IP addresses, ports, and even particular conversations. As you get more comfortable, you can start experimenting with complex filters to capture just the right data you need. For now, though, it's important to remember that filters are your best friend—they allow you to sift through mountains of data and find the golden nuggets of information you're seeking.

Another crucial part of your setup is configuring your capture preferences. This step may seem like a minor detail, but tweaking Wireshark's preferences can have a huge impact on your efficiency. For instance, adjusting the packet capture buffer size can help prevent packet loss during long captures, while enabling hardware acceleration can give you better performance on high-speed networks. Of course, these settings might not be necessary for everyone, but as you dive deeper into network analysis, you'll appreciate how small tweaks can make big differences in your capturing experience.

By now, you've installed Wireshark, configured your interfaces, and gotten a feel for the basics. You're officially on your way to becoming a packet-sniffing expert. But before we finish up this chapter, let's talk about some troubleshooting tips for those moments when things aren't going according to plan. First off, if Wireshark isn't capturing any data, make sure you've got the right interface selected. Wireshark won't capture traffic from an inactive or incorrect interface, so double-check that you're looking at the right one. Also, if you're on a Wi-Fi network, don't forget that some network cards require you to enable monitor mode to capture all wireless traffic. Make sure to consult your device's documentation for specifics on how to configure it properly.

Next, if you find that Wireshark isn't capturing enough traffic, or worse, is missing packets, it could be due to a low buffer size or packet drop. If this happens, adjust your buffer settings to accommodate the amount of traffic you expect to capture. You can also try decreasing the amount of traffic you're capturing by using more specific filters, as we discussed earlier. It's all about managing the flow of data to ensure that Wireshark has the resources to capture and store everything without overwhelming your system.

If you're encountering issues with permissions or network interfaces not showing up at all, don't panic. Double-check that you've run Wireshark with the necessary administrative privileges, as lacking the appropriate permissions can prevent the software from accessing your network interfaces. On Windows, running Wireshark as an administrator should solve this. On Linux or macOS, you may need to adjust user group settings or add your user to the appropriate network capture group. It's all part of the setup process, but once these permissions are sorted, everything should work seamlessly.

And just in case you're still wondering whether Wireshark is the right tool for you, here's the final word: absolutely. Wireshark is the Swiss Army knife of network analysis tools, capable of handling everything from basic packet capture to advanced protocol dissection. Whether you're a hobbyist looking to understand more about how networks work, or a professional troubleshooting complex issues, Wireshark is the tool that will help you get the job done. The best part? It's free, open-source, and constantly being updated by a passionate community of developers. You're not just using software—you're joining a global network of enthusiasts and professionals, all working to understand the digital world.

Now that you've got Wireshark installed and set up, it's time to start exploring the deeper aspects of packet analysis. In the following chapters, we'll dig into how to capture, filter, and analyze network traffic in more detail. We'll look at how to decode common protocols, spot network issues, and troubleshoot like a seasoned pro. But for now, take a moment to appreciate your success. You've just installed one of the most powerful network tools out there. Congratulations, and welcome to the wonderful world of Wireshark.

Chapter 3: Understanding the Wireshark Interface

Welcome to the beautiful, and occasionally bewildering, world of the Wireshark interface. If this is your first time opening Wireshark, you might be staring at your screen thinking, "What in the name of TCP/IP is all this?" Don't panic. The Wireshark interface might seem like a busy city street filled with vendors, street performers, and traffic jams, but I promise, once you know your way around, it's a breeze. Just like any new tool, it takes a little getting used to, but with a little guidance, you'll be navigating like a pro in no time.

First, let's break down the main window. When you open Wireshark, you're greeted with a few key sections: the toolbar, the packet list, the packet details, and the packet bytes pane. Each of these has a job to do, and together, they create a beautiful, chaotic symphony of network traffic. Think of the packet list as the stage where the action happens, and the packet details and bytes as the backstage crew, offering you all the fine details behind the scenes. The toolbar, meanwhile, is like your trusty toolbox — it has all the essential functions you need right at your fingertips.

Let's start with the toolbar. You'll find this at the top of the window, and it's packed with buttons that perform key actions, such as starting and stopping captures, opening files, and applying filters. It's like the control panel of a spaceship, and if you're not careful, you might accidentally launch yourself into the stratosphere of packet overload. But don't worry — these buttons are there to make your life easier. The start and stop buttons are pretty self-explanatory, but the real magic happens when you start diving into the filters and preferences, which we'll explore in a bit.

Below the toolbar, you'll find the packet list pane. This is where the real action happens, and it's what you'll spend most of your time looking at. When you start a packet capture, this is where the packets will appear, each row representing a single packet in your capture. It's like watching a flood of tiny data-filled envelopes zip by in a blur. Each packet in the list contains essential information like its number, timestamp, source, destination, protocol, and more. If this sounds like a lot, don't worry — we'll break it down piece by piece.

At the top of the packet list, you'll see a series of columns. These columns are your ticket to quickly scanning through the captured packets. The "No." column shows the packet number in the capture, which is helpful when you want to reference specific packets later. The "Time" column shows the timestamp for when the packet was captured, and it's displayed relative to the first packet's timestamp. You'll also see columns for the source and destination IP addresses, the protocol used (TCP, UDP, ICMP, etc.), the length of the packet, and an info column that gives a brief summary of the packet's contents.

If you're looking for more details, click on any packet in the list. This will expand the selected packet and reveal more information in the next section — the packet details pane. This is where things get interesting. The packet details section provides a breakdown of all the layers within a packet, from the Ethernet frame to the IP header, to the transport layer and the application data itself. It's like peeling back the layers of an onion — except, instead of tears, you'll be uncovering the secrets of the network.

Each layer is expandable, so you can drill down to see more detailed information about each field within the packet. For example, if you're looking at a TCP packet, you can expand the TCP section to see things like the sequence number, acknowledgment number, window size, and flags.

It's like getting a behind-the-scenes look at how data travels across the network. And the best part? You can see the actual values of each field, which is invaluable when you're troubleshooting network issues. The packet details pane is the meat and potatoes of Wireshark.

But wait, there's more! If you're feeling particularly adventurous, you can dive even deeper into the packet with the packet bytes pane, located at the bottom of the window. This pane shows you the raw data of the selected packet, byte by byte. If you're not fluent in hexadecimal, it might look like a bunch of cryptic symbols, but with a little practice, you'll start recognizing patterns and learning how to spot the relevant information you need. It's like reading an ancient text in a forgotten language—but once you've learned the code, it becomes second nature.

Now that we've covered the basic panes, let's talk about the filters. If the packet list is the main stage, then the filters are the spotlight that lets you zero in on specific actors. Filters are one of Wireshark's most powerful features, and they're essential for narrowing down large captures into something you can actually work with. Without filters, you'd be swimming in a sea of irrelevant data, desperately trying to find a needle in a haystack. But with filters, you can hone in on just the packets you care about—be it HTTP traffic, DNS queries, or something more niche like FTP control packets.

To apply a filter, simply type it into the filter bar at the top of the window. Wireshark uses a special syntax for filters, but don't be intimidated—once you get the hang of it, it's like having a superpower. You can filter by protocol, IP address, port number, and even by the contents of the packet itself. Want to find all the DNS requests in your capture? Just type in `dns` and hit enter. Need to track all HTTP traffic? Type `http` and watch the magic unfold. It's like having your own search engine for network traffic.

But what if you're not sure what to filter for? That's where Wireshark's auto-complete feature comes in handy. As you start typing a filter, Wireshark will offer suggestions based on the protocols and fields available in your capture. It's like having a network traffic expert sitting next to you, suggesting the best ways to narrow down your results. This is especially useful for beginners, who may not yet know all the correct filter syntax. With a little trial and error, you'll soon be filtering like a pro.

Let's talk about customizing your view. Wireshark is highly customizable, and the layout can be adjusted to suit your preferences. For example, you can resize the columns in the packet list pane to display more or less information, depending on what's most important to you. You can also add or remove columns by right-clicking on the column headers and selecting "Column Preferences." This allows you to tailor the interface to your workflow, ensuring that you see the data that matters most, and don't get bogged down by unnecessary information.

Another cool feature is the ability to bookmark packets. If you find a packet that's particularly interesting or relevant to your analysis, you can bookmark it by right-clicking on the packet and selecting "Add to Bookmark." This is great for tracking down specific packets you'll want to refer to later without having to scroll through the entire capture again. It's like sticking a post-it note on a page in a book—quick and easy, and it saves you time when you're going back for more details.

If you're feeling overwhelmed by the sheer amount of data in front of you, don't worry—Wireshark offers several ways to organize your captures. You can apply display filters to focus on specific types of traffic, use the "Statistics" menu for a high-level overview of your capture, or even export the data to a file for further analysis. There's no shortage of options for making your packet analysis more manageable.

And if you're a keyboard shortcut enthusiast (and who isn't?), Wireshark has a whole host of shortcuts to make navigating the interface faster. From starting and stopping captures to switching between panes, Wireshark lets you work more efficiently with just a few keystrokes. Once you get familiar with these shortcuts, you'll be navigating Wireshark like an old pro, impressing your colleagues with your lightning-fast packet analysis skills.

Before we wrap up this chapter, let's quickly touch on the "Capture Options" window, which you can access by clicking on the gear icon next to the capture button. This window lets you configure how your packet capture will behave. You can set options such as whether to capture on a specific interface, the maximum file size for your capture, and whether to capture in "promiscuous mode." It's like setting the rules for a game—you decide how the capture will play out.

At the end of the day, Wireshark's interface is all about giving you the tools to analyze your network traffic effectively. It's packed with features that help you capture, filter, analyze, and troubleshoot your network. With a little practice, the various panes and options will start feeling like second nature, and you'll begin to see the packet world in a whole new light. Don't be intimidated by all the options—take it one step at a time, and before you know it, you'll be navigating Wireshark like a pro.

Now that you've got a handle on the interface, you're ready to start capturing packets and diving into the real fun of network analysis. In the next chapters, we'll start using the Wireshark interface to capture specific types of traffic, filter out the noise, and interpret the data in meaningful ways. So buckle up—it's going to be a thrilling ride through the world of packet analysis!

As we continue exploring the Wireshark interface, let's take a moment to appreciate just how much power it gives you. Sure, it might feel a little overwhelming at first with all its buttons, columns, and tabs, but once you get the hang of it, you'll realize that Wireshark is like a magic window into the digital world. Every click, every filter, and every packet you analyze is a small step toward becoming a network detective of the highest order.

One of the truly remarkable aspects of Wireshark is its ability to present information in a way that's both accessible and detailed. Whether you're troubleshooting a network hiccup or just curious about how data flows through your home network, the interface is designed to provide you with the insights you need, without overwhelming you with complexity. The visual layout is intuitive, and as you become more familiar with the interface, you'll find yourself quickly honing in on the important data, all while ignoring the distractions.

One feature we haven't touched on yet is the "Statistics" menu. This is your ticket to high-level insights into the traffic you're capturing. With a few clicks, you can get an overview of protocol distributions, packet counts, and even network performance over time. It's like going from being in the weeds of packet analysis to getting an aerial view of the entire landscape. From the "Statistics" menu, you can pull up options like "Protocol Hierarchy," "IO Graphs," and "Conversations," all of which give you a broader picture of what's happening in your capture.

Let's not forget the importance of using "Follow TCP Stream." This is a function that will quickly make you feel like a network sleuth. By following a single stream, you can trace the entire conversation between two endpoints—whether it's a web browser and a server, or any other networked devices. The ability to track a conversation from start to finish, including all requests and responses, is invaluable when troubleshooting issues like slow load times or broken connections. This function is like having a trail of breadcrumbs that leads directly to the heart of the communication.

As you become more comfortable with the Wireshark interface, you'll notice that you can customize a lot of it to fit your workflow. For instance, you can create custom color rules to visually highlight certain types of packets. This is especially helpful when you're dealing with large captures, as it makes it easy to spot important traffic at a glance. You might choose to color HTTP packets in one shade and DNS queries in another, or perhaps you want to highlight any packets with errors or retransmissions. Customizing your view in this way not only makes Wireshark more visually appealing, but it also helps you analyze traffic more efficiently.

Wireshark also allows you to save and open capture files, which is great if you want to store your analysis for later or share it with colleagues. You can save your entire capture as a `.pcap` file, which can be opened again later in Wireshark for further investigation. This is perfect if you need to pause your analysis and return to it later, or if you're collaborating with a team and need to send them a snapshot of your packet capture. In this sense, Wireshark works like a digital time capsule—you can always go back and revisit the packets you've captured.

If you're the kind of person who likes to get their hands dirty, Wireshark even lets you dig into the raw packet data at the hexadecimal level. The packet bytes pane, located at the bottom of the window, provides you with the ability to see every byte of data that makes up a packet. This is essential for more advanced analysis, such as identifying malformed packets or uncovering hidden data that might not be immediately obvious. The hexadecimal view is definitely not for the faint of heart, but once you understand it, you'll have access to an entirely new world of insights.

While we're on the topic of advanced analysis, let's touch on the "Expert Info" feature. This is another powerful tool that can quickly help you spot potential issues in your network. The "Expert Info" window highlights packets that Wireshark deems to be "suspicious" or problematic, based on things like malformed headers, retransmissions, or unexpected flags. It's like having a built-in alarm system that alerts you when something goes wrong in your capture. If you ever feel overwhelmed by the amount of data, "Expert Info" helps you focus on the packets that require immediate attention.

Now that you've got a solid understanding of the interface, it's time to start thinking about how you want to organize your workflow. The interface is packed with features, but that doesn't mean you have to use every single one all at once. As you continue to explore Wireshark, you'll discover which features are most useful for the tasks at hand. For example, if you're troubleshooting a slow connection, you might lean heavily on the "Follow TCP Stream" function and the packet details pane. If you're analyzing a large dataset for trends, the "Statistics" menu and display filters will be your best friends.

As with any powerful tool, the key to mastering Wireshark is practice. The more you use it, the more natural it will feel. Eventually, you'll start recognizing packet patterns and anomalies, and it won't take long before you're spotting issues and fixing them like a seasoned professional. But even when you're comfortable with the interface, don't stop exploring. Wireshark is constantly evolving, and there's always something new to learn—whether it's a new feature, an updated protocol, or an improved way to organize your captures.

In this chapter, we've covered the basic layout of Wireshark and how to navigate its various panes and functions. The interface is designed to be intuitive, but it's packed with powerful tools that allow you to dive deep into packet analysis. With a little practice, you'll be capturing, filtering, and analyzing network traffic like a pro. Don't be intimidated by all the options—take your time and explore at your own pace. Before you know it, you'll be zooming through Wireshark with the confidence of a true network sleuth.

In the next chapters, we'll start putting all of this knowledge into practice. We'll explore how to capture specific types of traffic, use filters effectively, and decode common protocols to uncover issues and solve problems. But for now, take a moment to bask in your newfound Wireshark prowess. You've made it through the interface, and now, you're ready for the next big step in your journey to becoming a Wireshark expert. Happy sniffing!

Chapter 4: Capturing Your First Packets

Welcome to the thrilling world of packet capturing, where your network traffic is the stage, and Wireshark is the audience. This is where it all starts—the moment you hit that "Start" button and begin capturing packets. It's like opening the curtains on a magic show. You may not know exactly what's coming, but you're about to witness something incredible. Don't worry if you feel a little nervous at first—it's perfectly normal. But trust me, once you see those first packets start streaming in, you'll be hooked. It's the beginning of a long, fascinating journey into the depths of your network's inner workings.

Before we dive into the actual capturing, let's take a moment to check our setup. You've already installed Wireshark, configured your interface, and maybe even set up a few filters. Now, it's time to choose the network interface you want to capture from. This is the "door" through which all your network data flows, and it's where the action happens. Whether you're on a wired Ethernet connection, Wi-Fi, or even a virtual network, Wireshark needs to know which one to watch. You'll see a list of available interfaces when you launch Wireshark. Pick the one that matches your active network connection, and get ready for the show to begin.

Once you've selected the correct interface, you're almost ready to start capturing. But before you click that shiny green "Start" button, there's one crucial decision: promiscuous mode. Promiscuous mode allows Wireshark to capture *all* traffic on the selected interface, not just the traffic destined for your machine. It's like being able to eavesdrop on every conversation in the room instead of just listening to your own. This is especially useful when you want to analyze network traffic in general and not just the data that's specifically coming to your computer. Think of it as becoming a digital fly on the wall. You'll want to make sure this is enabled, so Wireshark doesn't miss a single byte.

Alright, now that we're all set, it's time to capture some packets! When you click "Start," Wireshark will begin to listen to everything happening on the network interface you've selected. It's like you've just cracked open a window into the bustling world of network traffic. Suddenly, packets start to pour in, one by one, flooding your packet list like a tide of data. At first, it might seem overwhelming, but that's just the nature of network traffic—it's happening constantly. In a typical network, there are thousands, even millions, of packets being sent and received every second. So don't worry if it seems like a lot—Wireshark is just doing its job of capturing it all.

But what kind of packets are we capturing? That's the beauty of Wireshark—it lets you see everything. You'll see packets that belong to all sorts of different protocols—HTTP, DNS, ARP, TCP, UDP, and more. If you're connected to the internet, you'll see requests and responses from websites, emails, or any online activity you're doing. It's like being in the audience at a theater and suddenly realizing you can see the entire script, including the actors' notes and behind-the-scenes directions. All of this is visible to you, and it's both thrilling and a little bit magical.

So, what exactly are you looking at? Each packet in the list represents a piece of network traffic, and it contains a wealth of information. The packet list pane shows a summary of each packet's details, including the source and destination IP addresses, the protocol used, and the length of the packet. It's like a snapshot of the network activity at that moment in time. Don't be overwhelmed by all the technical jargon at first—focus on the key parts, like the source and destination. This will help you understand the flow of traffic.

As packets stream in, you'll notice that they don't all look the same. Some will have more details than others, depending on the protocol and the type of communication taking place. For example, HTTP packets will contain the data being sent to or from a web server, while DNS packets will contain queries and responses for domain name resolution. It's like watching different types of vehicles on a highway—some are cars, some are trucks, and some are motorcycles. Each packet has its own role to play in the network traffic ecosystem.

When you click on a packet in the list, Wireshark opens up a more detailed view of that packet. This is where the real magic happens. The packet details pane shows you the layers of the packet, from the Ethernet header to the IP layer, and finally, the transport layer (e.g., TCP or UDP). Each layer contains its own set of information, like addresses, sequence numbers, and flags. It's like peeling back the layers of an onion, revealing the inner workings of the packet. As you get more familiar with the details, you'll start to recognize key pieces of information that help you understand the packet's purpose.

Let's take a quick look at an example. Suppose you're capturing HTTP traffic, and you see a packet that contains an HTTP GET request. This packet is essentially a request to retrieve a web page from a server. By examining the details in the packet, you can see the exact URL being requested, the HTTP headers, and even any cookies or other data sent along with the request. It's like peeking over someone's shoulder as they browse the web, except you have a front-row seat to all the technical details. It's a fascinating glimpse into how the internet works behind the scenes.

But wait, there's more! If you want to track a specific conversation, Wireshark has a nifty feature called "Follow TCP Stream." This allows you to see the entire communication between two devices. For example, if you're troubleshooting a slow connection to a web server, you can follow the TCP stream to see every request and response exchanged between your computer and the server. This feature is a game-changer for troubleshooting, as it lets you see the entire conversation in a single, continuous view.

Once you've captured some packets, you might want to stop the capture to focus on analyzing what you've got. You can click the red "Stop" button in the toolbar to halt the capture at any time. Wireshark will save the captured data in memory until you choose to save it to a file. You can then save the capture as a `.pcap` file, which you can open later for further analysis. This is great for when you want to analyze traffic over a longer period or share your findings with someone else. Think of it as saving your "network diary" for later reference.

But hold on—before you start analyzing, remember that Wireshark can capture a *lot* of data. If you don't filter out the noise, you could quickly become overwhelmed. That's where filters come in. Filters allow you to narrow down the traffic to focus on the packets that matter. For example, you can filter for only HTTP traffic or only packets from a specific IP address. Filters help you manage the flood of data and ensure you're only capturing what's relevant to your investigation. It's like having a net to catch just the fish you want while letting the rest of the sea flow freely.

One thing to keep in mind is that while capturing packets, Wireshark will show you *everything*— even packets that are not directly related to your current session. For example, you might capture packets from other devices on the same network, like a neighbor's smartphone or your printer. This is perfectly normal, as Wireshark is listening to all traffic on the selected interface. If you're just interested in traffic from your own machine, you can set up capture filters to exclude everything else. This is another reason why filters are so powerful—they help you fine-tune your analysis and focus on exactly what you need.

Let's take a quick detour into the concept of packet loss. If you notice that your capture is missing packets or that the data is incomplete, it could be a sign of packet loss. This can happen if the capture buffer is too small to hold all the incoming packets, or if there's too much network traffic for Wireshark to handle. In such cases, you may need to adjust your capture settings, such as increasing the buffer size or using more specific filters to reduce the volume of traffic. Don't let packet loss discourage you—it's a common issue that can usually be resolved with a few tweaks.

If you ever need to pause the capture, Wireshark makes that easy too. Simply click the "Pause" button, and Wireshark will stop capturing without closing the session. This is useful if you want to take a moment to analyze what you've captured so far without losing the data. You can resume the capture at any time by clicking "Resume." This flexibility is part of what makes Wireshark so powerful for both live troubleshooting and post-capture analysis.

Finally, let's talk about saving and sharing your captures. Once you've captured the packets you need, you can save the session as a `.pcap` file, which is the standard format for packet captures. This file can then be opened later in Wireshark or shared with other network professionals for analysis. If you're working in a team, sharing captures is a great way to collaborate on troubleshooting or network optimization. You can even export specific packets or summaries for detailed reports. Wireshark makes it easy to document your findings and communicate your results.

Congratulations! You've successfully captured your first packets. This is the first step in becoming a network analysis ninja. With each capture, you'll gain more experience, learn how to filter the noise, and decode the traffic flowing across your network. So go ahead—capture more packets, experiment with filters, and start analyzing. You've got the tools and knowledge to dig deeper into your network than ever before. Happy capturing!

Now that you've captured your first packets, you might feel like a network detective, peering into the underworld of digital communication. But don't get too comfortable yet—there's a lot more to uncover. Capturing packets is only the beginning; now, it's time to start understanding what you've caught in your net. The true power of Wireshark comes when you start decoding those packets, understanding the protocols behind them, and, ultimately, figuring out what's going right (or wrong) in your network.

As you continue to capture packets, you'll develop a sense for what normal traffic looks like versus what might be a problem. For example, when capturing HTTP traffic, a typical request might show a small data packet followed by a server response containing the requested web page. If you're capturing DNS traffic, you'll see requests and responses between clients and DNS servers. But if you see a packet that's unusually large or has an unexpected destination, that's a red flag worth investigating. Over time, you'll begin to spot these anomalies with ease, which is a major skill for anyone looking to become a networking expert.

Another important lesson in packet capturing is the realization that not all network traffic is equally important. Just because you see a packet doesn't mean it's critical to your analysis. There may be a whole lot of "background noise" that's not relevant to the issue you're investigating. In fact, capturing packets without applying filters can result in an overwhelming flood of data that makes it nearly impossible to find the issue. That's why filtering is essential—whether you're looking for a specific type of traffic, such as HTTP or DNS, or narrowing it down to packets from a particular IP address or port. Filters allow you to focus on the critical pieces of your packet capture, making your analysis more efficient and less time-consuming.

So, as you dive deeper into packet capturing, start thinking about your goals. Are you trying to troubleshoot a slow connection? Look for retransmissions and packet loss. Are you trying to monitor network performance? Look for patterns in the traffic volume, delays, or unusual spikes in activity. Are you simply exploring? Try capturing various types of traffic to get a sense of what flows through your network daily. With Wireshark at your fingertips, the possibilities for investigation are endless.

But even as you hone your skills, remember that packet capturing isn't just about gathering information. It's about asking the right questions. Why is a particular packet appearing at a specific time? What happens when packets don't arrive on time or get dropped? These are the kinds of questions that will lead you to meaningful insights. Whether you're diagnosing a problem or learning about network behavior, always approach packet capturing with curiosity and a detective's mindset.

While it's exciting to capture packets, it's also important to remember that packet captures can have limitations. For example, when capturing on a busy network, you might miss packets if the capture buffer is too small, or if there's just too much data flying by. This is one of the reasons why it's a good idea to limit your captures to a smaller window of time or apply filters to focus on the most relevant traffic. If you're running long-term captures or dealing with high-volume traffic, consider saving your capture data incrementally to avoid losing important packets.

If you're capturing on a wireless network, be aware that the behavior of wireless traffic is different from wired traffic. In Wi-Fi captures, you'll often see packets that are broadcasted to all devices on the network, such as ARP requests or DHCP discovery messages. These packets aren't always useful for troubleshooting but are part of the normal network conversation. If you're investigating wireless issues, keep in mind that certain tools or configurations might be required to capture packets effectively in monitor mode, as we discussed earlier. With Wireshark's flexibility, you can fine-tune your capture settings to suit your specific needs.

At some point, you may want to take your capturing skills to the next level. Once you're comfortable with basic packet capturing, try experimenting with advanced features like capturing on multiple interfaces simultaneously or setting up remote captures. Wireshark lets you capture traffic from several sources, which is especially useful in larger network environments where you might want to see traffic from multiple devices or locations. You can even use Wireshark to perform live captures over a network by using the "Remote Capture" option to connect to a machine on the network and start capturing remotely. This is a handy feature for network administrators who need to monitor devices without being physically present.

When you're analyzing the traffic, always remember that Wireshark doesn't *only* capture packets. It gives you the ability to interact with the data at a granular level. You can apply filters during the capture to zero in on specific packet types, or even use display filters to refine the data after it's been captured. Need to check for specific HTTP requests or packets containing particular text? Wireshark's filter syntax is there to help you. It's like having a magnifying glass over the packet stream, allowing you to zoom in on the exact packet you're interested in.

One powerful feature to experiment with is "Exporting Objects" from captured HTTP traffic. If you're capturing a webpage or other media, Wireshark allows you to extract elements like images, videos, or documents directly from the captured HTTP responses. It's a neat trick that lets you pull out embedded media from web traffic without the need for a browser. In the context of troubleshooting or digital forensics, this feature can be incredibly helpful when trying to recover assets or understand what data is being transferred over the network.

And let's not forget the importance of saving your captures. You might have the best analysis in the world, but if you don't save your data, it's like catching a fish and throwing it back in the water without taking a picture. Always save your captures with descriptive names, and keep track of the dates and times of your captures, so you can easily refer back to them later. If you're troubleshooting an issue, keeping a record of your captures can help you spot recurring patterns or show that a particular problem has been consistently happening over time. Wireshark's ability to save captures as `.pcap` files gives you a simple yet powerful way to store and share your work.

If you ever find yourself stuck, don't hesitate to look to the Wireshark community for help. There's an active and knowledgeable group of users, developers, and network engineers who are always willing to lend a hand. Wireshark's forums, mailing lists, and online resources are treasure troves of information that can help you overcome any obstacle you encounter. And if you discover something cool, don't be shy—share your findings with the community. Wireshark's open-source nature means that it thrives on collaboration, and there's always room for more people to contribute.

Ultimately, capturing packets is about more than just seeing the traffic—it's about understanding what's going on behind the scenes. With Wireshark, you're not just looking at numbers and protocols. You're seeing the lifeblood of the internet, the data that powers everything from simple web pages to complex applications. With every capture, you learn more about how your network works, and the more you learn, the better you'll be at diagnosing issues, optimizing performance, and securing your environment.

So, as you go forth and capture more packets, remember this: You're now part of an elite group of network explorers. Your journey has just begun, and with every packet you capture, you're uncovering secrets, solving puzzles, and making the digital world a little clearer. Keep practicing, keep experimenting, and don't forget to have fun. There's always more to learn, and with Wireshark, the possibilities are endless. Happy packet hunting!

Chapter 5: Filters: Your Search Engine for Packets

If you've ever tried to navigate a pile of data as vast as the one Wireshark collects, you know how quickly things can get chaotic. It's like trying to find a needle in a haystack—except the haystack is made up of billions of tiny needles, and some of them are glittering, others are rusty, and a few are even oddly shaped. Enter filters—the magical tool that makes your packet capturing life ten times easier and twenty times more organized. Think of them as your personal search engine for packet traffic, turning the wild, unstructured world of network data into a neat, searchable library.

Filters in Wireshark are powerful. They allow you to narrow down the flood of packets into exactly what you need, making it possible to analyze specific traffic without sifting through thousands of irrelevant packets. Want to look at just HTTP traffic? No problem. Looking for packets from a specific IP address? That's a breeze. Filters can be simple or complex, and once you get the hang of them, you'll wonder how you ever lived without them. In fact, filters are so important that you'll use them for nearly everything you do in Wireshark, from troubleshooting to performance monitoring.

Let's start with the basics—*display filters*. These are the filters that Wireshark uses to sift through captured packets and display only the data that matches the criteria you set. Display filters are applied after you've captured the data, so you can still see everything, but only the relevant packets will be highlighted. For example, if you're troubleshooting a web application and want to focus only on HTTP traffic, you can use the filter `http` and Wireshark will show you just the HTTP packets. It's like being able to read just the parts of a book that are relevant to your current chapter. No more flipping through irrelevant pages!

At this point, you may be wondering, "How do I actually create a filter?" The answer is simple: just type the filter into the display filter bar at the top of the Wireshark window. For example, if you want to see only traffic involving a specific IP address, you can use a filter like `ip.addr == 192.168.1.1`. This tells Wireshark, "Show me only packets where the source or destination IP address is 192.168.1.1." You can also specify both source and destination IP addresses using `ip.src` and `ip.dst`. Think of it as saying, "I'm only interested in packets that come from or go to this particular address." It's as if Wireshark is your butler, only bringing you packets that meet your exacting standards.

But hold on—what if you're dealing with more complex traffic? Not all packets are as straightforward as an IP address. For example, let's say you're trying to filter out TCP traffic. You can use the filter `tcp`, which will show only the TCP packets in your capture. What if you're trying to see HTTP traffic but only those packets that contain a specific host in the header? You can write a filter like `http.host == "example.com"`, and Wireshark will only display HTTP requests and responses to that host. This is where Wireshark's flexibility comes in—it can handle filters for a wide range of protocols and even specific fields within those protocols.

And just when you thought it couldn't get any cooler, Wireshark lets you combine multiple filters. This is where you enter the realm of logical operations. If you want to see both TCP and UDP traffic, you can use `tcp or udp`. Need to filter for traffic from a particular IP *and* a specific port? You'd write `ip.addr == 192.168.1.1 and tcp.port == 80`. Combining filters with logical operators like `and`, `or`, and `not` opens up a world of possibilities. It's like being a detective who can narrow down suspects using an exacting set of criteria—no more wild guesses!

But filters don't just stop at IP addresses and protocols. They get down to the nitty-gritty. For instance, you can filter based on flags in the TCP header. Want to see all the TCP packets with the SYN flag set? Use the filter `tcp.flags.syn == 1`. What about packets with the FIN flag? You can use `tcp.flags.fin == 1`. These filters help you focus on specific types of traffic, and they're especially useful when you're diagnosing network issues like connection resets or incomplete handshakes. Think of it as zooming in on a few select details in a very large, complex image.

You might be thinking, "I've seen some filters with `==` in them. What's the deal with that?" The double equals sign (`==`) is used to check for equality. So when you write `ip.addr == 192.168.1.1`, you're saying, "I want packets where the IP address is exactly 192.168.1.1." But what if you want to check if a field is not equal to something? That's where the exclamation mark (`!=`) comes in. For example, `ip.addr != 192.168.1.1` filters out all packets with that IP address. It's like saying, "Give me everything except this one thing." Think of it as keeping your eyes on the forest, not just that one tree.

Of course, some filters are more complicated than others. For example, what if you're dealing with an encrypted protocol like SSL/TLS? You may want to filter traffic based on the port number, but you don't want to see the individual encrypted packets. In cases like this, filters can help by showing you the handshake packets or the initial handshake request and response. Wireshark even has built-in dissectors for these protocols, so you can see more of the data, even if it's encrypted. It's like being able to read a secret code, even though you don't have the full decryption key.

So far, we've only covered display filters, but there's another type of filter you'll need to know about: *capture filters*. Capture filters are applied before you start capturing data, and they limit what Wireshark records in the first place. If you're capturing traffic on a busy network, applying a capture filter can save you a lot of time and space by excluding unnecessary packets. For example, if you're only interested in HTTP traffic, you can use a capture filter like `tcp port 80`, which ensures that Wireshark will only capture packets on port 80 (HTTP). It's like setting up a VIP guest list for your network traffic, only letting the important stuff in.

The main difference between capture and display filters is that capture filters are applied *before* the capture starts, while display filters are used after you've already captured the data. Capture filters are more efficient because they reduce the amount of data that's captured, making your Wireshark sessions run faster. Display filters, on the other hand, are more flexible, allowing you to sift through captured data with greater precision. So, depending on your needs, you might use one or both in combination to optimize your packet analysis.

If you're not sure how to write a filter, Wireshark has built-in filter expressions that you can use. You can access these by clicking on the "Expression" button next to the filter bar. This will open up a window that lets you build your filter by selecting from a list of available protocols, fields, and operators. It's like having a cheat sheet for creating filters, which is especially helpful if you're new to the filter syntax. Once you've selected the criteria you want, Wireshark will generate the filter for you. It's an easy way to get started if you're not quite ready to write filters from scratch.

One important thing to remember is that filters are case-sensitive. For example, `http` is not the same as `HTTP` in Wireshark. This means that when you're writing filters, you need to be precise about capitalization. If you accidentally use the wrong case, your filter may not work as expected, and you'll end up seeing the wrong data. It's like spelling a word incorrectly in a search engine—you might not find what you're looking for.

Wireshark also supports more advanced filtering, including the use of regular expressions. These are patterns that match specific sequences of characters, and they're incredibly powerful when you need to search for packets that match a complex string of text. For example, if you're looking for packets that contain a certain phrase or keyword, you can use a regular expression filter like `frame contains "example"`. This lets you capture packets with a particular string anywhere in the packet data, making it easier to track down specific information.

If you're working on a team or sharing your captures, it's useful to document your filters. Save the filters you use often as "Named Filters," so you can quickly apply them next time you need them. This is a huge time-saver if you're frequently troubleshooting or analyzing the same types of traffic. Instead of having to type out the entire filter each time, you can just click on your saved filter, and voila—instant packet analysis. It's like having a favorite playlist for your network traffic, ready to go at the push of a button.

So, after all this filtering talk, you might be thinking, "Is there ever a time when I don't need filters?" The answer is simple: probably not. Even in the simplest of captures, using filters makes your life easier. Whether you're focused on a single protocol or a specific IP address, filters are what keep your packet analysis from becoming a chaotic mess. They're your secret weapon for understanding what's really happening on your network.

Now that you've mastered the art of filtering, you're ready to tackle more complex analysis. In the upcoming chapters, we'll dive deeper into analyzing specific protocols, troubleshooting network issues, and using Wireshark's advanced features to make your life even easier. But before we move on, take a moment to play around with filters on your own. Capture some packets, apply different filters, and see how much clearer your data becomes. Filters are the backbone of efficient packet analysis, and the more you use them, the better you'll get at sniffing out problems and optimizing your network. Happy filtering!

As we wrap up this chapter on filters, it's clear that they're your ultimate tool in the Wireshark toolbox. Whether you're trying to catch a glimpse of a single conversation between two devices, focus on specific protocol traffic, or sift through a massive sea of data, filters are your best friend. You'll quickly find that Wireshark is a thousand times more powerful once you harness the full potential of filtering. The key takeaway? Filters aren't just a nice-to-have; they're a necessity for making sense of network traffic and finding the information you need without getting buried in a sea of irrelevant packets.

Let's be honest: when you're first starting out with Wireshark, the sheer amount of data can be overwhelming. It's like trying to read a novel where every page is filled with tiny, cryptic details about your network. Without filters, it's easy to get lost in the minutiae, frustrated by the lack of clarity. Filters allow you to zoom in on the important pages—skimming over the irrelevant bits and getting to the heart of the story. Once you start using them, you'll quickly realize that filtering isn't just about narrowing the data; it's about unlocking insights and understanding what's really happening behind the scenes.

Of course, as with anything in life, practice makes perfect. The more you work with filters, the more natural they'll feel. You'll become so familiar with the syntax and logic of filters that you'll be able to write them on the fly, adjusting them to meet your needs. One day, you'll look up and realize you've gone from struggling to remember how to filter for a specific protocol to effortlessly sifting through a massive capture with just a few keystrokes. That's the beauty of Wireshark—it's designed to grow with you as your expertise deepens.

Another thing to keep in mind is that filters can be as simple or as complex as you need them to be. You can use basic filters to isolate specific traffic, like `http` for web traffic or `ip.addr`

`== 192.168.1.1` for traffic from a particular device. But as you dive deeper into network analysis, you'll learn to write more sophisticated filters using logical operators, regular expressions, and field-specific criteria. As with any skill, you'll develop your own style and preferences when it comes to filtering. Some people like to build complex, multi-layered filters, while others prefer to keep it simple. Whatever your style, the important thing is that you're using filters to get the job done efficiently.

As you experiment with filters, don't forget that Wireshark has built-in filter expressions that can help guide you. If you're unsure of what to filter for, or if you're looking for a more complex expression, just click on the "Expression" button in the filter bar. This will bring up a list of available fields and operators, along with helpful descriptions. It's like having a cheat sheet for filtering, which can save you time when you're first starting out. Once you get comfortable with the basic filters, you can move on to more advanced ones, but the "Expression" button is a great way to start experimenting with Wireshark's powerful filtering capabilities.

And let's not forget about capture filters. While display filters are great for narrowing down your view after the capture, capture filters allow you to limit the data captured in the first place. When you're working with a busy network, applying a capture filter is an essential way to ensure you're not wasting time and memory by capturing unnecessary data. Whether you're capturing traffic on a specific port or filtering for a certain protocol, capture filters help you focus on what matters, ensuring that Wireshark doesn't waste valuable resources on irrelevant traffic. Just remember, capture filters are set before the capture starts, so make sure you've configured them properly before hitting "Start."

With all the filter options at your disposal, you're essentially in control of the entire packet-capturing process. Filters let you define your goals and zoom in on the precise data you need. No longer will you have to manually scroll through mountains of data, hoping to catch a glimpse of the packets that matter. With Wireshark's filtering capabilities, you can turn a chaotic flood of packets into a well-organized and manageable dataset, ready for analysis. The filter bar in Wireshark is your command center, and every time you apply a filter, you're issuing a command to get exactly what you want out of your network traffic.

If there's one thing that can save you hours of frustration in packet analysis, it's mastering filters. As you grow more comfortable with Wireshark, you'll find yourself using filters for everything, from simple tasks like isolating HTTP traffic to more complex challenges like tracking down intermittent network issues or debugging custom protocols. Filters are the key to unlocking the full potential of Wireshark, and they'll make your life a whole lot easier as you dive deeper into network analysis.

At the end of the day, filtering is about more than just making your job easier—it's about making your analysis smarter. With the right filters, you're not just skimming through data; you're pinpointing exactly what's important. You're seeing the forest through the trees, zeroing in on the most relevant traffic and ignoring the rest. That's the true power of Wireshark—and it's all thanks to filters. As you continue to practice, experiment, and refine your filter skills, you'll become more adept at navigating the world of network traffic and solving problems with precision and speed.

So, don't be afraid to experiment. Create filters, test them, and tweak them until you get the results you're looking for. And when you're not sure what to filter for, remember: Wireshark's documentation and community are always there to help. There's a wealth of knowledge out there, and by diving in and asking the right questions, you'll keep building your filtering expertise. The more you filter, the better you'll become at understanding network traffic, and the easier it will be to spot potential issues and optimize your network's performance.

In the next chapters, we'll put all of your newfound filtering knowledge into practice. We'll dive deeper into how to use filters for troubleshooting, performance monitoring, and even security analysis. But for now, take a moment to appreciate the power of filters. They're your personal search engine for packets, and with a little practice, you'll soon be using them like a pro. So, go ahead—capture more packets, apply some filters, and see how much clearer your network data becomes. You're well on your way to becoming a Wireshark wizard. Happy filtering!

Chapter 6: Packet Analysis 101

Welcome to the world of packet analysis, where data packets are your clues, and Wireshark is your magnifying glass. By now, you've captured some packets, applied a few filters, and maybe even started recognizing the basic structure of a packet. But now it's time to dive deeper and unravel the mysteries that lie within those packets. Think of packet analysis as a treasure hunt, where the more you look, the more secrets you uncover. It's like being a digital detective, sifting through clues to understand exactly what's going on in your network.

At its core, packet analysis is about understanding the structure of a packet and interpreting the information it contains. Every packet that flows across the network is a small, self-contained bundle of data, but within it lies a treasure trove of information. You'll find addresses, protocols, sequence numbers, flags, and more—each playing a critical role in how data is transmitted. Just like a detective who knows how to read body language and pick up on hidden cues, a skilled packet analyst knows how to interpret these little clues to figure out what's really going on in the network.

To begin, let's break down a typical network packet. The first thing you'll encounter in almost every packet is the *Ethernet frame*. This is the outermost layer of the packet, responsible for getting data from one device to another on the local network. The Ethernet frame contains essential information like the source and destination MAC addresses, which tell the network where the packet is coming from and where it's headed. It's like the address on an envelope— without it, the packet wouldn't know where to go.

Next, we move to the *IP header*. This is the part that tells us how the packet will be routed through the network. The IP header contains information such as the source and destination IP addresses, which identify the devices involved in the communication. Think of it as the postal system of the internet—once the packet leaves your local network, it's the IP header that guides it to its final destination, bouncing from router to router along the way. But it doesn't stop there —if you dig deeper, you'll also find fields like the TTL (Time To Live), which helps prevent packets from getting stuck in endless loops if a routing error occurs.

At this point, we arrive at the *transport layer*, where the packet gets a bit more interesting. This is where we find protocols like TCP and UDP. The transport layer is responsible for ensuring that data is delivered reliably and in the correct order (TCP) or quickly with minimal overhead (UDP). TCP is like a perfectly organized train schedule, making sure everything arrives on time and in the right order, while UDP is like an impromptu, high-speed car chase, delivering data as fast as possible, without worrying too much about order or reliability.

When you're analyzing a packet, the transport layer is often where the action is. If you're working with TCP, you'll see things like sequence numbers and acknowledgment numbers. These are the building blocks of a reliable data transmission. The sequence number tells the receiver which packet in the sequence this one is, and the acknowledgment number tells the sender that the receiver has received the previous packet. If you see a packet with an acknowledgment number that's out of order or not what you expected, that's a red flag—perhaps indicating packet loss, retransmissions, or even network congestion. Wireshark will even color these packets differently to highlight potential issues, so keep an eye out for anything that seems amiss.

One thing you'll quickly learn as you analyze packets is that there's often more to a packet than meets the eye. Take HTTP, for example. When you capture an HTTP packet, it's not just a simple "GET" request or a "200 OK" response. If you expand the HTTP layer in Wireshark, you'll see the headers, the method used (GET, POST, etc.), the host being requested, and even the length of the response. HTTP headers can contain valuable information, such as cookies, user-agent strings, and cache control directives. By looking closely at the details, you can start to understand the communication between the client and server on a deeper level.

As you get more comfortable with packet analysis, you'll begin to spot the patterns in network traffic. Some patterns are normal and expected, while others might indicate problems. For example, a simple, straightforward web browsing session might consist of a few HTTP GET requests and responses. But what happens if you start seeing repeated retransmissions or out-of-sequence packets? That's a sign that something's wrong, and it's time to dig deeper. Analyzing the timing and behavior of packets is one of the most important skills in packet analysis. For instance, if there's a delay between packets or if packets seem to be dropped and resent, you might be dealing with network congestion, faulty hardware, or even a misconfigured router.

Another key element of packet analysis is understanding the flags in the TCP header. These flags —such as SYN, ACK, FIN, and RST—are like signals that tell you what's happening with the connection. A SYN flag indicates the start of a TCP handshake, while an ACK flag shows that the receiving side is confirming receipt of a packet. The FIN flag marks the end of the connection, and the RST flag indicates that something went wrong and the connection should be reset. If you're troubleshooting a slow connection or a dropped session, understanding how these flags interact can be incredibly helpful.

Let's talk about analyzing packet flows. Sometimes, you'll want to trace the entire conversation between two devices. Wireshark makes this easy with the "Follow TCP Stream" feature. This feature lets you see all the packets exchanged between two endpoints, in order, so you can see the full context of a conversation. This is particularly useful when you're troubleshooting application issues, as it allows you to follow the request and response cycle from start to finish.

For example, if you're investigating a slow website, you can follow the HTTP stream to see exactly how long each step takes and where the bottlenecks are.

When analyzing packets, it's important to remember that packet analysis is often a process of elimination. If you're dealing with a network issue, you'll want to rule out different layers of the OSI model one by one. Start by checking the physical layer—are there any issues with cables or Wi-Fi signal strength? Next, check the data link layer—are there any problems with MAC addresses or Ethernet frames? Then move up to the network layer and check the IP addresses. If everything looks good at these lower layers, it's time to check the transport and application layers to see where things are going wrong.

As you analyze packets, it's also essential to keep an eye on performance metrics. Wireshark includes various statistics tools, such as I/O graphs and flow graphs, that give you an overview of network performance over time. These tools allow you to visualize things like packet throughput, round-trip times, and retransmissions. It's like stepping back from the microscope and looking at the big picture. By examining these high-level stats, you can get a sense of whether your network is performing optimally or if there are areas that need improvement.

Packet analysis isn't just for troubleshooting; it's also useful for security analysis. Malicious activity often leaves traces in network traffic, and Wireshark is an excellent tool for uncovering those traces. For example, if you're analyzing a network for signs of malware, you might look for suspicious outbound traffic, unusual DNS queries, or abnormal communication with known malicious IP addresses. Wireshark's powerful filtering and packet dissection capabilities can help you identify anomalies in the traffic, so you can spot potential security threats before they become serious problems.

Let's not forget about encrypted traffic. One of the most frustrating things for a packet analyst is encountering encrypted traffic, especially when you can't see the contents. SSL/TLS encryption is a common way to protect data, but it can make it difficult to analyze. However, there are ways around this, such as capturing the SSL/TLS handshake and using the appropriate decryption keys. Wireshark allows you to decrypt SSL/TLS traffic if you have access to the necessary keys, which can be a game-changer when trying to analyze secure connections.

When you're analyzing packets, it's also important to remember that context matters. Just like in detective work, understanding the bigger picture is key to interpreting individual clues. If you're troubleshooting a performance issue, for example, you need to know what's "normal" traffic looks like before you can spot anomalies. This is where experience comes in—over time, you'll start recognizing patterns and behaviors that signal something is wrong, whether it's a network bottleneck, a hardware failure, or a misconfigured device.

By now, you should have a basic understanding of how to analyze packets and identify potential issues in your network. But this is just the beginning. Packet analysis is a deep and fascinating field that you can continue to explore for years. The more you work with Wireshark, the more proficient you'll become at identifying and troubleshooting network problems. As you build your skills, you'll find yourself diving deeper into the various protocols, learning to decode and understand them with ease.

In the next chapters, we'll explore how to troubleshoot common network issues using packet analysis, dig deeper into specific protocols, and leverage advanced Wireshark features to optimize your network. But for now, take some time to practice your packet analysis skills. The more you analyze, the more confident you'll become in your ability to understand the traffic flowing across your network and solve any issues that arise. Happy analyzing!

As you continue honing your packet analysis skills, you'll soon discover that the real value of this process isn't just in identifying individual packets or specific protocols, but in understanding how they all work together to maintain a functioning network. Each packet is a small, but essential part of a larger communication system, and learning how to interpret those packets will give you the insight you need to troubleshoot problems, optimize performance, and even secure your network.

One of the most rewarding aspects of packet analysis is the ability to make educated guesses based on the information at hand. Just like a detective piecing together clues to solve a crime, you'll find that packets often leave traces of behavior that tell a larger story. For example, seeing repeated TCP retransmissions could indicate a network bottleneck or a faulty connection. A series of unexpected resets or incomplete handshakes could suggest that a service or server is unavailable, and those little details provide invaluable clues when trying to diagnose a network issue.

Packet analysis is also about knowing how to use the tools at your disposal effectively. In Wireshark, there are plenty of built-in tools to help you analyze packets in various ways. Beyond just following a stream or isolating a specific protocol, you have the option to generate graphs, calculate round-trip times, or even compare two separate captures to see how traffic has changed over time. These features help you visualize data and trends that might otherwise be invisible in raw packet data. This ability to "zoom out" and gain a holistic view of the network's behavior is one of the reasons why Wireshark is such a powerful tool.

As you move forward in your analysis journey, don't be discouraged if things seem complex or overwhelming at times. Just like learning a new language, mastering packet analysis takes practice. At first, you might feel like you're staring at a bunch of indecipherable hex codes, but over time, the patterns will begin to emerge. You'll start seeing things like protocol headers, flags, and sequence numbers, not as abstract concepts, but as familiar pieces of a larger puzzle that you can read and understand.

Another important lesson to learn is that no two packets are the same. Even when analyzing seemingly similar traffic, there are always nuances that make each packet unique. This is particularly true when you start working with more complex network setups or encrypted traffic. Understanding these subtleties will give you the edge in uncovering hidden issues, such as misconfigurations or performance problems, which can be incredibly tricky to spot without a keen eye for detail.

As you work with more advanced protocols, you'll find that some packets are better understood when you have context. For example, analyzing HTTP packets is relatively straightforward when you know the web pages being accessed or the applications involved. However, with more complex traffic like VoIP calls or file-sharing protocols, understanding the context behind the traffic will often require knowledge of the application itself. It's like being able to understand the conversation only if you know the characters involved and the plot of the story.

Along with these technical skills, packet analysis also involves a certain level of curiosity. You may find yourself asking, "What's causing this delay?" or "Why is this packet being sent at this specific time?" Those questions drive the process and help you uncover the answers that lead to solutions. The best packet analysts don't just look at packets—they look for patterns, they question what they see, and they dig deeper until they find the root cause.

Now, let's talk about some of the common issues you might encounter while analyzing packets. One of the most frequent problems is network congestion. If the network becomes congested, you'll see delayed packets, retransmissions, and timeouts. In Wireshark, these issues often manifest as gaps between packets or a flurry of retransmissions as devices attempt to resend missing data. If you're dealing with congestion, it's important to analyze traffic patterns over time to see where the bottleneck is happening. Is there too much traffic on one particular link? Or is a device or server struggling to handle requests? Understanding congestion is critical for optimizing network performance.

Another issue you might encounter is packet loss, which can happen for various reasons, including poor network conditions, hardware failures, or misconfigured devices. Packet loss is often easy to spot in Wireshark because it causes disruptions in the flow of traffic, including out-of-sequence packets or duplicate packets being retransmitted. If you're troubleshooting packet loss, look for areas where the flow is interrupted or where packets don't arrive in the expected order. This can help pinpoint the source of the issue, whether it's a faulty cable, an overloaded router, or an issue at the application layer.

When analyzing TCP connections specifically, you'll often come across connection resets (RST) or unexpected terminations. These can be a sign of either a normal closure of a session or something more problematic, like an application or server error. RST packets usually appear when a connection is forcibly closed, which can happen if the server crashes, the client is disconnected unexpectedly, or there's a protocol mismatch. If you see a series of RST packets in the middle of an active connection, that's a signal that something went wrong and it's time to dig deeper.

For those of you focusing on network security, packet analysis is your first line of defense. Malicious activity can often be detected in packets, such as unusual traffic patterns, unexpected open ports, or suspicious DNS queries. Wireshark allows you to spot these anomalies and take action before they escalate into full-blown security threats. For example, an attack like DNS spoofing might involve suspicious DNS queries from unknown devices or queries to a non-standard port. By analyzing these packets, you can identify potential intruders or signs of a breach, giving you the upper hand in securing your network.

Understanding how to use Wireshark to its full potential also means knowing how to deal with encrypted traffic. While encrypted packets can be challenging to analyze, especially when you're dealing with protocols like SSL/TLS, there are ways to capture enough information to gain insight into what's happening. If you have access to the necessary decryption keys or use tools like session keys, you can decrypt the traffic and view the plaintext. Without this ability, though, you can still analyze metadata, such as packet sizes, timing, and the sequence of the handshakes, to get a sense of the encrypted traffic's behavior.

When troubleshooting a network, it's important to remember that packet analysis isn't a magic bullet. It's a tool to help you gather clues, but it's up to you to piece those clues together and make sense of the bigger picture. You may uncover packet loss or retransmissions, but those clues are only valuable if you understand what's causing them. Often, you'll need to combine packet analysis with other diagnostic tools, such as ping tests or traceroutes, to get a full picture of the network's health.

As you gain more experience with packet analysis, you'll also learn to recognize the common behaviors that occur under normal conditions. For example, a healthy TCP connection will have well-ordered packets, predictable sequence numbers, and regular acknowledgments. When things go wrong, those patterns will break, and it's your job to notice those breaks and figure out why they're happening. Whether it's a slow application, a network congestion issue, or a misbehaving server, understanding what constitutes "normal" behavior is key to identifying problems.

Finally, remember that packet analysis is a skill that improves with time and practice. The more packets you analyze, the better you'll get at spotting patterns, identifying problems, and even predicting network behavior. It's a bit like learning to read music—you start by recognizing the basic notes, and over time, you start to understand the flow of the melody. As you become more proficient with Wireshark and packet analysis, you'll begin to see the larger structure of the network in ways that were previously invisible. You won't just be analyzing packets—you'll be understanding the story they're telling, and with that knowledge, you'll be able to make smarter decisions and solve problems more efficiently.

With your foundational knowledge in packet analysis, you're now ready to dive into specific troubleshooting methods, security analysis, and advanced packet dissection in the chapters to come. But for now, take a moment to reflect on the power you've unlocked. Packet analysis is not only about diagnosing issues; it's about gaining deeper insights into your network's behavior and making informed decisions to keep everything running smoothly. Keep practicing, and soon enough, you'll be the network detective who can uncover the answers hidden in the packets. Happy analyzing!

Chapter 7: Decoding Protocols

Welcome to the wonderful world of protocols! Think of them as the unwritten rules of the internet—how data is packaged, transmitted, and understood. Protocols are the backbone of communication between devices, and understanding how they work is crucial for troubleshooting, optimizing, and securing your network. The packet captures you've been analyzing? They're all full of protocol traffic. Some of these protocols are simple, others are complex, and some are downright quirky. In this chapter, we'll take a journey through some of the most common protocols you'll encounter in packet analysis and decode what they're really saying.

Let's start with the king of all protocols—**IP (Internet Protocol)**. IP is like the postal system of the internet. It's responsible for addressing and routing packets between devices. Every device on the internet has an IP address, just like a house has a physical address. When you send data, it's like sending a letter to a friend, but instead of using a street address, you use an IP address to guide the packet through the maze of routers and switches. In Wireshark, you'll see both the source and destination IP addresses for each packet, and these are your key clues for understanding who's talking to whom on the network.

But IP isn't perfect—it's just the delivery system. It doesn't guarantee that the data will arrive intact, in the right order, or at all. That's where **TCP (Transmission Control Protocol)** comes in. Think of TCP as the reliable postman who ensures that your package not only gets delivered but is also tracked and ordered. When you look at a TCP packet in Wireshark, you'll see things like sequence numbers, acknowledgment numbers, and flags. The sequence number tells you where the packet fits in the overall stream, and the acknowledgment number confirms that the recipient has received a packet and is ready for the next one. It's like having a tracking number for each delivery, and if the package doesn't arrive, TCP will send a new one. If you're troubleshooting a network issue and see a lot of retransmissions, that's a sign that something's wrong with the delivery process.

Then we have **UDP (User Datagram Protocol)**, which is the polar opposite of TCP. If TCP is the overly organized postman, UDP is the rebellious one who's just trying to get things done as quickly as possible. UDP doesn't guarantee delivery, ordering, or integrity. It just throws packets out there and hopes for the best. While this makes UDP faster, it can also cause problems in applications where reliability is important—such as video streaming or VoIP. When you're analyzing UDP packets in Wireshark, you'll notice there's no sequence number or acknowledgment. It's like sending a letter without asking for confirmation that it was received. That doesn't mean UDP is bad—it's just a different tool for different jobs. For instance, UDP is perfect for real-time applications where speed is more important than perfection.

Of course, HTTP is the protocol that fuels the web, and it's one of the most common protocols you'll encounter. HTTP is how browsers talk to web servers, and it's the language of everything from loading a simple webpage to streaming videos. When you analyze HTTP packets in Wireshark, you'll see GET requests, POST requests, and responses like "HTTP/1.1 200 OK" or "HTTP/2 404 Not Found". GET requests are like asking a server to send you a webpage, while POST requests are used when you're submitting data, like filling out a form. HTTP is a text-based protocol, which means it's human-readable, so you can often see things like headers, cookies, and URLs in the packet details. If you're analyzing web traffic, this is your bread and butter.

Then, there's **DNS (Domain Name System)**, which is like the phone book of the internet. DNS resolves human-readable domain names (like www.example.com) into machine-readable IP addresses (like 192.168.1.1). Without DNS, the internet would be a confusing mess of numbers instead of a seamless browsing experience. When you're troubleshooting a website that's not loading, DNS is often where the problem lies. A failed DNS query can stop a website from being found in the first place. In Wireshark, you'll see DNS queries and responses, and they'll typically involve records like A (address) or MX (mail exchange). If you see repeated DNS queries but no responses, that could indicate a misconfigured DNS server.

Next up is **ARP (Address Resolution Protocol)**, which is the protocol that maps an IP address to a MAC address on the local network. Think of ARP as the internal phone directory of a network—while IP addresses help devices communicate across networks, MAC addresses are used for communication within a local network. When a device wants to send a packet to another device on the same local network, it uses ARP to figure out the recipient's MAC address. In Wireshark, ARP packets appear as requests and replies, where a device says, "Who has this IP address?" and another device replies, "That's me! Here's my MAC address." If you see a lot of ARP requests without responses, you might have a network misconfiguration.

Then there's **ICMP (Internet Control Message Protocol)**, which is like the network's "emergency services." ICMP is used for diagnostic purposes, such as sending a "ping" to check if a device is reachable. When you run the `ping` command, you're sending ICMP Echo Request packets, and the device on the other side replies with ICMP Echo Reply packets. Wireshark makes it easy to spot ICMP packets because they're typically small and contain a simple message like "echo request" or "echo reply." ICMP is crucial for troubleshooting, especially when diagnosing network connectivity issues. If you're pinging a device and seeing no reply, you know something's wrong with the network connection.

Let's not forget **SMTP (Simple Mail Transfer Protocol)**, which is the protocol used for sending email. SMTP is responsible for transferring email messages from the sender's mail server to the recipient's mail server. When you capture SMTP traffic in Wireshark, you'll often see commands like "HELO", "MAIL FROM", and "RCPT TO" as part of the email exchange process. SMTP is a text-based protocol, so you can easily read the headers and the body of the email being transmitted. However, it doesn't actually handle email retrieval; for that, you'd need protocols like POP3 or IMAP, which are used for accessing email. Analyzing SMTP traffic is essential for diagnosing email delivery issues or spotting suspicious activity in your inbox.

Speaking of email, let's take a look at **POP3 (Post Office Protocol 3)** and **IMAP (Internet Message Access Protocol)**, the two protocols used for retrieving email. POP3 is more simplistic —it downloads email from the server and removes it, while IMAP allows you to keep your email on the server and manage it remotely. If you're analyzing email traffic, POP3 and IMAP packets will give you a glimpse of how emails are being accessed and managed. IMAP is generally the more modern choice because it allows for synchronization across multiple devices, making it ideal for mobile and desktop use.

Let's talk about **FTP (File Transfer Protocol)** next. FTP is the protocol used for transferring files between devices on a network. It operates on two separate channels: a command channel for sending instructions (like "get" or "put") and a data channel for transferring the actual files. FTP packets in Wireshark can be identified by their specific command codes, such as `RETR` (retrieve) and `STOR` (store). FTP is great for transferring large files, but it's not the most secure option, which is why many people prefer using **SFTP (Secure File Transfer Protocol)** or **FTPS (FTP Secure)**, both of which encrypt the file transfer process.

As you analyze more protocols, you'll encounter **TLS (Transport Layer Security)**, the protocol that keeps your web browsing, email, and other data secure. TLS is responsible for encrypting communication between clients and servers, ensuring that sensitive data—like passwords, credit card numbers, and emails—stays private. When you capture TLS traffic in Wireshark, it may appear encrypted, but you can still see the handshake process. The TLS handshake involves the client and server agreeing on encryption methods, exchanging keys, and verifying identities. Without the ability to decrypt the traffic, you won't be able to see the actual content of the messages, but understanding the handshake is still crucial for troubleshooting SSL/TLS-related issues.

Now, let's wrap things up with **SSH (Secure Shell)**, a protocol used for securely logging into remote systems and executing commands. SSH encrypts the entire communication between the client and server, providing a secure tunnel for transmitting commands and data. SSH is widely used by network administrators and system administrators for managing servers. In Wireshark, you won't be able to see the actual commands being executed over SSH because they're encrypted. However, the initial connection and authentication process are visible, and this can provide valuable information about the security of the remote session.

By now, you should have a solid understanding of some of the most common protocols you'll encounter in packet analysis. But remember, this is just the beginning. There are hundreds of other protocols out there, and each one has its own quirks and intricacies. As you continue to capture and analyze packets, you'll begin to recognize the patterns and behaviors of each protocol, and you'll become more adept at troubleshooting, optimizing, and securing your network. So, grab your magnifying glass, dive into the packets, and start decoding the mysteries of the network!

As you continue your journey through the world of packet analysis, one of the most exciting things is the ability to truly "speak" the language of the network. With each protocol you decode, you unlock more insight into how devices communicate, how data flows, and where problems might arise. The beauty of protocol analysis is that each packet tells a story, and your job is to interpret it correctly. Whether you're troubleshooting a slow connection, optimizing network performance, or securing your infrastructure, understanding the protocols that drive network traffic is essential to solving problems and making informed decisions.

One key takeaway from this chapter is that not all protocols are created equal. Some protocols are designed for speed and simplicity, like UDP, while others prioritize reliability, like TCP. Some are human-readable, like HTTP, which makes it easier to dive into their details, while others, like SSL/TLS, encrypt their content to ensure privacy. As you work with different types of network traffic, you'll begin to understand why certain protocols are used in specific contexts, and why they might behave the way they do. This deeper understanding allows you to troubleshoot more efficiently and recognize the symptoms of various network issues, from congestion to protocol misconfigurations.

It's also important to remember that packet analysis isn't just about decoding individual packets in isolation. The real power of protocol analysis comes when you look at the overall flow of traffic and understand how different protocols interact with each other. For example, an HTTP request relies on TCP for reliable delivery, while DNS queries rely on UDP for speed. By analyzing the interactions between protocols, you can get a better sense of how each one contributes to the overall network experience. It's like being able to see how all the parts of a machine work together—when one part fails, it can have a ripple effect on the rest of the system.

Another fascinating aspect of decoding protocols is the ever-evolving nature of the internet. New protocols are continuously developed to meet the needs of emerging technologies, while older ones are updated to become more efficient or secure. For instance, HTTP/2 and HTTP/3 have been developed to speed up web browsing and reduce latency, while older versions of FTP are being phased out in favor of more secure protocols like SFTP. As a network analyst, it's crucial to stay up to date on the latest protocols and their changes, so you can recognize them in your captures and adapt to the ever-changing digital landscape.

In addition to understanding the technical aspects of protocols, analyzing network traffic also requires a level of curiosity and problem-solving. You'll often encounter strange or unexpected behavior in your packet captures, and it's up to you to figure out why. For example, if you notice a series of TCP retransmissions, it could indicate network congestion or packet loss. If you're seeing repeated DNS queries without responses, that could signal a DNS server issue. As you become more experienced with protocol analysis, you'll develop the skills needed to recognize these anomalies quickly and pinpoint the root cause of the problem.

One of the most rewarding aspects of decoding protocols is that it allows you to uncover security vulnerabilities. Many network-based attacks leave traces in the packet traffic, and by analyzing the behavior of protocols, you can spot signs of malicious activity. For instance, a man-in-the-middle attack might involve tampering with HTTP packets to inject malicious content, or an attacker might use a protocol like DNS to redirect traffic to a malicious server. By understanding how protocols are supposed to behave, you can spot deviations from the norm and take steps to mitigate risks.

Let's not forget that packet analysis is not just for network professionals—it's a valuable skill for anyone who wants to understand how the internet works. Whether you're an IT professional troubleshooting network issues, a security analyst looking for threats, or simply someone who's curious about how data flows across the web, decoding protocols is an essential skill. In fact, one of the most fun parts of packet analysis is the "a-ha" moment when you figure out what's causing an issue or how a protocol is functioning behind the scenes. It's like being able to peek behind the curtain of the internet and see the gears turning.

As you continue to develop your packet analysis skills, you'll find that protocols are just the beginning. The real fun comes when you start combining knowledge of multiple protocols to troubleshoot complex issues or optimize network performance. For example, you might need to analyze TCP traffic and correlate it with DNS or HTTP traffic to understand why a website is loading slowly. Or, you might use packet analysis to identify inefficient protocols that are consuming too much bandwidth and recommend more efficient alternatives. The possibilities are endless, and the more protocols you learn, the more versatile you become as a network analyst.

With Wireshark, you have an incredibly powerful tool at your disposal, but it's up to you to explore and experiment. Every capture is an opportunity to decode new protocols, troubleshoot network problems, and even discover hidden issues you didn't know existed. The key is to keep practicing, stay curious, and continue learning about the many protocols that make up the vast network of communication we use every day. As you dive deeper into the world of packet analysis, you'll begin to see patterns, recognize behaviors, and develop an intuitive understanding of how networks function.

In the next chapters, we'll continue our exploration of protocols and dive deeper into how you can use this knowledge to troubleshoot specific issues, optimize network performance, and enhance security. But for now, take a moment to reflect on what you've learned. You've unlocked the ability to decode some of the most common protocols that drive the internet, and with each new protocol you explore, you're becoming more proficient at understanding the intricate web of data that makes modern communication possible. The world of packet analysis is vast and ever-changing, but with the skills you've developed, you're well on your way to becoming a network expert.

So, grab your Wireshark hat, dive into those captures, and keep decoding. Each packet you analyze is another step toward mastering the art of network traffic analysis. Keep learning, keep practicing, and most importantly, keep having fun with it—because in the world of packet analysis, the journey is just as exciting as the destination. Happy decoding!

Chapter 8: Mastering Packet Capture Best Practices

Welcome to the world of packet capturing, where every bit of data is precious, and every packet is a clue to unraveling the mysteries of your network. But before you dive in and start capturing packets like a wild, unchecked data collector, let's slow down a bit. As with any powerful tool, there are best practices that'll help you make the most out of your captures, without drowning in a sea of irrelevant information. Think of packet capturing like fishing—you don't want to cast your net too wide, but you also don't want to miss the good catch by being too selective. Mastering the art of packet capturing is about knowing when to cast, how wide to spread the net, and how to reel in exactly what you need.

First things first, let's talk about **choosing the right network interface**. When you launch Wireshark, you're presented with a list of network interfaces to capture from. Choosing the correct one is key—after all, you can't catch a fish in the wrong pond. If you're on a wired connection, you'll want to select the Ethernet adapter, and if you're using Wi-Fi, pick your wireless adapter. If you're capturing traffic from a virtual machine or remote host, there may be additional interfaces to consider. You'll want to ensure you're capturing on the right interface to avoid unnecessary data and ensure that you're capturing the traffic you need.

Next, consider **filtering your captures from the start**. It's tempting to just hit "Start" and let Wireshark capture everything, but unless you're hunting for *everything* (which, let's be honest, you're probably not), filters will save you from drowning in packet overload. By applying capture filters, you limit the traffic being captured at the very source, saving you from the hassle of filtering through unnecessary packets later. For example, if you're troubleshooting a website issue, use a filter like `tcp port 80` to capture only HTTP traffic. This reduces your workload and ensures that you're focusing on the right packets right from the start.

Limit the capture duration to avoid capturing too much data. We've all been there—you hit "Start," walk away, and come back hours later to find that your capture file has bloated to gigabytes. While it may seem tempting to capture everything in hopes of catching the elusive network bug, long captures can lead to performance problems and large, unmanageable files. Instead, try to capture traffic in smaller time windows, ideally in intervals when the issue you're troubleshooting is most likely to happen. This not only helps you avoid massive files but also ensures that the capture data is more relevant to the problem at hand.

Set a capture filter that's specific to your problem, and avoid capturing everything you can see. It's tempting to set a catch-all filter like "any," but this is where it's easy to fall into the trap of capturing far more data than you need. If you're troubleshooting DNS, use `udp port 53` as your filter. For HTTP traffic, use `tcp port 80`. By focusing your captures on specific protocols or traffic types, you'll spend less time sifting through irrelevant packets and more time analyzing the ones that matter.

Enable promiscuous mode only when necessary. Promiscuous mode allows Wireshark to capture all packets on the network, not just those addressed to your machine. While this is useful when you need to see everything, it's not always necessary. If you're troubleshooting a specific issue on your machine, there's no need to enable promiscuous mode. Enabling promiscuous mode for unnecessary captures increases the amount of traffic Wireshark processes, and that can slow things down, especially on busy networks.

Once you've got your filters set, you'll want to keep **an eye on your capture file size**. Large capture files are like trying to carry a suitcase that's far too big for what you actually need. Over time, a huge file can slow down your computer and make it difficult to find the key information you're looking for. If you're capturing for a long time, use Wireshark's option to limit the file size. For example, you could set it to stop capturing once the file reaches 100MB. This will prevent you from hitting the dreaded file size cap, while still capturing all the necessary packets.

Consider using ring buffers for long captures. If you're capturing for an extended period, especially in environments like production networks, ring buffers allow you to limit the size of the capture file. As one file fills up, Wireshark automatically creates a new file, keeping your capture manageable. It's like having a series of small, bite-sized data files instead of one massive log that you can't even open. Ring buffers are a great way to manage long-term packet captures without worrying about the data growing too large to handle.

Now, let's talk about **reducing capture noise**. The world of networking is noisy—there's a lot of unnecessary traffic that can distract you from the problem you're trying to solve. These can include things like ARP requests, broadcasts, or even your printer chatting away on the network. Use Wireshark's filtering capabilities to cut out this unwanted noise and focus only on what's relevant. The better you filter out the irrelevant traffic, the quicker you'll be able to spot the issue and move on to solving it.

Don't forget to **monitor the capture process**. While Wireshark is working its magic in the background, it's easy to get distracted by other tasks. But if you're capturing for an extended period, it's important to check in periodically. Make sure your capture hasn't filled up, and ensure the data still looks relevant. If you're capturing data for an issue that's intermittent, it's best to keep an eye on it and stop the capture once you've gotten the data you need.

Label your captures thoughtfully. You wouldn't name a book "Untitled," right? Well, the same goes for packet captures. It's crucial to give each capture a clear and descriptive name so you can identify it later. This is especially important if you're capturing over an extended period or working with multiple captures. Instead of "Capture1," name it something more specific, like "WiFi Slowness – 2023-04-08." This way, when you need to go back and reference the data, you'll know exactly what you're looking at. Trust me, you'll thank yourself later.

Avoid capturing too much metadata. Every packet in your capture file has additional metadata, like timestamps and protocol info. While this data is useful, it can also add unnecessary bulk to your capture. By limiting the amount of metadata you capture (such as packet length, IP addresses, and so on), you can reduce the file size and improve performance. You don't need every tiny detail about every packet—you just need the relevant bits to troubleshoot your issue.

If you're dealing with high-speed networks, **adjust the capture buffer size**. High-speed networks can generate packets at a blistering pace, and Wireshark's default buffer might not be able to handle the volume. If you find that your capture is missing packets or that packets are being dropped, it's time to increase the buffer size. This ensures that your system can store all the packets, even under high traffic conditions. You want to make sure your capture is as complete as possible, so adjusting this setting is a key move.

As you get more comfortable with packet capturing, you'll also begin to **fine-tune your capture settings** for specific protocols. For example, capturing VoIP traffic might require a different approach than capturing web traffic. For VoIP, you might want to capture packets that include the RTP (Real-time Transport Protocol), which handles audio and video streams. By tailoring your capture settings for each type of traffic, you can ensure that you're capturing all the relevant packets for your analysis.

In case things go wrong, **know how to handle capture corruption**. Capturing large amounts of data over long periods of time can sometimes result in file corruption. While this is relatively rare, it's essential to have a backup plan. Wireshark offers tools to verify the integrity of the capture file, and if corruption does occur, it's often possible to recover at least part of the data. Having a strategy in place to handle corruption will save you a lot of headaches if the worst happens.

A less exciting but crucial part of packet capture is **securing your captures**. Packet captures often contain sensitive data, especially if you're dealing with protocols like HTTP, DNS, or even unencrypted email. It's essential to keep your capture files secure, especially if you're working in a professional or enterprise environment. Never leave them lying around in plain view, and if possible, use encryption to protect the data in your captures. It's about keeping your analysis secure, so that unauthorized users can't gain access to sensitive network traffic.

Lastly, let's talk about **regular cleanup**. As you capture packets and gather data, your disk will fill up quickly. Regularly cleaning up unnecessary capture files ensures you don't end up with a storage nightmare. After completing a capture session, go through your files and delete any that aren't essential to your work. It's a small but important habit that will keep your system running smoothly and your workspace organized.

By following these best practices, you'll be capturing packets like a pro in no time. The more you refine your technique, the more efficient and effective your packet captures will be. You'll spend less time digging through irrelevant data and more time solving the actual network issues at hand. So, now that you're armed with the knowledge of packet capture best practices, go forth and capture with confidence. Your network awaits!

With all these packet capture best practices in your toolkit, you're now ready to approach network analysis with precision and efficiency. The process of capturing network traffic isn't just about blindly collecting data—it's about being strategic, organized, and purposeful in your approach. Whether you're troubleshooting a slow network, diagnosing connection issues, or just observing traffic for analysis, following these best practices ensures that your captures are clean, manageable, and highly relevant to the problem you're investigating.

By focusing on filtering your captures from the start, you avoid unnecessary clutter and make your data more manageable. This practice not only saves you time but also helps ensure that your captures are targeted and specific to the issue you're facing. If you're dealing with high volumes of data, capturing in shorter windows or with tighter filters ensures that you stay on task and aren't overwhelmed by endless packets that aren't relevant to your analysis.

It's important to remember that **data integrity is key**. Whether you're working with sensitive traffic or trying to pinpoint a critical issue, maintaining the integrity of your capture files should be one of your top priorities. Backing up your data and securing your captures is crucial in professional environments, where data leakage or corruption can lead to significant issues. Keep your capture files organized, secure, and clean, and you'll find that the network analysis process is far more streamlined and effective.

As you gain experience, **customizing your capture settings** for different protocols will become second nature. Each type of network traffic has its own quirks, and knowing how to tweak Wireshark's settings for VoIP traffic, HTTP sessions, or DNS queries can drastically improve the quality of your captures. It's like knowing how to use the right tool for the job—whether you're catching a rare fish or diagnosing a rogue packet, having the right settings ensures that you're not missing out on vital data.

One of the most empowering aspects of packet capturing is **developing your own efficient workflow**. Once you've mastered the best practices, you'll start creating your own set of procedures for common issues. You'll know exactly how to configure your filters, adjust capture settings, and organize your files for easy retrieval. A solid workflow will help you reduce the time spent on capturing data, leaving more time to focus on analyzing packets and resolving issues.

As you progress, don't forget about the potential for **real-time analysis**. Sometimes, a live capture is the only way to catch an issue as it happens. For example, if a user is experiencing network slowness, you can start a real-time capture and watch for any anomalies or bottlenecks while they're occurring. By applying filters on the fly, you can focus in on specific traffic and identify issues immediately, without needing to sift through hours of captured data later. Real-time packet captures are an invaluable skill that can make your troubleshooting efforts faster and more efficient.

In addition to real-time analysis, **using Wireshark's advanced features** can dramatically speed up your analysis process. Features like "Follow TCP Stream," "Statistics," and "Expert Info" are indispensable when analyzing complex traffic patterns. "Follow TCP Stream" lets you trace an entire conversation between two devices, which is especially helpful for diagnosing application-layer issues like slow website load times or dropped connections. Meanwhile, "Expert Info" highlights anomalies in your capture, pointing out potential issues like retransmissions, misconfigurations, or abnormal connection terminations.

As you dive deeper into packet captures, **be mindful of network security**. Capturing network traffic can expose sensitive data, such as passwords, cookies, and unencrypted emails, so it's essential to always consider the security implications of your work. Whether you're working in an enterprise environment or on a personal project, it's important to secure your capture files and be aware of the data you're handling. This includes using encryption where necessary and ensuring that your packet analysis activities comply with relevant security policies and regulations.

Finally, **don't forget to document your captures and findings**. Just as you wouldn't build a house without blueprints, don't perform a packet capture without keeping clear notes on what you're trying to analyze and what you've found. Not only does this help keep your analysis organized, but it also enables you to track the progress of troubleshooting efforts and share findings with others. Whether it's exporting packets for further analysis, taking notes on potential issues, or creating a report for stakeholders, proper documentation is key to maintaining clarity and improving team collaboration.

The goal of packet capturing is to solve problems efficiently and effectively. By following best practices, you eliminate much of the guesswork and streamline the entire process. From setting filters that refine your captures to organizing your data, every step you take toward mastering packet capture helps you become more proficient in solving network issues. Keep refining your process, stay organized, and be disciplined in your approach, and soon enough, packet capturing will become second nature.

In the next chapters, we'll take all of this knowledge and apply it to specific use cases, such as troubleshooting complex network issues, analyzing specific protocols, and using advanced Wireshark features. By building on these best practices, you'll be able to troubleshoot faster, optimize performance, and enhance your security posture. But for now, take a moment to appreciate the power of a good capture. With the right practices in place, you're well on your way to becoming a network analysis master. Happy capturing!

Chapter 9: Wireshark Statistics Tools

Welcome to the world of Wireshark's statistics tools—where raw packet data transforms into meaningful insights. If packet capturing is the art of collecting information, then statistics is the science of making sense of it. While Wireshark's main interface is excellent for diving deep into individual packets, the statistics tools take a step back and let you see the forest for the trees. Think of these tools as your trusty map, guiding you through the vast jungle of network traffic, and helping you identify areas that need attention. If you're a network detective, the statistics tools are like your magnifying glass, highlighting patterns and anomalies that you wouldn't see by just looking at individual packets.

Let's kick things off with **I/O Graphs**, one of the most powerful statistical tools Wireshark offers. I/O graphs let you visualize packet flow over time, which can be invaluable when you're troubleshooting performance issues or trying to see how traffic changes during specific events. With I/O graphs, you can track packets per second, bytes per second, or even the rate of protocol-specific traffic over time. It's like having a time-lapse view of your network traffic—what might look like a chaotic mess of packets in the capture window suddenly becomes clear when you see the peaks and valleys on a graph. This is especially helpful for spotting bottlenecks or bursts of traffic that might not be immediately obvious in a packet-by-packet view.

I/O graphs are also highly customizable. You can choose what data to track, adjust the time window, and apply filters to focus on the exact traffic you're interested in. Whether you're looking to monitor HTTP traffic spikes, identify periods of high latency, or investigate sudden drops in throughput, I/O graphs give you the ability to see exactly how your network is behaving over time. They provide a visual representation of the data, making it easier to spot trends and anomalies that you can then investigate in more detail. They're like the network version of a radar—always scanning for something interesting.

Next up, we have **Protocol Hierarchy**, another gem in Wireshark's statistics toolkit. The Protocol Hierarchy tool gives you a high-level overview of all the protocols present in your packet capture, broken down by the percentage of traffic each protocol represents. It's like reading the contents of a buffet laid out before you, where each dish represents a different protocol. You can see how much of your traffic is HTTP, how much is DNS, and how much is other protocols like ARP or TCP. This is incredibly useful if you're trying to identify which protocols are dominating the network and whether that's expected or problematic. For example, if you're troubleshooting web traffic and see that DNS traffic is disproportionately high, it could be a sign of DNS resolution issues, which would be the next area to investigate.

The Protocol Hierarchy tool also gives you the ability to dig deeper into individual protocols. Once you've seen that HTTP makes up 40% of your traffic, you can expand it to get a breakdown of the HTTP methods, like GET or POST requests, and even track which URLs are being requested the most. This level of insight is invaluable for troubleshooting network performance or diagnosing web application issues. It's like having a microscope that zooms in to reveal all the tiny details behind the bigger picture.

If you're dealing with complex network behavior or a high volume of traffic, **Conversations** can be a lifesaver. The Conversations tool groups packets by conversation, allowing you to see the total amount of traffic exchanged between specific pairs of devices. It's like having a detailed list of every phone call made between two people, with each call showing the duration, number of packets exchanged, and the amount of data transferred. Conversations can help you pinpoint which devices are communicating the most, and this is useful for finding outliers or unexpected communication patterns that might be causing issues.

The Conversations tool isn't just for TCP traffic—it can also track other protocols like UDP, HTTP, and even Bluetooth traffic. This makes it an incredibly versatile tool for analyzing all kinds of network communication. Whether you're troubleshooting slow downloads, identifying rogue devices, or investigating security concerns, the Conversations tool helps you focus on the traffic between specific devices, allowing for more targeted troubleshooting. It's like having a detailed log of all the "conversations" your network devices are having, with all the important metrics neatly summarized in one place.

Want to go even deeper? The **Endpoints** tool allows you to see the communication stats for each device on your network. This tool lists all devices involved in the capture, showing you how much traffic each device has sent and received. It's a great way to identify which devices are using the most bandwidth or causing traffic spikes. Think of it like a leaderboard of network activity, where you can see the top talkers in terms of traffic volume. If you're investigating a network slowdown, this tool will help you quickly identify the devices that might be consuming all the available bandwidth. You can even drill down into each device's traffic to see what protocols and ports it's using, helping you uncover the source of any performance problems.

Now, let's talk about **Flow Graphs**, which take the concept of analyzing conversations a step further. Flow Graphs give you a visual representation of packet exchanges between two devices, showing you the flow of data between them. Each node represents a device, and the edges between them represent the packets being sent. This is a fantastic tool when you need to understand the sequence of events in a particular network conversation. For example, you can use Flow Graphs to visualize a TCP handshake and see the exchange of SYN, SYN-ACK, and ACK packets. It's like watching a series of events unfold in slow motion, helping you spot any missteps in the protocol flow that might be causing problems.

Flow Graphs also let you track round-trip times and retransmissions, which are crucial metrics when you're troubleshooting network performance. By identifying the time delays between packets and spotting any retransmissions, you can pinpoint network latency or packet loss issues. These visual tools are great for those who prefer seeing their data in a graphical format rather than just scrolling through lines of text. It's like having a network detective's magnifying glass, giving you a detailed look at the sequence of events that lead up to an issue.

Let's not forget about **Statistics for specific protocols**, which provide insights into the individual performance of different protocols in your network. Wireshark offers protocol-specific statistics for TCP, HTTP, DNS, and more. For example, the TCP statistics tool shows you things like the number of retransmissions, the number of connections, and the amount of data transferred. This is incredibly useful for identifying problems with protocol performance, such as slow connection setups, connection resets, or high retransmission rates. It's like having a health check for each protocol, allowing you to spot any protocol-specific issues that might be affecting your network.

For instance, HTTP statistics can tell you how many HTTP requests and responses occurred during the capture, as well as the total size of the data transferred. This can help you determine if a website or application is consuming more bandwidth than expected. DNS statistics, on the other hand, can show you how many DNS queries were made, whether they were resolved successfully, and how long it took to resolve them. If you're seeing a large number of unresolved DNS queries, that could indicate a DNS server problem that needs your attention. These protocol-specific statistics give you a deep dive into the performance and behavior of each protocol, which is invaluable when troubleshooting specific issues.

Don't overlook **TCP Stream Analysis**—it's a quick way to follow the entire conversation between two endpoints. This tool lets you isolate and analyze individual TCP streams, making it easier to track issues with specific connections. Whether you're troubleshooting a slow web page load or analyzing a file transfer, TCP Stream Analysis will show you all the packets exchanged between two devices in a particular stream. This is especially helpful for spotting anomalies, such as retransmissions, delays, or connection resets that might be causing performance issues.

If you're more interested in **packet loss or delays**, Wireshark offers the **TCP Analysis** tool to help you track these issues across your capture. It highlights signs of packet loss and provides round-trip time statistics, helping you identify network congestion or other issues that might be causing delays. This is invaluable when dealing with slow connections or unreliable networks, as it helps pinpoint exactly where the bottleneck is occurring. By isolating where the delays or losses are happening, you can take targeted steps to resolve the issue.

Finally, remember that **Wireshark's statistics tools are a treasure trove of information**, but they're most effective when combined with your packet analysis skills. Using statistics tools in conjunction with the detailed packet view allows you to gain a complete understanding of what's happening on your network. These tools aren't just about visualizing data—they're about providing you with actionable insights that help you solve problems faster, whether you're diagnosing a slow network, optimizing performance, or ensuring network security.

In the next chapters, we'll delve deeper into how you can use these statistics tools for real-world troubleshooting and optimization. For now, take some time to explore Wireshark's various statistics tools. Play with the graphs, dive into the flow charts, and get comfortable with the data Wireshark is giving you. The more familiar you become with these tools, the better equipped you'll be to solve complex network problems and get your network running at its best. Happy analyzing!

Now that we've explored the wide range of **Wireshark's statistics tools**, you should be feeling much more confident in your ability to harness their full potential. These tools give you a powerful lens through which you can view your network traffic, uncover patterns, and troubleshoot issues. The beauty of Wireshark's statistics is that they transform raw, chaotic packet data into something you can analyze and act upon. Whether you're trying to fix a slow connection, investigate security concerns, or optimize your network's performance, these tools provide the clarity and insight you need.

One of the great things about Wireshark is that its statistics tools are customizable. You can choose which metrics are most relevant to your analysis and configure Wireshark to focus on them. This level of flexibility makes Wireshark a tool that can be tailored to your specific needs —whether you're a network engineer monitoring traffic in real time or a security analyst looking for signs of malicious activity. By experimenting with the different statistics tools, you can develop your own workflow, making packet analysis faster, more efficient, and more intuitive.

Of course, the best way to truly master Wireshark's statistics tools is through practice. Don't be afraid to dive into different capture files and play with the graphs and charts. The more you explore, the more patterns and trends you'll recognize, and soon enough, you'll be able to identify network issues at a glance. Whether it's spotting a bottleneck in an I/O graph or noticing an unusual spike in DNS traffic, these tools are your key to unlocking the story behind the data.

Another important takeaway is that **Wireshark's statistics tools are not just for troubleshooting—they can also be used for proactive network monitoring**. By regularly using the I/O graphs, protocol hierarchy, and flow analysis tools, you can stay ahead of potential issues and address them before they escalate into serious problems. This proactive approach helps you maintain a healthy, efficient network, minimizing downtime and optimizing performance. Think of it as a digital fitness tracker for your network—it lets you monitor performance over time and catch problems early.

As you continue your journey through Wireshark's statistics, remember that each tool serves a different purpose, and the more you understand them, the more powerful your network analysis becomes. While some tools are excellent for high-level overviews, like the protocol hierarchy or endpoint statistics, others—like TCP stream analysis and flow graphs—are better suited for detailed, low-level analysis. Understanding when to use each tool is a vital part of becoming proficient at packet analysis.

It's also worth noting that **Wireshark's statistics tools are invaluable for troubleshooting both small-scale and large-scale networks**. For instance, if you're working on a small home network, a quick look at the protocol hierarchy might show that a particular device is sending too many DNS requests, which could be a sign of a misconfiguration. On a larger enterprise network, these same tools can help you spot communication issues between servers, monitor traffic across different subnets, or even track down security breaches. In both scenarios, Wireshark's statistics allow you to analyze traffic in a way that's both comprehensive and granular.

Now, it's time to take all of this knowledge and apply it to real-world scenarios. In future chapters, we'll be focusing on how you can leverage Wireshark's statistics tools to troubleshoot specific network problems, optimize performance, and even enhance your security posture. You'll learn how to use these tools in combination with other diagnostic methods, such as ping tests, traceroutes, and firewall logs, to develop a more holistic approach to network analysis. This will help you become the go-to person for network troubleshooting in any environment, whether it's a home network or a corporate data center.

But for now, take a moment to appreciate the power you now have at your fingertips. Wireshark's statistics tools give you the ability to view your network traffic through a microscope or a telescope, depending on the situation. Whether you need to analyze one packet in detail or observe network-wide trends, these tools are there to help you see the full picture. The more you practice with them, the sharper your skills will become, and soon enough, you'll be identifying and resolving network issues faster than you can say "packet loss."

So, go ahead—open up a new capture, explore the statistics tools, and get familiar with the various views they offer. As you dive deeper into the world of network analysis, you'll realize that these tools aren't just useful—they're essential. From pinpointing performance issues to uncovering security threats, Wireshark's statistics tools will be your trusted sidekick, helping you make informed decisions and keep your network running smoothly. Happy capturing, analyzing, and troubleshooting! Your network adventure is just beginning.

Chapter 10: TCP Troubleshooting

Ah, TCP—the reliable, well-behaved cousin of network protocols. If you've spent much time in the world of networking, you've probably heard of TCP. It's the protocol that makes sure data gets to where it needs to go, in order, with all the necessary acknowledgments, handshakes, and checks along the way. It's like that friend who double-checks that you've received their text, waits for your thumbs-up, and then gives you a summary of what's going on, just to be sure. But even this meticulous protocol can get into trouble from time to time. And when it does, you're going to want to know how to diagnose and fix it. This chapter is all about learning how to troubleshoot TCP problems using Wireshark.

TCP is known for being a reliable, connection-oriented protocol, which means it takes care of things like packet order and retransmissions. So, when something goes wrong, it's usually pretty clear—like a postal service that forgets to deliver your package, or worse, delivers it to the wrong address. One of the first things to look for when diagnosing TCP issues is the **three-way handshake**. The handshake is the foundation of any TCP connection, and it happens when two devices agree on how they'll communicate. When the handshake fails, it's like someone showing up at the door to deliver a package but forgetting the delivery instructions—nothing gets through.

In Wireshark, if you don't see a full three-way handshake (SYN, SYN-ACK, ACK), you've probably got a connection issue. A successful handshake goes like this: The sender sends a **SYN** packet, the receiver responds with a **SYN-ACK**, and the sender replies with an **ACK**. If one of these packets is missing, something is blocking the connection. You'll often see this if a firewall is filtering out traffic or if there's a network configuration issue, preventing the devices from communicating. The handshake is the dance that starts the connection, and if it's interrupted, no data can be sent.

Another thing to keep an eye on is **TCP resets (RST)**. If you see a lot of **RST** flags in your capture, it's like a computer slamming the door in someone's face during the handshake process. A **TCP RST** packet is a way for a device to terminate a connection immediately. It's sent by either party to force the closure of a connection, typically due to an error or misconfiguration. If you're troubleshooting a TCP issue and you see RST packets being sent unexpectedly, it means one side is refusing to continue the conversation. This could indicate a server that's overloaded, an application error, or a misconfigured router dropping the connection.

Next, let's talk about **TCP retransmissions**. If you see packets being resent over and over again, that's a sign that the network isn't working as smoothly as it should be. TCP is a "reliable" protocol, which means it's designed to resend packets if it doesn't receive an acknowledgment within a certain time. This is useful for ensuring that no data is lost, but it can also indicate network congestion, faulty cables, or router issues when it happens too frequently. In Wireshark, retransmitted packets are easy to spot because they often have a "TCP Retransmission" label. If you're seeing a lot of retransmissions, it's time to start investigating the network infrastructure for problems.

Another issue you'll encounter when troubleshooting TCP is **out-of-order packets**. TCP is designed to guarantee that packets arrive in the right order. However, sometimes packets get delayed or rerouted and arrive out of sequence. This can cause delays or problems in application performance. Wireshark makes it easy to spot out-of-order packets by displaying a "TCP Out-Of-Order" message. These packets are usually part of a larger communication sequence, so if you see them frequently, it could indicate congestion, a misconfigured router, or a failing network device that's messing with the flow.

Window size is another crucial factor when troubleshooting TCP. The window size defines how much data can be sent before an acknowledgment is required. A small window size can lead to slow data transfers because it forces frequent acknowledgments, causing more round trips. In Wireshark, you can examine the TCP window size to see how much data is being sent before the receiver must acknowledge it. If you notice that the window size is unusually small, it might be time to look into the sender's buffer settings or investigate if there's any network delay causing the window size to shrink.

When troubleshooting TCP performance, **delayed acknowledgments** can also cause problems. TCP is designed to use efficient mechanisms to acknowledge received packets, but sometimes those acknowledgments can get delayed, which results in slower data transfer rates. If you see delayed ACKs in Wireshark, it might mean that either the sender or receiver is overwhelmed or that there's a bottleneck somewhere in the network. This is a common issue in networks with high traffic, so if you're seeing delays, it's worth investigating congestion points or looking into the configuration of network devices.

Next, let's consider **TCP keep-alive packets**, which help maintain an open connection between two devices. If your capture reveals a lot of keep-alive packets being sent and received, it could mean that the connection is having trouble staying active. These packets are usually small and sent periodically to ensure that the connection hasn't timed out. If you see an unusual number of keep-alive packets, it might indicate that a device is struggling to maintain a connection due to network instability or an idle timeout setting that's too aggressive.

Speaking of timeouts, **TCP connection timeouts** are another big indicator of issues. If you're troubleshooting a service that isn't responding, a connection timeout in the TCP stream can tell you exactly where the process breaks down. Wireshark can help you spot timeouts by highlighting them in the stream view, which will allow you to see which side of the connection isn't responding. If you're seeing frequent timeouts, it's likely that the server or device you're trying to reach is overwhelmed, down, or having network routing issues.

One of the most elusive TCP issues to troubleshoot is **network congestion**. When there's too much traffic on the network, packets get delayed, retransmitted, or dropped altogether. This can result in TCP delays and slow data transfer rates. The easiest way to spot network congestion in Wireshark is by looking for long delays between packets and repeated retransmissions. If you're seeing slowdowns that don't have an obvious cause, it might be time to check the overall health of the network, including bandwidth usage and latency.

TCP is also prone to **buffer overflow problems**, especially in high-traffic environments. When a device's buffer fills up, it can't accept any more data until it processes what it already has. This results in delayed ACKs and retransmissions as TCP tries to resend data. In Wireshark, buffer issues can often be spotted by looking at the sequence of events and identifying places where the flow of data stops for longer than expected. If you see these gaps, especially on the server-side, it could mean that the buffer size needs to be adjusted or that the device is overloaded.

You'll also want to keep an eye on **duplicate ACKs**, which are often a sign of packet loss. When a device receives out-of-order packets, it sends a duplicate acknowledgment to indicate that it's waiting for the missing packet. This is Wireshark's way of signaling that something went wrong, and the network is trying to recover. If you're seeing a high number of duplicate ACKs, it's worth investigating for packet loss, which can be caused by faulty hardware, congestion, or even a poor wireless connection.

As a **TCP troubleshooter**, it's important to remember that Wireshark isn't always going to give you a clear answer with a big red flag that says "problem here." Often, you have to piece together clues from various events in the packet stream. Retransmissions, out-of-order packets, timeouts, and RST flags—each of these can be part of the puzzle. Sometimes, you need to analyze the sequence of packets over time, correlate them with other network activity, and follow your intuition to uncover the issue.

You also want to pay attention to **window scaling** when troubleshooting high-speed networks. The window size and scaling factor determine how much data can be sent before an acknowledgment is required. On modern high-speed networks, window scaling is critical for ensuring fast data transfer. If the window size is too small or the scaling factor is incorrectly configured, the network will underperform. Wireshark lets you view these settings, so you can check whether window scaling is enabled and whether the scaling factor is appropriate for your network's speed.

Now, let's talk about **TCP sequence and acknowledgment numbers**. These are the DNA of a TCP connection—they help the sender and receiver keep track of what data has been sent and acknowledged. If the sequence or acknowledgment numbers don't line up properly, it can be a sign of packet loss or corruption. In Wireshark, you can trace these numbers to follow the flow of data and identify where things go wrong. Sequence number mismatches or unexpected gaps in the sequence are strong indicators of transmission problems.

Finally, **trace your TCP streams** using Wireshark's "Follow TCP Stream" feature. This tool lets you view the entire conversation between two devices, which is incredibly useful when debugging applications or services that rely on TCP connections. By isolating the stream and following the sequence of events, you can see exactly how the connection is behaving from start to finish, helping you pinpoint delays, resets, or protocol mismatches.

TCP troubleshooting is both an art and a science—understanding the sequence of events, analyzing patterns, and knowing when to apply the right tool can make all the difference. With Wireshark at your side, you have the ability to diagnose and fix TCP-related problems like a seasoned network detective. The next time you're faced with a slow connection, unexpected drops, or sluggish performance, you'll have the skills to dive in, dig through the data, and bring the problem to light.

As you gain more experience with TCP troubleshooting, you'll find that the key to solving problems lies in developing a keen eye for the subtle clues that Wireshark's packet captures provide. Think of it like solving a mystery—each packet is a small detail that, when combined with others, leads you closer to the culprit. From analyzing three-way handshakes to inspecting retransmissions and out-of-order packets, every piece of data has a story to tell. It's all about learning how to connect those dots.

One thing to always keep in mind is that TCP problems don't exist in a vacuum. They often occur alongside other network issues, such as congestion or faulty hardware. For example, a slow connection might not just be a problem with the server; it could be a result of network congestion or even a bad cable somewhere between the sender and receiver. This is why **cross-referencing data from multiple sources** is crucial. Use your Wireshark packet captures in tandem with other network tools, like ping tests, traceroutes, or system logs, to build a fuller picture of what's going wrong.

Let's not forget that TCP troubleshooting often involves a bit of trial and error. While Wireshark can give you detailed insight into what's happening, sometimes the solution involves making adjustments to network settings or hardware and seeing how the problem changes. If you're troubleshooting high latency or slow performance, for instance, you might start by adjusting buffer sizes or changing TCP window sizes. Small tweaks can have a big impact, but the process is often iterative. As you experiment, Wireshark will continue to guide you, showing you how the changes you make are reflected in the network traffic.

It's also important to understand that **TCP performance issues are not always about technical misconfigurations**. Sometimes, they're a result of network load or the sheer volume of traffic being processed. If you're dealing with a sudden surge in data or high application demand, the issue might not be with the protocol itself but with how your network is handling that volume. By examining the flow of data and pinpointing areas where congestion is occurring, you can identify whether performance issues are the result of an overload or if there's something more insidious at play, like a broken device or misconfigured routing.

If you're looking to improve your troubleshooting efficiency, **develop a systematic approach**. Start by focusing on the most basic and obvious causes—like ensuring the three-way handshake completes properly—then work your way down to the more complex potential issues, such as TCP window sizes, retransmissions, or advanced flow control settings. You'll find that, over time, you develop an intuitive sense of where to look first, making the troubleshooting process faster and more effective. Building this routine will help you handle even the trickiest TCP issues without breaking a sweat.

Don't underestimate the value of learning from past troubleshooting sessions. Wireshark captures are invaluable tools, and reviewing previous captures from past incidents can provide insight into recurring problems. By identifying patterns or behaviors that have cropped up before, you can solve new issues faster and more accurately. It's like keeping a troubleshooting journal—you learn from each experience, and that knowledge helps you work smarter the next time a problem arises.

And while we're on the topic of learning from experience, let's not forget about **advanced network troubleshooting tools** that can complement your packet captures. Sometimes, Wireshark might not give you the full picture if there are other external factors at play, such as DNS resolution issues, security protocols, or application-level problems. By using additional tools like NetFlow, SNMP, or network performance monitoring solutions, you can gain even more visibility into how traffic is being handled across your network. These tools can provide real-time insights into your network's performance, helping you correlate what's happening at the packet level with broader network behavior.

As you dig into TCP troubleshooting, it's also important to develop an understanding of **network congestion management techniques**. TCP congestion control is responsible for preventing a network from becoming overwhelmed with data. When the network experiences congestion, the TCP window size may shrink, which can lead to performance slowdowns. Understanding how different congestion control algorithms work, such as **slow start**, **congestion avoidance**, and **fast recovery**, can help you spot potential issues with TCP traffic under heavy load and guide your troubleshooting efforts.

Another valuable skill to develop is the ability to **interpret application behavior** in the context of TCP. Many applications rely heavily on TCP for data transmission, so performance problems in these applications can often be traced back to TCP inefficiencies. For example, an HTTP request that's running slowly may not be a result of the application itself but rather an issue with how the underlying TCP connection is being established or maintained. By viewing application traffic within the context of TCP, you can often identify the root cause of slow application performance.

Don't forget the importance of documenting your findings. One of the most powerful things you can do as a TCP troubleshooter is to keep a record of your analysis process. Whether it's through annotated captures, summary reports, or just taking notes on the specific behaviors you've observed, documentation ensures that you can reference past issues in the future. It also helps your team stay aligned and ensures that everyone involved in troubleshooting has a clear understanding of the issue and the steps taken to resolve it. This documentation becomes invaluable when similar problems arise again, providing a solid reference point for quicker resolution.

In many cases, **TCP troubleshooting is not a one-time job**. Once you've solved the immediate issue, it's important to monitor the network to ensure that the fix holds and doesn't cause new problems. For instance, if you've adjusted the TCP window size or fixed retransmissions, monitor the network over the next few days or weeks to ensure that performance improves and remains stable. Use tools like Wireshark's statistics or external monitoring systems to ensure the network continues to run smoothly. Preventative monitoring can often catch issues before they escalate, saving you from more serious headaches later.

As you continue troubleshooting TCP, don't be afraid to **get comfortable with advanced Wireshark features**. Features like TCP Stream analysis, expert information, and even advanced filters can help you zero in on exactly what's happening in the connection. These tools give you a level of control that's indispensable when dealing with more complex TCP issues, such as fine-tuning the behavior of a particular stream or analyzing the performance of a specific TCP connection over time.

Finally, remember that **TCP troubleshooting is an art, not a science**. While Wireshark gives you an incredible level of insight, sometimes solving the problem requires creativity. It's about knowing how to interpret the data, applying your troubleshooting knowledge, and experimenting with different fixes until you find the solution that works. Over time, you'll develop an intuitive understanding of how TCP works, what behaviors are normal, and where things are likely to go wrong. And when you solve that elusive TCP issue that's been causing headaches, you'll feel like a networking superhero.

TCP troubleshooting isn't just about identifying problems—it's about solving them. By applying the skills you've learned in this chapter, you'll become a more confident and effective troubleshooter. With Wireshark as your sidekick, you'll be ready to dive into any TCP issue, dissect it with precision, and come out the other side with a solution that makes your network run smoother than ever. Happy troubleshooting!

Chapter 11: Exploring UDP and Other Protocols

Ah, UDP—the wild child of networking protocols. Unlike its more disciplined cousin TCP, which insists on reliability and order, UDP is carefree, fast, and often a bit reckless. UDP, or User Datagram Protocol, is used when speed is more important than ensuring that every packet is received in order, acknowledged, or retransmitted. If TCP is the overprotective parent, UDP is the rebellious teenager who's more interested in getting to the party than making sure every invitation is accepted. In this chapter, we'll dive into the world of UDP and other protocols, exploring how they differ from TCP and how to troubleshoot issues related to them.

Let's start with **UDP's signature trait: simplicity**. Unlike TCP, which requires a handshake and a long series of acknowledgments to establish a connection, UDP skips all of that. It's like sending a postcard without worrying about whether it gets to the recipient. This makes UDP incredibly fast, but it also means that if a packet is lost, there's no automatic retransmission to recover it. For applications that require real-time performance, like video streaming or VoIP, the simplicity of UDP makes it an ideal choice, even if some data loss is inevitable. The tradeoff is that while UDP is fast, it's also more error-prone, and that's where your packet analysis skills come in.

When analyzing **UDP traffic in Wireshark**, you'll notice it's much more straightforward than TCP traffic. There are no sequence numbers, window sizes, or acknowledgment numbers to deal with. Instead, you'll typically see the source and destination port numbers, which are used to identify the application layer protocols. It's like walking into a crowded room where everyone's talking but no one's keeping track of who's saying what to whom. This lack of structure can make troubleshooting tricky, but if you're looking at an application that uses UDP, such as DNS or VoIP, you'll quickly realize how useful it is to understand how these applications behave within the context of UDP.

Speaking of **DNS (Domain Name System)**, let's take a moment to appreciate this protocol, which relies on UDP for its quick and simple requests. DNS queries are typically small and require fast resolution, so using UDP is a perfect fit. When you're troubleshooting a DNS issue, the first thing to look for is whether you're seeing **UDP packets** that contain DNS queries and responses. If DNS queries aren't being answered or if you're seeing a lot of retransmissions, it could indicate a problem with the DNS server or network connectivity. In Wireshark, DNS queries and responses are easily identified by the protocol label, and you'll also be able to view the queried domain names, which are especially useful when troubleshooting domain resolution issues.

Next, let's talk about **VoIP (Voice over IP)**, another heavyweight that uses UDP. If you've ever used a service like Skype or Zoom, you've used VoIP. VoIP relies on UDP because it prioritizes real-time performance over absolute reliability. In the world of voice communication, delays and jitter are worse than losing a few packets. When you're analyzing VoIP traffic in Wireshark, you'll typically see **RTP (Real-time Transport Protocol)** packets carried over UDP. RTP ensures that voice packets are sent with a timestamp so that they can be played back in the correct order, despite the inherent disorder of UDP. If you're troubleshooting VoIP quality, such as poor voice quality or dropped calls, Wireshark's ability to filter by **RTP** is invaluable.

Let's shift gears and talk about **HTTP/2 and HTTP/3**—two protocols that aim to improve the speed and efficiency of web traffic. HTTP/2, which is already widely adopted, enhances HTTP by enabling multiplexing, meaning multiple requests and responses can be sent over a single TCP connection. HTTP/3, however, takes it a step further by switching from TCP to **QUIC (Quick UDP Internet Connections)**, which uses UDP for even faster performance. The shift from TCP to UDP in HTTP/3 is designed to eliminate the connection setup time of TCP and improve web performance, especially in environments with high latency or packet loss. If you're analyzing HTTP/2 or HTTP/3 traffic in Wireshark, you'll notice the difference in behavior—specifically with HTTP/3, which uses **QUIC** packets over UDP. Understanding this shift is important as we move toward faster and more efficient web technologies.

While **HTTP/2 and HTTP/3** make use of UDP in some instances, most web traffic still uses **TCP**. However, it's important to note that while TCP and UDP are the two most commonly used transport protocols, there are others worth exploring. For instance, **FTP** (File Transfer Protocol) is used for transferring files between devices, often in data-heavy environments like servers and cloud storage systems. FTP typically uses **TCP** for reliability, ensuring that large files are transferred without losing data. However, in modern environments, **SFTP** (Secure FTP) is becoming more popular due to its added security layers via **SSH** (Secure Shell).

Speaking of security, another protocol you should be familiar with is **SSL/TLS (Secure Sockets Layer/Transport Layer Security)**. This protocol secures communications on the internet, often used in HTTPS to protect web traffic. SSL/TLS essentially wraps TCP traffic in an encrypted layer, ensuring that data sent between a web server and a client is kept private and secure. In Wireshark, SSL/TLS packets can be tricky because they're encrypted, but you can still analyze handshake information to see if any issues are occurring during the establishment of a secure connection. If you see problems with SSL/TLS handshakes, it could be a sign of an expired certificate, an unsupported encryption algorithm, or an issue with the certificate authority.

Let's take a moment to discuss **ICMP (Internet Control Message Protocol)**, another critical protocol that often gets overshadowed by TCP and UDP. ICMP is used for diagnostic purposes, such as with the "ping" command. While it's not usually used for transmitting regular data, it plays a critical role in network troubleshooting. When you run a ping test, for example, you're generating ICMP Echo Request and Echo Reply packets. In Wireshark, you can capture ICMP traffic to analyze network reachability, check for packet loss, and measure round-trip times. It's a simple protocol, but understanding ICMP can be crucial when diagnosing basic connectivity issues or network instability.

Another protocol worth mentioning is **SMTP (Simple Mail Transfer Protocol)**, which is used for sending emails. SMTP usually operates over TCP, and analyzing its packets can reveal a lot about how email traffic is flowing across your network. Wireshark allows you to examine SMTP sessions, including the sender and recipient information, the mail server's responses, and the email's size. If you're having trouble with email delivery or spam, looking at SMTP traffic in Wireshark can help identify issues related to mail servers, email routing, or blocked ports.

Let's not forget **DNS over HTTPS (DoH)**, an innovation in internet security that encrypts DNS queries via HTTPS. This provides enhanced privacy compared to traditional DNS requests, which are typically sent over UDP in plaintext. While DoH is still relatively new, its growing adoption is important for securing users' privacy by preventing eavesdropping or manipulation of DNS queries. When analyzing DoH traffic in Wireshark, you'll see DNS queries wrapped in HTTPS packets. This can be a bit more challenging to analyze compared to traditional DNS over UDP, but understanding DoH is important if you're focused on network security or privacy.

Speaking of privacy, another protocol gaining traction is **Tor (The Onion Router)**. Tor is a privacy-focused network that anonymizes your internet traffic by routing it through a series of volunteer-run servers, making it much harder to trace. It uses a variety of protocols, including **TCP**, but the real magic happens in how it creates anonymous circuits for routing traffic. While Tor isn't something you'll see frequently in everyday network traffic, being aware of how it works is important for analyzing network traffic that might be obfuscated or hidden. If you're trying to troubleshoot traffic on a network with Tor running, it can be tricky, since the traffic is deliberately disguised.

Let's circle back to **RTP** (Real-time Transport Protocol), which we briefly mentioned earlier. RTP is used in real-time communications like voice and video calls, and it typically runs over UDP. Unlike traditional packet-based protocols, RTP is optimized for real-time performance, meaning that it doesn't guarantee packet delivery or order. This tradeoff allows it to work more efficiently for live communications, where speed is paramount. When analyzing RTP in Wireshark, you'll want to check for **jitter** and **packet loss**, as these can significantly degrade voice or video quality. Wireshark's ability to analyze and visualize RTP streams makes it invaluable for troubleshooting VoIP or streaming issues.

Lastly, we come to **SNMP (Simple Network Management Protocol)**, a protocol used for managing devices on a network, such as routers, switches, and printers. SNMP allows you to monitor network devices, check their health, and gather performance data. In Wireshark, SNMP traffic appears as requests and responses between a management system and the devices it's monitoring. Troubleshooting SNMP involves looking at these packets to check if devices are sending the right information and if there are any problems with communication between the manager and the devices. If devices aren't reporting correctly, it's likely an issue with SNMP configuration or network connectivity.

The internet is full of protocols, each serving a different purpose, and while TCP and UDP are the heavy hitters, understanding how to troubleshoot and analyze other protocols like DNS, VoIP,

SMTP, and even SSL/TLS will make you a more complete network analyst. By expanding your knowledge of these protocols and knowing where to look when issues arise, you'll be better equipped to diagnose a wide variety of network problems. In the end, networking is all about understanding how data moves and how different protocols interact with each other—so the more you know, the more you'll be able to troubleshoot with confidence. Happy analyzing!

As you continue exploring **UDP and other protocols**, you'll begin to realize that troubleshooting isn't a one-size-fits-all process. Each protocol has its quirks and strengths, and understanding them allows you to diagnose issues with precision. While TCP is known for its reliability and order, UDP's speed and simplicity make it ideal for time-sensitive applications, even though it sacrifices the safety net of retransmission and ordering. Whether it's DNS queries flying fast and loose over UDP or RTP streams filling the airwaves with voice and video, Wireshark helps you capture, filter, and analyze all these protocols in ways that are invaluable for troubleshooting.

Understanding **UDP's unique role** in network communication will allow you to spot common issues, like packet loss, jitter, and latency, that could affect the performance of real-time applications. Unlike TCP, where retransmissions or sequence numbers can help identify problems, UDP leaves much more to chance. So, when you're troubleshooting UDP traffic, you're not just analyzing packets—you're learning to anticipate problems based on real-time behavior. Whether you're dealing with slow web requests, laggy VoIP calls, or dropped video streams, your packet analysis toolkit—complete with an understanding of UDP's quirks—will help you find the culprit and improve the experience.

It's also important to recognize that protocols like **HTTP, DNS, FTP, and others** are often just the tip of the iceberg. They rely on **TCP or UDP** to function, and without a deep understanding of how these transport protocols work, it can be difficult to diagnose performance issues accurately. For example, if a web page is loading slowly, the issue could be related to HTTP over TCP, but it could also be caused by DNS lookups via UDP, packet loss, or network congestion somewhere in the middle. The true magic of packet analysis happens when you connect the dots between the various protocols in the stack. That's when you unlock the power of Wireshark's ability to not just capture data, but tell you exactly where the traffic is flowing and why it's behaving the way it is.

You'll also find that **security concerns** come up with UDP and some of these other protocols. Unlike TCP, which ensures reliable connections and data integrity, UDP offers no such guarantees. This makes it a prime target for malicious activity, including DDoS attacks, DNS spoofing, and UDP floods. As you analyze network traffic, it's essential to keep an eye out for suspicious behavior that could indicate a security breach. This could be anything from unusual spikes in UDP traffic to malformed packets that suggest an attempt to exploit vulnerabilities in the network. Wireshark's expert info tool, along with your newfound understanding of UDP, will help you quickly identify anything that's out of the ordinary and take action before things escalate.

When it comes to analyzing **VoIP and RTP**, the complexity of real-time data transmission adds another layer to your analysis. RTP packets, which transport voice and video data, are often vulnerable to issues like jitter, packet loss, and latency, which can degrade the user experience.

Wireshark's ability to capture and analyze RTP streams lets you see these problems in real-time, helping you pinpoint where things are going wrong. It might be a matter of improper buffer settings, network congestion, or even codec mismatch. Being able to see the conversation between devices in Wireshark helps you understand the behavior of these applications, which is key to troubleshooting quality-of-service issues in VoIP.

Security protocols, like SSL/TLS, are yet another area that requires specific attention when troubleshooting. While they encrypt data, making it difficult to inspect directly, SSL/TLS traffic still reveals valuable information in Wireshark's packet captures, especially during the handshake process. By focusing on SSL/TLS handshakes, you can identify potential issues with certificate mismatches, unsupported encryption algorithms, or failed negotiations. If you're analyzing web traffic over HTTPS and it's slow or intermittent, checking the SSL/TLS handshake in Wireshark could provide insight into what's going wrong.

Another protocol that has an important role in **network management and monitoring** is **SNMP**. As simple as it sounds, SNMP allows you to manage and monitor devices such as routers, switches, and even printers across the network. When troubleshooting network devices, you can use Wireshark to capture SNMP requests and responses, and check whether the devices are responding properly to management commands. This is a great tool for network administrators, as it allows them to keep an eye on devices and spot potential failures before they affect the entire network. Whether you're troubleshooting slow devices, checking for unauthorized access, or analyzing overall network health, SNMP captures can provide key insights.

We can't talk about **protocols** without mentioning **FTP**—the File Transfer Protocol, which is often used in business and enterprise environments for transferring large files. FTP operates over TCP and has its own set of quirks that can make it tricky to troubleshoot, especially when file transfers are slow or interrupted. Wireshark helps you break down FTP commands, responses, and data transfers so you can see exactly where the bottleneck occurs—whether it's with the control channel, data channel, or somewhere in between. Once you've captured the traffic, you can examine the details of the commands and responses, which can reveal problems like port blocking, file permissions, or inefficient configurations.

Understanding the layers of network communication—from the physical layer up to the application layer—gives you the knowledge you need to troubleshoot complex problems that span multiple protocols. When you analyze a packet, you're seeing not just the data being transmitted but the behaviors and interactions of the various protocols in play. Take, for example, an **HTTP** request—while HTTP itself is easy to analyze, it relies on the **TCP** layer for reliable delivery, **DNS** for domain name resolution, and potentially even **SSL/TLS** for encryption. Understanding how each of these protocols fits into the overall communication picture allows you to see the root cause of an issue when things go wrong, whether it's a failed connection, a server misconfiguration, or an attack on the network.

In summary, exploring **UDP and other protocols** is about expanding your understanding of how data flows across the network and how different protocols interact to make things happen. Whether it's the real-time speed of UDP, the reliability of TCP, or the specialized behavior of protocols like DNS, VoIP, or SSL/TLS, understanding the inner workings of these protocols helps you become a better network troubleshooter. Wireshark is your go-to tool for analyzing all these protocols, from the ground up. As you continue to hone your skills, you'll find that the more protocols you explore, the better you get at spotting problems and resolving them swiftly.

So go ahead—capture more packets, dive into those UDP flows, and start identifying how your network traffic is behaving. Whether you're diagnosing a VoIP call that's too jittery, an FTP transfer that's too slow, or a DNS query that won't resolve, Wireshark gives you the tools to break down the problem, step by step. The world of networking protocols is vast, but with Wireshark by your side, you're well on your way to mastering the art of troubleshooting and becoming a network hero. Happy analyzing!

Chapter 12: Dealing with Encryption

Ah, encryption. The knight in shining armor of the internet, protecting your data from prying eyes and making sure that when you send your credit card info, no one but the intended recipient can read it. It's also the reason why packet analysis can sometimes feel like trying to solve a puzzle with half the pieces missing. When you're dealing with encrypted traffic, your usual tricks for dissecting packets won't give you the whole picture. In this chapter, we'll explore how to handle encrypted traffic in Wireshark and still get valuable insights without feeling like you're banging your head against the wall.

Let's start with **SSL/TLS**, which is the encryption protocol used by many applications, especially HTTPS. HTTPS is what keeps your online banking, shopping, and social media accounts safe from hackers and the nosy neighbor. When a website uses HTTPS, your browser and the web server establish an encrypted SSL/TLS connection before any data is transmitted. Wireshark can capture the handshake process and give you valuable information, like the version of SSL/TLS being used and which cipher suites were negotiated, but it won't show you the actual data unless you have the decryption key. It's like you can see the envelope, but you can't read the letter inside.

So, how do you get around this? **SSL decryption** in Wireshark is your key to reading encrypted traffic. The idea is simple: if you have access to the **private key** used in the SSL/TLS handshake, Wireshark can use it to decrypt the encrypted data and show you exactly what's going on inside. This works well if you're analyzing your own traffic, but let's face it—you're probably not going to have access to a website's private key. For your own traffic, though, you can configure your browser to log the session keys, which Wireshark can then use to decrypt the traffic. This is like getting a secret decoder ring that helps you unlock the hidden message.

If you don't have access to the private key, you might feel like you're in the middle of an encrypted blackout. But fear not! There are other ways to **analyze encrypted traffic** without decrypting it. One method is to examine the SSL/TLS handshake, which is not encrypted. This handshake gives you valuable insight into how the connection was established, including the protocols and cipher suites used. By examining the handshake, you can often figure out if there are issues with the SSL/TLS configuration, like an unsupported cipher or an expired certificate. Think of it as reading the cover letter to an encrypted message—you might not know what's inside, but you get an idea of how the communication started.

When it comes to **TLS 1.3**, the latest version of the protocol, there are a few added complications. TLS 1.3 uses **forward secrecy**, which means that the session keys used to encrypt the communication are not stored, making it harder to decrypt the traffic later. While this adds an extra layer of security, it also means that if you're trying to decrypt TLS 1.3 traffic in Wireshark, you might be out of luck unless you have access to the session keys during the communication. TLS 1.3 is the future of secure web traffic, and while it's excellent for security, it's also a bit of a headache for packet analysts who want to see inside the encrypted sessions.

But don't despair. Even when you can't decrypt the traffic, **Wireshark still gives you valuable information**. You can look at the size of the encrypted packets and the timing of their arrival, which can give you an idea of the network's performance. If you're troubleshooting a slow HTTPS connection, the encrypted packets may help you spot issues like latency or congestion, even though you can't see the contents of the traffic. It's like being able to measure the traffic jam without knowing exactly what cars are stuck in it.

Another thing to keep in mind when analyzing encrypted traffic is that **encrypted protocols can hide problems**. For example, if you're troubleshooting an issue with a website and the traffic is encrypted, you won't be able to see HTTP-level errors like a 404 or a 500. This can make troubleshooting trickier because you have to rely on other methods, like examining the SSL handshake or checking server-side logs. In a way, encryption can act like a security blanket that hides the real issues from view, but with the right tools and techniques, you can still get the answers you need.

When it comes to **Wi-Fi encryption**, the scenario is a bit different. Wi-Fi networks use encryption protocols like WPA2 or WPA3 to protect your wireless traffic. If you're capturing traffic on a Wi-Fi network, you might find that packets are encrypted using the Wi-Fi security protocol. To analyze this traffic, you'll need the Wi-Fi password or, in some cases, a **pre-shared key** (PSK). Once you've got that, Wireshark can decrypt the traffic for you, allowing you to see everything from HTTP requests to DNS queries. Without the key, though, it's like trying to listen to a conversation in another language without a translator.

In environments with **VPNs (Virtual Private Networks)**, things get even trickier. VPNs encrypt all traffic between your device and the VPN server, which means that any data being sent over the network is encrypted by the VPN tunnel. If you're capturing packets on a VPN, you won't be able to see the contents of the traffic unless you have access to the VPN's keys or the traffic is being tunneled in an unencrypted protocol, which is increasingly rare. VPNs are great for protecting privacy, but they also make it more difficult to analyze traffic without access to the decryption keys. However, VPN traffic itself can sometimes be identified in Wireshark, as it often uses specific protocols like **IPsec** or **OpenVPN**.

There's also the challenge of **HTTP over TLS/SSL** when analyzing **web traffic**. While HTTPS is great for protecting the integrity and privacy of communications, it also complicates your ability to perform deep packet inspection (DPI). One common trick is to set up a **man-in-the-middle (MITM)** proxy for testing purposes. Tools like **Wireshark** and **Fiddler** can be used to decrypt traffic on your local machine, allowing you to view and analyze encrypted packets as they are decrypted by the proxy. This method is helpful for developers and network administrators, but it's worth noting that **MITM proxies** should only be used in controlled environments and with the right ethical considerations.

When you're analyzing traffic from **encrypted websites** that you don't control, the next best thing is to look at the **metadata**. While you may not be able to see the contents of the HTTP requests and responses, you can still gather information about the size, timing, and frequency of packets. For example, if you're troubleshooting slow performance with a secure website, you can measure how long it takes to establish the connection or how many retransmissions are happening during the handshake. By examining the **timing** of the encrypted packets, you can still spot delays, bottlenecks, or performance issues in the network layer.

Let's talk about **DNS over HTTPS (DoH)**, which is another way encryption can sneak in and hide your network traffic. DNS over HTTPS encrypts DNS queries, preventing eavesdropping or man-in-the-middle attacks on DNS lookups. While this adds privacy benefits, it also means that traditional methods of monitoring DNS traffic (like sniffing packets for DNS queries) won't work. If you want to monitor DoH traffic, you'll need to capture and analyze the HTTPS traffic itself, which can be tricky. Again, this comes down to the fact that even though you can see the DNS queries in Wireshark, they're wrapped up in the encrypted HTTPS packets. Fortunately, tools that decrypt HTTPS traffic can help you see these encrypted DNS requests and responses.

If you're dealing with **TLS and SSL traffic** but don't have the decryption keys, you're essentially flying blind. However, **SSL handshake analysis** can still provide valuable insights. The handshake packets, although encrypted, contain useful details about the encryption methods being used, the certificate chains, and the protocol versions. These packets can give you clues about whether the issue lies with outdated certificates, unsupported cipher suites, or a mismatch in protocol versions. Understanding how to interpret these handshakes can help you diagnose issues without needing to decrypt the entire session.

Finally, **certificate validation** plays a huge role in encrypted traffic. If a certificate is expired, invalid, or not properly signed, it can prevent the establishment of an encrypted connection. Wireshark provides detailed information about certificates during the SSL/TLS handshake, so if you're dealing with connection errors, checking the certificate details in Wireshark can help you identify if certificate-related issues are the culprit.

In conclusion, while **encryption** adds a layer of complexity to packet analysis, it doesn't mean you're completely in the dark. With the right tools, knowledge, and access to keys, you can decrypt the data or at least gather valuable metadata that will guide your troubleshooting efforts. Whether it's SSL/TLS, VPNs, Wi-Fi encryption, or HTTPS, Wireshark gives you the capabilities to analyze encrypted traffic and uncover the truth hidden behind those cryptographic shields. Keep sharpening your skills, and soon you'll be a master at handling encrypted traffic—because in the world of packet analysis, nothing stays hidden for long! Happy decrypting!

As you continue to explore the complexities of encryption in packet analysis, you'll start to realize that while encryption is designed to protect data, it also presents a significant challenge for those trying to diagnose network issues. Fortunately, even though encryption hides the content of your traffic, there are still ways to glean valuable insights from encrypted sessions.

Whether it's through analyzing handshakes, inspecting metadata, or leveraging decryption keys, there's always something to learn from encrypted traffic—even if it isn't the full picture.

Another key to understanding encryption in network traffic is **network security best practices**. As encryption becomes more widespread, network administrators are finding that securing the network infrastructure is just as important as protecting the data itself. For example, making sure that **TLS certificates** are valid and up to date can prevent issues with failed encrypted connections. In Wireshark, you can examine the certificate information presented during the handshake to determine if there are any issues with the certificate chain or if it's been expired. Problems with certificates are often at the root of connectivity issues, and having the ability to spot these in your captures can save you from unnecessary troubleshooting.

On the topic of encryption, **SSL/TLS session reuse** is another concept worth exploring. When two devices communicate over SSL/TLS, they can sometimes reuse previously established sessions to avoid the time-consuming handshake process. While this improves performance by skipping the full handshake, it can sometimes create problems in environments where security policies require fresh sessions for every communication. If you suspect that session reuse is causing issues, Wireshark can help you identify when and how session resumption occurs. This can be crucial when analyzing performance problems in secure connections.

Additionally, **network segmentation** and **firewalls** can influence how encryption behaves in a network. Often, security devices and firewalls will terminate SSL/TLS connections for inspection before re-encrypting the traffic to the destination. This is known as **SSL/TLS interception** or **decryption proxies**. In these cases, Wireshark can capture the decrypted traffic between the proxy and the client but not the encrypted traffic between the client and the original destination. Understanding how these systems work and configuring your packet capture accordingly is key to making sure you're capturing the right data.

The real-world application of **Wireshark's decryption features** often involves working with **SSL/TLS keys** for your own traffic. For example, if you're managing a website or a server and need to troubleshoot SSL/TLS issues, having access to the private key used in your server's SSL/TLS configuration lets you decrypt traffic and pinpoint problems with handshakes, cipher suites, or certificate validity. However, as we mentioned earlier, gaining access to private keys for third-party services or websites is not feasible. This is where capturing **session keys** from your browser or application becomes a game-changer. For browsers like Chrome and Firefox, it's possible to configure the browser to log the session keys, which can then be used in Wireshark to decrypt the traffic. This process requires some technical know-how, but it's a valuable method for inspecting encrypted web traffic when you have the right access.

It's also crucial to recognize that encrypted traffic, especially **VPN traffic**, often presents unique challenges for packet analysis. VPNs encrypt all your traffic, and when they are used with protocols like **IPsec** or **OpenVPN**, they make it nearly impossible to inspect the contents of the traffic without the decryption keys. Fortunately, Wireshark can still provide insights into the **protocols used** (like IPsec or OpenVPN) and the **tunnel creation process**, which can be useful for diagnosing network routing issues, high latency, or VPN disconnects. If you're troubleshooting VPN traffic, knowing how to capture and analyze the handshake between the client and the server is your first step toward understanding any problems.

One of the more advanced methods for dealing with encrypted traffic is **using a man-in-the-middle (MITM) proxy**. This is a method commonly used for testing in controlled environments. The MITM proxy decrypts the traffic as it flows between the client and the server, allowing you to analyze the traffic in its decrypted form. This method is particularly helpful for debugging HTTPS or analyzing the behavior of applications over SSL/TLS. However, it's essential to be aware of the ethical and security considerations of using a MITM proxy, as it can expose sensitive data if misused. It's vital to ensure that your analysis is limited to environments where you have permission to inspect the traffic.

But sometimes, you don't need full decryption to diagnose issues. **Metadata**—such as packet sizes, timing, and the flow of the traffic—can give you enough information to identify where problems might lie. For example, if you notice an unusually high number of **SSL/TLS handshake failures**, this could indicate that the client and server are unable to negotiate a secure connection, possibly due to mismatched cipher suites or expired certificates. You may not be able to see the full handshake, but by analyzing the timing and pattern of these failed attempts, you can infer what's going wrong.

Another important skill to develop is the ability to **interpret the different SSL/TLS versions and cipher suites** used in the handshake. For example, older SSL versions (like SSLv3) are considered insecure, and many modern websites no longer support them. If you're troubleshooting SSL/TLS traffic, Wireshark will show you which version and cipher suites were chosen for the session. If you see that outdated or insecure versions are being used, it's a sign that you should update your server's configuration or enforce more modern encryption standards. Knowing how to spot these versions and suites is crucial in maintaining the security of your network.

While **SSL/TLS** is the most common form of encryption you'll encounter, there are other encrypted protocols, such as **IPsec** for site-to-site VPNs or **SSH** for secure remote shell access. These protocols also rely on encryption, but they operate differently from SSL/TLS, and their analysis requires different techniques. For instance, **IPsec** typically operates at the network layer and uses protocols like **ESP (Encapsulating Security Payload)** and **AH (Authentication Header)**. Wireshark can capture and display IPsec traffic, but without the proper keys or configuration, you won't be able to decrypt the actual payload.

The **SSH protocol** is another encrypted communication method that's often used for remote access to servers. Unlike SSL/TLS, SSH is designed for terminal-based access and can carry encrypted traffic for things like file transfers or command execution. If you're analyzing SSH traffic in Wireshark, it's important to understand that while the connection setup and authentication steps can be captured, the payload data (commands and responses) will be encrypted. To properly troubleshoot SSH-related issues, you may need to access server logs or use other diagnostic tools to complement your Wireshark analysis.

While encryption certainly complicates packet analysis, it's not an insurmountable barrier. In fact, the more you learn about the different encryption methods and how to deal with them in Wireshark, the more confident you'll become in your troubleshooting skills. By analyzing metadata, examining handshakes, and leveraging your knowledge of SSL/TLS, VPNs, and other encrypted protocols, you can still glean valuable insights from your captures. Even when you can't decrypt the data, Wireshark's expert info and packet analysis tools give you enough information to diagnose issues and identify potential weaknesses.

In conclusion, dealing with encryption requires a mixture of technical knowledge, creativity, and the right tools. As you gain more experience analyzing encrypted traffic, you'll become adept at navigating the encrypted layers and uncovering the underlying issues without needing to see every detail of the payload. Whether you're dealing with SSL/TLS, VPNs, SSH, or other encrypted traffic, Wireshark is a powerful tool in your arsenal that can help you make sense of encrypted networks and solve problems efficiently. Keep exploring, keep decrypting (when you can!), and stay on top of your network security game—because in the world of encryption, there's always more than meets the eye.

Chapter 13: Wireshark Colorization: Visual Aid for Packet Analysis

If you've ever been knee-deep in a packet capture, scrolling through thousands of packets, you know that the sea of data can feel like trying to read a book with no chapters, headings, or page numbers. Sure, it's useful information, but it's not exactly user-friendly. Enter **Wireshark's colorization**—a feature that transforms that intimidating wall of text into something much more digestible. In this chapter, we're going to explore how colorization works in Wireshark and why it's one of the best tools in your packet analysis toolbox.

First things first, **what is colorization?** Think of it as a packet traffic traffic light. In Wireshark, colorization uses different colors to highlight specific types of packets or behaviors, making it easy to spot important patterns or issues. Whether it's a suspicious packet, a retransmission, or a handshake, colorizing your capture can help you quickly find the stuff that matters without having to scan line by line. It's like having a map with all the roads clearly marked, instead of relying on a pile of directions that might or might not lead you to your destination.

Let's get a little practical. By default, Wireshark assigns a color scheme to different packet types. For example, **TCP packets** might appear in a specific color, while **DNS requests** are in another. These default colors give you immediate feedback as to what's going on in the capture. You can even adjust Wireshark's **color rules** to match your preferences. If you prefer DNS requests to be bright green instead of yellow, go ahead and make it happen. With colorization, you're not just reading packets—you're *interpreting* them visually, making it easier to spot patterns or irregularities.

One of the most **useful aspects of colorization** is that it highlights unusual or out-of-the-ordinary events. For example, if you're looking for retransmissions, Wireshark can highlight those packets in red, making them impossible to miss. This is particularly helpful when you're dealing with **network congestion** or **packet loss**. When a retransmission happens, it's often a sign that something is wrong—whether it's a broken connection, slow network, or some rogue device. Colorizing these packets lets you zero in on these issues with lightning speed, without having to dig through a sea of "normal" traffic.

You don't have to settle for Wireshark's default color scheme if you don't like it. In fact, Wireshark allows you to customize **your color rules** to meet your specific needs. Have a particular protocol or issue you want to stand out? You can adjust the colorization settings to apply a unique color to packets based on specific attributes, such as **protocol type**, **IP address**, **port number**, or even **packet flags**. Custom color rules mean you can focus on exactly the traffic that interests you—whether that's **HTTP requests**, **SYN packets**, or even **specific network devices**.

Another great feature of Wireshark colorization is **the ability to visualize protocol interactions**. For example, you might want to see the difference between **SYN packets** and **SYN-ACK packets** in a TCP handshake. Wireshark's colorization will automatically color each packet type differently, helping you visually trace the sequence of events as the connection is established. This makes it easier to spot problems, such as **handshake failures**, **dropped connections**, or **delayed packets**. It's a quick way to understand the flow of a conversation between two devices without having to read every packet.

Colorization isn't just about making things pretty—it's about making your packet analysis **more efficient**. It helps you **organize** the chaos of a packet capture and focus on what's relevant. For example, if you're troubleshooting a network issue, you can colorize the packets that match your filter criteria, instantly drawing your attention to the packets you need to analyze. Rather than manually sorting through packets or looking for certain values, the colors do the work for you, pointing you to areas that might need further investigation.

Now, let's talk about **Wireshark's built-in color filters**. When you start a packet capture, Wireshark automatically colorizes packets based on specific **display filters**—for instance, packets containing the protocol **HTTP** might show up in one color, while **DNS** packets are in another. You can tweak these default filters or create your own to match your specific needs. Want to see just packets from a particular IP address or port? Set up a custom rule and, just like that, Wireshark will highlight those packets in a color of your choice. You can make your capture as colorful as a rainbow, but still keep it organized and efficient.

If you're trying to troubleshoot **specific packet types**, colorization is a game-changer. For example, if you're dealing with **large payloads**, Wireshark's colorization can highlight packets with big chunks of data in a different color. This allows you to quickly differentiate between **header-only packets** and those that carry a significant payload. Whether you're analyzing traffic volume, investigating slow transfers, or pinpointing payload-related issues, colorization will help you zoom in on the packets that matter.

One cool feature of Wireshark is that it lets you **create multiple color rules** based on different packet fields. This means you can color packets based on a combination of criteria—say, a specific IP address and a certain port. This is perfect for when you need to analyze traffic from a specific service, device, or application. By setting up custom color rules, you can ensure that packets relevant to your analysis stand out without any distraction.

Speaking of distractions, let's talk about **packet noise**. When you're analyzing a busy network, there's always the potential for unwanted traffic, like **broadcast packets** or **ARP requests**. These can clutter up your capture and make it hard to focus on the important traffic. With colorization, you can assign muted or neutral colors to less important traffic, like ARP or ICMP packets, and assign brighter, more vibrant colors to traffic you're actively investigating. This allows you to declutter your capture and keep your focus on the traffic that matters.

TCP retransmissions, which we've touched on earlier, are another prime candidate for colorization. Wireshark can automatically highlight these in **bright red**, making them instantly recognizable. Retransmissions happen when packets are lost or delayed in transit, and spotting them quickly can save you a lot of time in troubleshooting. By focusing on these red packets, you can quickly identify problem areas in the network, whether they're due to congestion, faulty hardware, or routing issues.

Speaking of **faulty hardware**, colorization is an excellent tool for diagnosing issues like **network interface failures**. If a network card starts having trouble or drops packets, Wireshark can be configured to highlight any **out-of-sequence packets** or **errors** that occur. This makes it easy to spot when something's off, even if you're not looking at the underlying data. As your network grows in size and complexity, the ability to visually identify network hardware problems using colorized packets becomes essential for efficient troubleshooting.

Filters and colorization go hand in hand, allowing you to hone in on the exact packets you want to analyze. If you're troubleshooting an issue with a **specific service**, you can apply a filter for that service—like **HTTP**, **DNS**, or **FTP**—and then colorize the resulting packets. This is especially useful when working with multiple protocols or services simultaneously, as it allows you to visually differentiate between the various types of traffic without confusion. You can focus on exactly what you need to see, without the distraction of irrelevant data.

Colorization isn't limited to just packet analysis—**Wireshark also uses colorization to indicate warnings and errors**. If there's a problem with a packet, Wireshark might highlight it in **bold red** or another attention-grabbing color. These packets could indicate things like **checksum errors**, **duplicate packets**, or **malformed packets**. With colorization, Wireshark makes it easy to spot these red flags and immediately dive deeper into the packet to understand what's going wrong.

Another way to use colorization is for **layered analysis**. For instance, you might color packets by protocol to visually separate **Ethernet**, **IP**, **TCP**, and **application layer protocols**. This allows you to see how each layer is behaving in real time, and it's particularly useful for troubleshooting **protocol handshakes** or **interoperability issues**. By visually separating the layers with different colors, you can track how the packet flows from one layer to another, and where potential breakdowns occur.

If you're dealing with **complex captures**, Wireshark's colorization capabilities can help break things down into manageable chunks. You can assign colors based on **time intervals** to see when certain packets were sent. This is particularly useful when troubleshooting intermittent issues, such as **network congestion** or **latency spikes**, as it lets you identify patterns in timing and packet flow.

Finally, **colorizing your packet captures** isn't just about adding flair—it's about making your analysis more **efficient** and **effective**. Instead of combing through endless rows of packet data, Wireshark's colorization allows you to quickly identify patterns, spot anomalies, and focus on the traffic that matters most. Whether you're a seasoned network administrator or just starting out, learning to use Wireshark's colorization features will streamline your troubleshooting process and help you work smarter, not harder.

In conclusion, **Wireshark colorization** is more than just a way to make your packet captures look pretty—it's a powerful visual aid that enhances your packet analysis skills. By helping you differentiate between protocols, identify problem areas, and highlight important traffic, colorization allows you to perform more targeted, efficient, and effective troubleshooting. So go ahead—tune up those colors, customize your capture to match your needs, and start navigating your packet captures like a pro. Because in the world of network analysis, a little color can go a long way! Happy packet hunting!

As you continue to experiment with **Wireshark's colorization features**, you'll find that they not only save you time, but also help you approach packet analysis from a more strategic, high-level perspective. Instead of getting lost in the weeds of endless packets, colorization enables you to **scan your capture quickly**, identify patterns, and dive into the areas that require the most attention. It's like having a visual cheat sheet that makes complex data far more accessible—sort of like having a GPS for navigating a dense forest of packets.

One more tip when using **colorization effectively** is to customize the rules to fit your specific **troubleshooting goals**. If you know you're dealing with a **network congestion issue**, for example, you might colorize **large packets** in a bright color to quickly identify which large payloads are being transferred. If you're troubleshooting a **network attack** or unusual traffic patterns, you can set up custom color rules to highlight things like **suspicious IP addresses**, **high packet rates**, or **unauthorized ports**. This gives you a targeted, immediate overview of potential problem areas that you can focus on as you dig deeper into the capture.

Speaking of **attacks**, colorization also comes in handy when looking for **security vulnerabilities**. Many types of malicious network activity can be easily identified once you know what to look for. For instance, if you're analyzing traffic for signs of **DoS (Denial of Service)** or **DDoS (Distributed Denial of Service)** attacks, you might want to colorize high-frequency traffic from a single source or a group of IPs in a way that jumps out at you. If you're investigating **spoofing attempts**, such as ARP or DNS spoofing, you can colorize **unexpected responses** or **out-of-sequence packets** to catch these in the act. With colorization, spotting the early signs of malicious activity becomes more intuitive and faster, so you can react before the situation escalates.

One of the greatest advantages of Wireshark's colorization feature is that it doesn't just stop at packets—it extends to **protocols, flags, and even specific patterns** within packets. For instance, if you're debugging a **handshake failure** in a TCP connection, you can colorize **SYN packets**, **ACK packets**, and **SYN-ACK responses** in different colors to visually follow the progress of the handshake. When something goes wrong and the handshake doesn't complete, the colorized packets will immediately stand out, letting you know exactly where the problem lies. You can also highlight **connection resets (RST)** or **duplicate acknowledgments (ACK)**—two common symptoms of failed connections—by assigning them a color that alerts you to something breaking down in the handshake process.

As you start to **experiment with the colorization options**, you'll discover that certain color rules can become part of your **standard workflow**. For example, if you consistently troubleshoot DNS-related issues, you can create a custom rule that highlights all DNS queries and responses in a bright, noticeable color. This allows you to quickly spot when there's an issue with DNS resolution—such as **timeouts** or **unexpected responses**—without having to manually sift through all of the traffic. It's all about making your packet analysis more intuitive, so you can troubleshoot more efficiently.

When you're working on a **busy network**, especially with high traffic loads or long capture sessions, **colorization becomes an essential tool**. It allows you to quickly sift through thousands or even millions of packets and pick out the ones that are relevant to your investigation. Imagine being able to spot the **problematic packets** in a few seconds, without having to manually scroll through endless lines of information. It's like a searchlight cutting through the darkness, helping you navigate the vast ocean of data to find the islands of interest. Colorization helps make the process faster, more precise, and less stressful.

Another great aspect of Wireshark's colorization feature is that it is **dynamic**—meaning it updates in real-time as new packets are captured. This is especially useful during live captures or while analyzing traffic in response to an ongoing network event. As packets are captured, the colorization rules you've set up will immediately highlight the most relevant packets as they appear. If a specific pattern or event occurs, Wireshark will highlight it without you having to constantly change your focus or filters. It's like a network radar that alerts you when something unusual is happening, letting you stay ahead of the game.

Sometimes, **colorization can also help you see trends over time**. For instance, if you're analyzing **HTTP traffic** during a specific time frame and suspect a sudden increase in requests, you can set up color rules to highlight **HTTP GET requests** or **POST requests**. As more traffic is captured, you'll see if the pattern holds true. This is invaluable for **performance monitoring** —whether you're looking for spikes in traffic, detecting slow server responses, or trying to track down **server overloads**. By keeping a constant watch on the packets as they come in, you can spot trends that could indicate underlying issues.

While **default color rules** are helpful, sometimes they just don't cut it. That's why Wireshark gives you the ability to fine-tune the **filters and conditions** that control colorization. For instance, if you're investigating a specific **network device** and want to see traffic from that device in a specific color, you can configure the rules to highlight packets that match the device's **IP address** or **MAC address**. This allows you to hone in on exactly what you're looking for, whether it's a device generating excessive traffic or a host with a potential security issue.

When you're dealing with **multiple protocols** running on the network, colorization provides an excellent way to visually **separate the traffic** and understand the role of each protocol in the overall communication. If you're capturing traffic from a mix of **HTTP, FTP, DNS**, and **SMB**, you can assign each protocol its own color. This helps you quickly identify which protocol is dominating the traffic and allows you to prioritize your troubleshooting. For instance, if you notice that HTTP traffic is taking up more bandwidth than expected, you can zoom in and investigate whether there are any issues with **website performance**, **excessive image sizes**, or a **misconfigured web server**.

Another neat feature is the ability to **export colorized packets** for reporting purposes. If you're working in a team or need to share your findings with others, you can export your capture file with the colorization intact, so the person reviewing it will also see the same color-coded packets you've analyzed. This can save a lot of time and confusion when you need to communicate key insights, especially if the packet data is complex and requires visual cues to make sense of the analysis. It's like creating a visual report of your findings, ensuring that anyone reviewing the data can easily follow your analysis.

Lastly, **colorization is also an educational tool** for newcomers to packet analysis. When you're just starting out, it can be overwhelming to navigate through a full packet capture. But with colorization, you can immediately see what type of traffic you're dealing with, and get a sense of the patterns in the data. It helps you develop an intuition for how network communication flows and where things can go wrong. If you're mentoring someone or teaching a class, Wireshark's colorization can be an excellent tool to visually demonstrate the key concepts of network traffic.

In conclusion, Wireshark's **colorization feature** is much more than just a visual gimmick—it's a powerful tool that enhances your packet analysis, improves your efficiency, and makes troubleshooting more intuitive. Whether you're dealing with a busy network, diagnosing performance issues, or investigating security threats, colorizing your packets helps you quickly spot important patterns and anomalies. By customizing your color rules and leveraging this feature effectively, you'll make your packet analysis not only faster but also more insightful. So, go ahead—add some color to your captures and see just how much easier packet analysis can be. Happy analyzing!

Chapter 14: Wireshark and Security Analysis

Ah, security—every network administrator's favorite topic and every hacker's playground. In the world of network traffic analysis, **Wireshark** is your magnifying glass, allowing you to sift through packets and find those pesky security issues hiding in plain sight. Whether you're defending against an attack or trying to understand what went wrong after one, Wireshark provides you with the tools you need to identify vulnerabilities, track malicious activity, and patch up those security holes. In this chapter, we're going to dive into how to use Wireshark for security analysis, from detecting attacks to securing your network.

Let's start with the basics: **what makes Wireshark so great for security analysis?** Unlike traditional firewalls or intrusion detection systems, Wireshark gives you a window into **all** of your network traffic—every byte of data that's sent and received across your network. It allows you to see exactly what's happening on the network, including potential security threats. With Wireshark, you don't just know when something is wrong—you can see **why** it's wrong. Whether it's an unauthorized connection, a suspicious IP address, or malicious data packets, Wireshark can expose them all. It's like being a digital detective, but instead of a magnifying glass, you have a packet sniffer.

One of the **first steps in security analysis** with Wireshark is recognizing **unusual traffic patterns**. This is one of the most basic yet powerful things you can look for when performing a security audit. For example, an abnormally high volume of requests to a particular port could be a sign of a **DDoS (Distributed Denial of Service)** attack. If you notice packets being sent to ports that shouldn't be open, it could indicate a **port scan**. Wireshark's colorization and filtering features make it incredibly easy to spot such suspicious activity. It's like setting up a radar system that pings every suspicious movement on your network and gives you a bright red warning.

Speaking of **DDoS attacks**, let's take a closer look at how **Wireshark** helps detect them. A **DDoS attack** involves overwhelming a target system with a flood of traffic, causing it to crash or become unresponsive. Wireshark helps you track this flood of traffic by allowing you to analyze traffic patterns over time. You can use Wireshark's **I/O graphs** to visualize the volume of traffic and detect sudden spikes. If you notice a massive increase in packets from a particular source or group of sources, you might be dealing with a DDoS attack. With colorization, you can highlight these bursts in traffic and track the IP addresses causing the overload.

Another classic security threat that Wireshark can help with is **ARP spoofing**. In **ARP spoofing**, an attacker sends fake **ARP (Address Resolution Protocol)** messages to associate their MAC address with a target IP address. This causes traffic to be misdirected, allowing the attacker to intercept data or launch a **man-in-the-middle attack**. In Wireshark, **ARP requests** and **ARP replies** are easy to spot. If you notice duplicate **ARP responses** from different MAC addresses for the same IP address, it could be a sign of ARP spoofing. Wireshark allows you to quickly analyze ARP traffic, identify anomalies, and take action before the attacker can escalate the attack.

But ARP spoofing isn't the only type of **man-in-the-middle (MITM) attacks** Wireshark can help with. These types of attacks occur when an attacker intercepts or alters communication between two parties, often without either party realizing. In Wireshark, MITM attacks often manifest as **SSL/TLS handshake anomalies**. If you're dealing with **HTTPS traffic**, the first thing to do is examine the **SSL/TLS handshake**. Look for mismatches in certificate details, unsupported cipher suites, or the presence of **self-signed certificates** where you expect trusted ones. If anything looks suspicious, that's your first clue that someone might be intercepting the connection.

DNS spoofing is another network security concern that Wireshark can help you investigate. In DNS spoofing, an attacker manipulates DNS queries and responses to redirect users to malicious websites. Wireshark helps by capturing **DNS traffic**, which is typically sent over **UDP port 53**. If you notice multiple DNS requests to a **non-authoritative DNS server**, or suspicious responses with an **incorrect IP address**, it could be a sign of DNS poisoning. Wireshark's **filtering capabilities** allow you to isolate DNS queries, track the sources, and verify the integrity of the responses to identify whether an attacker is tampering with your DNS traffic.

Another key area in **security analysis** is **packet sniffing**, where attackers capture and analyze network traffic to steal sensitive information, like usernames, passwords, or credit card numbers. This can be a serious risk on networks that aren't encrypted. With Wireshark, you can quickly spot **unencrypted traffic**. Look for protocols like **HTTP** (instead of HTTPS) or **FTP** (instead of SFTP) that transmit data in plaintext. Wireshark can also highlight **passwords** and other sensitive data if they are transmitted without encryption. If you see unencrypted sensitive information, it's a good indicator that your network or application security needs a major overhaul.

TLS/SSL certificate analysis is crucial when dealing with encrypted communication. If you're investigating potential MITM attacks or other security threats in **encrypted traffic**, checking the

SSL/TLS certificates involved in the handshake is key. Look for any **expired certificates**, **self-signed certificates**, or **weak cipher suites**. Wireshark provides details about the certificates presented during the handshake, and if something seems out of place, it could be a red flag. Many network vulnerabilities stem from weak or misconfigured SSL/TLS settings, so it's vital to identify and address them as early as possible.

You can also use Wireshark to investigate **unauthorized network access**. This could be an attacker trying to sneak into your network by exploiting open ports or weak access controls. By capturing **authentication traffic** (like **Telnet** or **FTP** logins), Wireshark can show you usernames, passwords, and failed login attempts. It can also help identify **brute-force attacks**, where an attacker attempts to guess a password by trying many combinations. If you see a large number of **failed login attempts** in a short time period, it's a sign that someone is trying to crack into your system.

One of the more **subtle security threats** that Wireshark can help detect is **suspicious traffic patterns** in **VPN connections**. VPNs are designed to encrypt traffic, but if not configured properly, they can still be vulnerable to attacks. For example, if you see unusual traffic patterns within your VPN tunnel or notice **IPsec handshakes** being abruptly terminated, it could indicate a security problem. Wireshark allows you to analyze VPN protocols and ensure that they are operating as expected. If something seems amiss, such as packets being sent in plain text or strange packet sizes, it's time to investigate further.

Let's talk about **network access control**. **Wireshark** can be used to help assess whether your network is enforcing proper access policies. If an attacker gains access to a restricted network segment, you may see them attempting to communicate with devices or services that they shouldn't have access to. By analyzing the packet capture, you can quickly spot suspicious **ARP traffic** or **unauthorized IP addresses** attempting to connect to your internal network. If an attacker is bypassing access controls, Wireshark will help you track their activity, potentially saving your network from more severe damage.

Another area where Wireshark shines is in detecting **malware infections**. Malware often communicates with remote servers, sending stolen data or receiving commands. By analyzing **outbound traffic**, you can spot patterns indicative of malware activity. For example, if you notice **large amounts of traffic** going to an **unusual external IP address**, especially over an unencrypted protocol, it could be a sign that malware is sending data to a remote server. Wireshark can also help you identify suspicious **DNS queries** that might be used for **domain generation algorithms (DGAs)**, which many malware variants use to communicate with their command and control servers.

Traffic anomalies are another key indicator of malicious activity, and Wireshark makes it easy to spot them. For example, if an internal device is suddenly sending large amounts of traffic to external IP addresses or if you see **ports being accessed unexpectedly**, these could be signs of an intrusion. By applying **filters** to your capture, you can isolate unusual traffic and track down the source of the problem. Once you've identified the device or IP address responsible, you can block it from the network and take additional steps to mitigate the attack.

Advanced persistent threats (APTs) are another security concern that Wireshark can help investigate. APTs are typically long-term, sophisticated attacks where the attacker maintains a foothold in the network. These attacks often use stealthy techniques to avoid detection, making them difficult to spot. By using Wireshark to capture traffic over extended periods, you can look for small, **slow-and-low traffic patterns** that could indicate an APT in action. Anomalies in **data flow** or **repeated access to specific resources** over time are key indicators that something is amiss, and Wireshark can help you uncover those subtleties.

Finally, **Wireshark and security analysis** go hand in hand. Whether you're investigating network attacks, ensuring encrypted communication, or hunting down malware, Wireshark provides the power and flexibility to monitor, capture, and analyze your network traffic. Its ability to decode thousands of different protocols, apply filters, and present traffic visually makes it an invaluable tool for anyone serious about network security. With Wireshark in your arsenal, you'll have the ability to catch attacks before they escalate, pinpoint vulnerabilities in your network, and keep your infrastructure safe and sound. Stay vigilant, stay secure, and keep analyzing with Wireshark! Happy hunting!

As you continue exploring **Wireshark's capabilities in security analysis**, you'll realize that the more you practice, the better you get at detecting even the most subtle threats. Network security is a game of attention to detail, and with Wireshark, you can sharpen your detective skills and develop an eye for things that others might miss. The beauty of Wireshark is that it gives you a microscope through which you can examine every single packet in your network—nothing slips by unnoticed.

Real-time monitoring is a critical aspect of security analysis, and Wireshark's ability to capture and analyze packets as they happen makes it an invaluable tool in active defense strategies. When you're on the lookout for an attack, you don't have the luxury of time—you need to detect the anomaly **as it's happening**. With Wireshark, you can run real-time captures and set up filters that immediately alert you when suspicious activity occurs, whether that's **unexpected IP traffic**, **unusual protocols**, or **suspicious ports** being accessed. This instant feedback loop allows you to act quickly, blocking malicious traffic before it can cause significant damage.

One of the most rewarding aspects of using Wireshark for security analysis is the ability to **learn from past attacks**. By capturing traffic during or after an attack, you can review the steps the attacker took, from the initial breach to their actions on the network. These captured packets often reveal the attacker's **command and control servers**, methods of exploitation, and even the tools they used. It's like having a behind-the-scenes view of an attack, allowing you to learn from it and fortify your network against future threats. Security isn't just about reacting to attacks—it's about learning from them and becoming more resilient over time.

Intrusion Detection Systems (IDS) and **Intrusion Prevention Systems (IPS)** are often used alongside Wireshark to monitor network activity for suspicious behavior. While IDS/IPS systems are automated and look for known attack signatures, Wireshark can be your backup system, allowing you to manually analyze packets when the IDS/IPS system alerts you to something unusual. Using both systems in tandem provides a layered defense, where automation catches common attacks and Wireshark gives you the flexibility to investigate and respond to **new or unknown threats** that may slip past the automated systems.

The versatility of **Wireshark** means that it's not just limited to detecting external threats. It's also great for **internal network security**, helping you detect unauthorized access or activity within your own organization. For instance, **shadow IT**, where employees use unauthorized devices or software, can be spotted by Wireshark. If you notice **unknown devices** or **unapproved applications** communicating on the network, Wireshark allows you to trace the source and investigate. Whether it's a rogue employee or an unauthorized device on your network, Wireshark can help you spot these vulnerabilities before they lead to a larger breach.

Let's not forget about **Wi-Fi security**. When analyzing a wireless network, **Wi-Fi encryption protocols** like **WPA2** and **WPA3** are essential for protecting data in transit. If your network isn't using the right encryption, or if an attacker is sniffing unencrypted packets, it's a clear vulnerability. Wireshark can help you assess your Wi-Fi traffic, highlighting any weak or unencrypted packets that could expose sensitive information. It also lets you analyze **handshakes** in **WPA/WPA2** to ensure that no one is trying to crack your Wi-Fi password through a **brute-force attack**. By analyzing the encryption status and handshake process, you can confirm that your wireless network is properly secured.

Vulnerability scanning is another area where Wireshark shines. Although Wireshark is not a vulnerability scanner by itself, it works well in conjunction with other security tools. By capturing network traffic during a vulnerability scan, you can see exactly which services are being probed for weaknesses. Wireshark can give you a closer look at the scanning process, showing you which ports are being targeted, what types of requests are being sent, and whether any unauthorized services are being accessed. This insight can be crucial for reinforcing your security posture by identifying unpatched vulnerabilities and ensuring that your defense mechanisms are properly configured.

As a **security analyst**, you can also use Wireshark to analyze **encrypted traffic** for potential weaknesses in your encryption protocols. For example, if you're using SSL/TLS encryption, but your cipher suite configuration is weak or outdated, an attacker could exploit this to decrypt your traffic. Wireshark can show you the SSL/TLS handshake, the chosen cipher suite, and whether **forward secrecy** is enabled. This gives you the ability to evaluate the strength of your encryption and make necessary adjustments to ensure that sensitive data is protected. By regularly reviewing encryption settings with Wireshark, you can ensure that your network is protected against attackers who might be trying to exploit weak encryption.

Another great use case for Wireshark in security analysis is its ability to help **analyze suspicious payloads**. If you suspect that a malicious payload has been injected into a packet, Wireshark allows you to carefully inspect the packet's contents. It can even highlight **malformed packets**, which often indicate that an attack is taking place, such as in the case of a **buffer overflow attack**. By drilling down into suspicious packets, you can analyze their contents and determine whether they contain malicious code or payloads designed to exploit vulnerabilities in your system.

Wireshark also excels in incident response, allowing you to quickly capture and analyze the traffic leading up to, during, and after a security incident. By collecting packets during an attack, you can build a detailed timeline of the event. You can identify how the attack was executed, which systems were targeted, and whether any data was exfiltrated. Once the attack is over, you can use Wireshark to clean up and make sure the attack hasn't left any backdoors open. Whether it's a **ransomware attack**, **data exfiltration**, or any other type of breach, Wireshark helps you piece together the puzzle, understand the attack vectors, and recover from the incident.

With **Wireshark's powerful filtering capabilities**, you can isolate traffic related to a **specific user** or **device** involved in the security incident. If an employee's machine is compromised or a specific device is being targeted, Wireshark allows you to follow the traffic related to that device. This helps you trace the **lateral movement** of the attack, identify which systems were compromised, and stop the attacker from spreading further. By isolating suspicious activity to a single device or user, you can contain the breach and prevent further damage.

Wireshark's ability to analyze **DNS traffic** also plays a crucial role in security analysis. Many attackers use **DNS tunneling** to exfiltrate data or communicate with remote servers. DNS tunneling encodes data in DNS queries and responses, which are often overlooked by security filters. With Wireshark, you can capture DNS traffic and analyze it for unusual patterns, such as **high-frequency DNS requests** to external, suspicious domains or **unusually large DNS responses**. By monitoring DNS traffic, you can quickly identify data exfiltration attempts or other malicious activity that is hiding in plain sight.

For those dealing with **IoT (Internet of Things)** security, Wireshark is an excellent tool for sniffing out insecure IoT devices. These devices are often vulnerable to **default passwords**, unencrypted communication, and other flaws that make them easy targets for attackers. By analyzing the traffic between IoT devices and their associated networks, you can quickly spot **unusual behavior** or insecure protocols, such as **Telnet** or **HTTP**. If you see IoT devices sending data in **plaintext**, it's a sign that they need to be secured with stronger encryption.

Finally, one of the best things about **Wireshark in security analysis** is that it's an **open-source tool**. This means that, unlike some proprietary tools, you're not limited by expensive licenses or vendor lock-ins. Anyone can access Wireshark's source code, contribute to its development, and use it to defend their networks. Whether you're a seasoned professional or just getting started, Wireshark offers an accessible, powerful platform for network security analysis. The more you use it, the more you'll uncover, making it an invaluable tool for anyone looking to safeguard their network.

In conclusion, **Wireshark's security analysis capabilities** are vast and incredibly powerful. By helping you capture, filter, and analyze network traffic, it enables you to uncover malicious activity, detect security breaches, and improve your overall network security posture. Whether you're investigating a DDoS attack, hunting down malware, or analyzing encrypted traffic, Wireshark provides the insight you need to respond quickly and effectively. With the right knowledge, Wireshark becomes your ultimate tool in securing your network, protecting your data, and keeping cyber threats at bay. Happy analyzing and stay secure!

Chapter 15: Wireshark for VoIP Troubleshooting

Ah, VoIP—Voice over IP, the great enabler of modern communication. Whether you're making a quick call on Skype, attending a Zoom meeting, or talking to a colleague over a corporate IP phone system, **VoIP** is how we keep in touch in the digital age. But like any technology, VoIP isn't immune to problems. Calls drop, there's echo, sound quality dips, and sometimes it feels like the audio is coming from a tunnel. Luckily, Wireshark is here to be your detective when things go wrong. In this chapter, we'll explore how to use Wireshark for **VoIP troubleshooting** —from jitter and packet loss to call setup failures and codec issues.

Let's start with the basics—**what makes VoIP traffic different** from regular internet traffic? Unlike traditional phone systems, VoIP sends voice data over the internet in the form of small packets. These packets travel through routers, switches, and firewalls to reach their destination. The key difference here is that **real-time voice** requires **low latency** and **high reliability**. If packets are delayed or dropped, you'll hear it in the form of poor voice quality, lag, or dropped calls. This is where Wireshark comes in—it allows you to capture these packets and **inspect the traffic** to find out where the problem is happening.

The first step in troubleshooting VoIP calls is to capture the traffic. This usually involves analyzing the **RTP (Real-time Transport Protocol)** packets that carry the voice data. In Wireshark, you can filter out **RTP streams** by looking for UDP packets with specific ports used for VoIP, like **5060** for SIP or **16384-32767** for RTP. If you're capturing traffic and see a steady stream of these packets, congratulations—your VoIP call is happening. If the flow seems choppy or inconsistent, then you've found the start of your investigation.

Packet loss is one of the most common issues in VoIP calls. It occurs when some of the voice data packets don't make it to their destination, and you can hear the effects immediately— dropped syllables, stuttering, or silences. When troubleshooting packet loss, Wireshark can help you identify **lost RTP packets** by checking for **sequence number gaps**. Each RTP packet has a sequence number that helps the receiver reorder packets if they arrive out of sequence. If you notice a **gap** in these numbers, it means that packets were dropped during transmission. Packet loss often points to network congestion or unreliable connections, and Wireshark's analysis will help you isolate the problem.

Another common issue is **jitter**, which is a fancy word for **packet delay variation**. When packets are delivered at uneven intervals, it causes distortion in the voice call, making it sound robotic or echoey. Jitter can occur if there's congestion in the network, or if the call's routing path changes during the conversation. In Wireshark, you can analyze jitter by examining the **inter-arrival times** between consecutive RTP packets. If the times are inconsistent, it's a sign that jitter is affecting the quality of the call. You can use Wireshark's **RTP stream analysis** to calculate **jitter statistics** and determine if the levels are acceptable for the call.

Now, let's talk about **call setup failures**, which are often caused by issues in the **SIP (Session Initiation Protocol)** signaling. SIP is used to set up and terminate VoIP calls, and if it's misconfigured or encounters problems, the call can fail before it even begins. In Wireshark, you can filter **SIP packets** (usually on **port 5060**) and analyze the **call flow**. If you see **SIP error messages** like "SIP 404 Not Found" or "SIP 503 Service Unavailable," it means that there's an issue with the call setup process. This could be due to incorrect server configuration, a wrong user address, or even an issue with your network's DNS resolution. Wireshark will help you find where the call is being dropped in the signaling process.

Another potential problem when troubleshooting VoIP is **codec mismatch**. VoIP uses different **audio codecs** to compress and decompress voice data. If the caller and receiver don't have a common codec, the call won't work properly, and you'll hear garbled or no audio. In Wireshark, you can check the **SIP INVITE** message to see which codecs were offered by the caller and accepted by the receiver. If there's a codec mismatch, Wireshark will show you the **SIP messages** with the specific codec parameters. Solving codec issues might involve ensuring that both devices support the same codecs or adjusting the codec settings on your VoIP servers.

NAT (Network Address Translation) issues are another headache when it comes to VoIP troubleshooting. NAT is used to map private IP addresses to public ones, but it can break VoIP calls by modifying the headers of RTP or SIP packets, making them unreadable by the receiving party. Wireshark is great for spotting **NAT traversal problems** by showing you the **source and destination IP addresses** in your packets. If the destination IP addresses don't match the expected public IP address of the VoIP server, it's a sign that NAT is causing issues. Solutions often involve configuring **SIP ALG (Application Layer Gateway)** on routers or using **STUN (Session Traversal Utilities for NAT)** to help the devices communicate correctly.

Let's not forget about **firewall issues**, which can block VoIP traffic altogether. Many firewalls are configured to block SIP and RTP traffic for security reasons, especially when they are running on non-standard ports. If you're troubleshooting a VoIP call that won't connect or experiences **audio dropouts**, it's worth checking the **firewall logs** and **Wireshark captures** to see if the relevant ports are being blocked. In Wireshark, you can filter for **SIP and RTP traffic** and analyze whether the packets are being dropped or if there are **TCP resets** that are preventing the connection. If a firewall is the culprit, you may need to adjust your **firewall rules** to allow VoIP traffic.

One-way audio is a frustrating issue in VoIP calls where one party can hear the other, but not vice versa. This can be caused by issues like **incorrect NAT configuration**, **firewall blocking**, or **SIP misconfigurations**. In Wireshark, you can isolate the **RTP streams** of both parties to see whether one direction of traffic is being blocked or dropped. By examining the flow of packets, you'll likely spot where the issue lies. If you see **no RTP packets** from one side, it's an indication that the **audio stream** isn't reaching the other party, and it's likely being blocked by a firewall or misconfigured NAT.

When analyzing **VoIP call quality**, you can use Wireshark to evaluate the **MOS (Mean Opinion Score)**, which is a numerical measurement of call quality. The higher the MOS score, the better the quality of the call. Wireshark provides **RTP analysis tools** that allow you to calculate the **MOS score** based on packet loss, jitter, and latency. If the MOS score is low, it points to poor voice quality, and you can drill down into the **RTP streams** to find the root cause, whether it's **packet loss**, **jitter**, or **high latency**.

You can also use **Wireshark's "Follow RTP Stream"** feature to isolate a particular VoIP call and view the raw audio packets. By following the RTP stream, you can listen to the call directly in Wireshark and evaluate the voice quality firsthand. If the call quality is poor, you'll hear it directly through the capture. This allows you to identify issues like **echo**, **garbled speech**, or **silence**, which are common in low-quality VoIP calls. Once you've identified the issue, you can work backward through the capture to find out what's causing it.

VoIP network performance often depends on the overall health of your **local area network (LAN)** and **wide area network (WAN)**. If you're dealing with VoIP issues, it's important to evaluate the entire network's performance. Wireshark can help you track **network congestion**, **latency**, and **packet loss**, all of which can severely impact VoIP quality. By analyzing **I/O graphs** and **round-trip times** in Wireshark, you can identify where the network is becoming slow or overloaded. If you see spikes in **latency** or **packet loss**, it's time to investigate whether the issue lies with the physical network or the **QoS (Quality of Service)** settings.

To wrap things up, **Wireshark's VoIP troubleshooting tools** are a **game-changer** for network engineers, system administrators, or anyone involved in maintaining VoIP infrastructure. From call setup failures and codec mismatches to jitter, packet loss, and firewall issues, Wireshark gives you the power to capture and analyze VoIP traffic in ways that would be impossible without it. Armed with the knowledge in this chapter, you're now ready to tackle any VoIP issue that comes your way. So go ahead, start capturing those packets, troubleshoot like a pro, and get those calls sounding crystal clear again! Happy VoIP troubleshooting!

As you become more comfortable with **Wireshark for VoIP troubleshooting**, you'll notice that the ability to **analyze network traffic in real time** gives you a massive advantage when troubleshooting issues quickly and efficiently. While you might have a good understanding of how VoIP works on paper, nothing compares to seeing the live interaction of packets, protocols, and real-world problems. The ability to dive deep into the **RTP stream**, check **SIP signaling**, and monitor **network performance** gives you a unique edge in diagnosing VoIP issues faster and more accurately than relying solely on theoretical knowledge or external tools.

One thing to always keep in mind is that **VoIP is a delicate ecosystem** that requires **constant monitoring** to ensure optimal performance. Because voice data is sensitive to delays, packet loss, and jitter, it's important to check not just the quality of the individual calls but also the **overall network health**. By using Wireshark to track trends in call performance, you can spot potential problems before they become full-fledged issues. If you notice patterns such as **degraded audio quality** during certain times of the day or **repeated call drops**, you can focus your efforts on finding the root cause—whether it's network congestion, insufficient bandwidth, or a server issue.

Wireshark's diagnostic tools, like **RTP stream analysis**, are excellent for diagnosing more specific **audio quality issues**. Whether you're dealing with **echoes**, **one-way audio**, or **garbled voice**, these tools allow you to listen to the call itself, providing a direct feedback loop for analyzing the audio quality. By isolating the **problematic stream** and listening to it in Wireshark, you can identify exactly where the audio is breaking down. Listening to a VoIP call in Wireshark lets you make a diagnosis of the **quality issues**, and knowing the exact cause allows you to implement more targeted fixes—whether it's adjusting codec settings or ensuring better network routing.

It's also crucial to consider **VoIP scalability** when performing your analysis. **Small-scale VoIP implementations** may work fine on basic network setups, but as the number of calls increases, the network must be capable of handling the additional load. **Wireshark's ability to capture large volumes of traffic** allows you to understand how your network performs under stress and identify bottlenecks or areas of congestion. By looking at **call setup times**, **network delays**, and

throughput, you can gain a clear picture of how well your network supports VoIP as the demand grows. Wireshark helps you visualize these patterns over time and make adjustments before your system hits its capacity.

When you're troubleshooting **multiple VoIP services** or **complex deployments**, Wireshark can also help with **interoperability testing**. VoIP deployments often involve different vendors, codecs, and devices, and understanding how they communicate with each other is key. Wireshark gives you the ability to compare different devices and services to see if they are properly interworking. Whether you're troubleshooting issues related to codec compatibility, call routing, or even issues with **proprietary protocols**, Wireshark helps break down the barriers between disparate systems and makes it easier to find solutions.

Additionally, **Wireshark can reveal hidden security threats** in your VoIP network, such as unauthorized access attempts, **suspicious traffic patterns**, or even **fraudulent calls**. VoIP is an attractive target for attackers because it combines voice data with the flexibility of the internet. By using **Wireshark to capture signaling traffic**, you can spot anything suspicious, like **SIP INVITE flooding** (a type of DoS attack), or **unwanted IP addresses** attempting to register with your VoIP server. Understanding the flow of signaling and call data through Wireshark can give you an early warning if your network is under attack, allowing you to act swiftly to prevent further damage.

A useful feature when dealing with **large-scale VoIP infrastructures** is **Wireshark's ability to analyze historical data**. In many enterprise environments, network performance degradation may not be immediately visible during live troubleshooting sessions. However, capturing and saving data over a longer period provides a way to analyze trends and pinpoint recurring issues. For instance, you might observe a pattern of intermittent **call drops** or **poor quality** only during peak hours. By analyzing the traffic over time in Wireshark, you can correlate performance degradation with specific network events, such as **increased bandwidth consumption** or **high utilization of network hardware**.

Moreover, if you're analyzing **VoIP over a VPN**, Wireshark can help you track **VPN-related issues** that affect call quality. VoIP traffic is sensitive to latency, and VPNs can introduce significant delays, which may impact the call quality. By analyzing the **VPN tunnel's behavior** in Wireshark and comparing it with normal VoIP traffic, you can spot any issues caused by VPN configuration problems or misalignment between the **encryption overhead** and **real-time communication**. If you're noticing delays or jitter on encrypted calls, it's time to dive into the VPN configuration and analyze how the **encryption overhead** might be affecting the quality of the calls.

As a final tip, it's essential to be familiar with **VoIP monitoring tools** and how they complement Wireshark. Tools like **PRTG** or **SolarWinds** are excellent for **ongoing network monitoring** and can provide alerts when something goes wrong in real-time. Wireshark, on the other hand, is your go-to tool when you need to **analyze specific packets** in detail, especially during troubleshooting sessions or incident responses. By combining the strengths of both, you can continuously monitor your network for **VoIP-related issues** while also having a powerful tool for diving deep into **packet-level analysis** when needed.

If you are ever unsure whether an issue is related to VoIP or the network itself, **Wireshark's ability to separate out specific protocols** is a huge help. By filtering for VoIP traffic specifically (whether it's **SIP**, **RTP**, or other protocols), you can easily pinpoint whether the problem lies in the **signaling layer** or the **media layer**. This helps you avoid wasting time chasing down network issues that aren't related to your VoIP setup. With proper use of filters and protocol identification, Wireshark allows you to **focus your troubleshooting efforts** on exactly what matters.

In conclusion, **Wireshark for VoIP troubleshooting** is an indispensable tool for anyone working with VoIP technologies. Whether you're dealing with jitter, packet loss, codec mismatches, call setup failures, or network congestion, Wireshark's deep packet analysis gives you the power to see what's going on under the hood. It's like having a **digital magnifying glass** that lets you inspect every packet of a VoIP call, no matter how complex the setup. By understanding how VoIP works on a packet level and using Wireshark's powerful filtering, analysis, and visualization tools, you can resolve issues quickly and improve the overall quality of your VoIP calls. So, the next time you're dealing with an issue, remember: Wireshark is your go-to detective for getting the job done. Happy troubleshooting!

Chapter 16: Analyzing Wireless Networks

Welcome to the exciting, and often chaotic, world of wireless networks. There's something magical about Wi-Fi, isn't there? You can sit on your couch, stare out the window, and still browse cat videos—without a single wire in sight. But behind that magic is a world of fluctuating signals, interference, and sometimes, downright inexplicable performance issues. Whether it's the buffer circle of doom on Netflix or Wi-Fi dropping in the middle of a Zoom call, wireless networks bring their own unique set of challenges. But don't worry, **Wireshark** is here to help you dive deep into those invisible waves and solve your wireless woes. In this chapter, we're going to explore how to use Wireshark for analyzing **wireless networks** and troubleshooting those frustrating connectivity issues.

The first thing you need to know is that **wireless networks are inherently different** from wired ones. Unlike Ethernet cables, where data travels down a neat, predictable path, **wireless signals bounce around like hyperactive children** at a birthday party. They can be reflected, refracted, and absorbed by walls, furniture, or your neighbor's microwave. Because of this unpredictability, troubleshooting wireless networks requires a different approach. **Wireshark** helps by giving you a window into the packet traffic that flows through the air, enabling you to spot interference, misconfigurations, or congestion that might be causing issues. So, let's break down how to analyze wireless traffic using Wireshark and make your Wi-Fi behave like a well-mannered guest.

To get started, you'll need a **Wi-Fi adapter** capable of **monitor mode**. This is crucial because, in order to analyze wireless packets, you need to capture everything that's flying through the air, including traffic that's not necessarily destined for your device. A standard adapter in regular mode will only show traffic directed to and from your computer, but **monitor mode** allows you to eavesdrop on the entire wireless network. Think of it like a spy in the middle of a conversation—**Wireshark** can show you everything, even the secrets the network is keeping. Once you've got the right hardware, you're ready to capture those packets and start analyzing them.

One of the first things you'll notice when analyzing **wireless traffic** in Wireshark is the **802.11** protocol. This is the core standard for Wi-Fi communication, and it contains several frames that are key to understanding the behavior of your network. The most important frames to look at are **Beacon frames** and **Probe Request/Response frames**. Beacon frames are like the broadcasted "hey, I'm here!" messages from your access point (AP), letting devices know about the network's existence. **Probe Requests and Responses** are the way devices try to find a particular network or ask the AP for details about available networks. Wireshark allows you to filter for these specific frames, making it easier to see how devices are interacting with your access point.

Now, let's talk about **signal strength** and how it impacts your wireless network. **Wi-Fi signal strength** is typically measured in decibels (dBm), and the stronger the signal, the better the connection. Unfortunately, signals aren't always strong. **Distance** from the access point, **walls**, and even **microwave ovens** can degrade the signal. Wireshark can capture **802.11 frames** and display the signal strength for each packet, helping you identify **weak spots** in your network coverage. By monitoring the **RSSI (Received Signal Strength Indicator)**, you can pinpoint where your network is suffering and where you might need to install **additional access points** or move your router for better coverage.

Interference is another common culprit when it comes to wireless network issues. Many people don't realize that Wi-Fi operates in the same frequency range as other devices, such as **microwave ovens, Bluetooth devices**, and **baby monitors**. If you've ever tried to stream a movie only to be interrupted by static and buffering, interference could be the culprit. Wireshark allows you to identify which channels your **Wi-Fi network** and other devices are using. You can easily filter Wi-Fi traffic by channel and see if there's overlap with other nearby networks. The goal is to find a **clear channel**, away from interference, to improve your signal quality. If your current channel is crowded, you can try switching to a less congested one.

When troubleshooting **low-speed connections** or **high latency** in wireless networks, it's essential to understand how the Wi-Fi network is behaving at a **protocol level**. In **Wi-Fi communication**, data is sent in **frames**—and these frames can include a variety of issues that affect performance. One issue you may see in Wireshark is **frame retransmissions**, which occur when a packet is lost and needs to be sent again. A high rate of retransmissions indicates that something is interfering with the signal or the connection is unstable. You can use Wireshark to monitor the number of retransmissions and identify if your network is underperforming due to these issues.

In addition to retransmissions, **Wireshark** can help you analyze **network throughput** in real-time. Throughput refers to the rate at which data is successfully transmitted over the network. If your wireless network isn't performing as expected, it could be due to **bandwidth limitations**, **interference**, or **poor signal quality**. By analyzing the **data packets** in Wireshark, you can calculate the **throughput** and compare it against expected speeds. If you notice that your throughput is consistently low, it might be time to check your router's configuration or upgrade to a higher-performance device.

Sometimes, the issue isn't with the **Wi-Fi network itself** but with **network congestion**. If you're in an environment where many devices are connected to the same access point—like an office or apartment building—the network can become congested. Wireshark allows you to capture **802.11**

management frames, which can give you insight into **how many devices** are connected to the AP and how they're interacting with each other. If you see excessive **association requests** or **retries**, it could mean the network is overloaded and needs to be optimized for better performance. In extreme cases, you may need to consider **load balancing** or **upgrading to more powerful access points** to accommodate the volume of traffic.

Speaking of **optimizing the network**, one of the best things you can do for your wireless setup is **configure Quality of Service (QoS)**. QoS helps prioritize traffic on the network, ensuring that **real-time applications** like **VoIP** and **video conferencing** get the bandwidth they need. When troubleshooting, Wireshark lets you see how well your QoS settings are being applied by analyzing the **Ethernet frame** headers for **priority tags**. You can also track **latency** and **jitter** in Wireshark to see how well the network is handling prioritized traffic. If you notice that high-priority traffic is being delayed, it might be time to revisit your QoS configuration.

One of the trickier problems you might run into is **handshake failures** in **802.11 wireless security**. If you're using **WPA2** or **WPA3** encryption, Wireshark can capture the **handshake process** and display potential issues. Problems with the **WPA key exchange** can cause devices to fail to connect, or even worse, fall back to **weaker encryption protocols**. Wireshark allows you to capture the four-way handshake process and verify if the **pairwise master key (PMK)** is being correctly derived. If you see issues in the handshake, it might indicate that your router's security settings need to be adjusted or that your devices are having trouble with the encryption method.

Another hidden issue in wireless networks is **overlapping channels**, which can cause **channel contention** and degrade performance. In Wi-Fi networks, especially in dense environments, multiple access points may be operating on the same or overlapping channels. Wireshark allows you to **scan the 2.4 GHz and 5 GHz bands** and identify which channels are being used by neighboring access points. By identifying the **channel overlap**, you can manually adjust the channels on your access points to reduce interference and improve performance. Ideally, you want to avoid using the same channel as a neighboring AP to minimize the risk of interference.

When you're analyzing a **large wireless network**, you'll likely encounter a mix of **different Wi-Fi standards**—**802.11a**, **802.11b/g/n**, and the newer **802.11ac** or **802.11ax (Wi-Fi 6)**. Different standards offer varying performance levels, with Wi-Fi 6 being the **most efficient** for handling high-density environments. Wireshark can help you identify which Wi-Fi standard is being used in each frame, so you can assess whether your network is operating at peak performance. If you notice that your devices are stuck on an older standard, it might be time to upgrade your access points and client devices for better speeds and efficiency.

Let's talk about **Wi-Fi roaming**—an issue that often frustrates users in large networks. Roaming happens when a client device moves from one access point to another, and if not done correctly, it can result in **dropped connections** or **lag**. When troubleshooting roaming issues, Wireshark can capture the **association requests** and **authentication frames** between the device and access points. By analyzing these frames, you can see whether the device is having trouble transitioning between access points, and determine whether it's a **configuration issue** or a **signal strength problem**.

Lastly, **Wireshark's ability to analyze the **802.11 management frames** is crucial for understanding **network performance** at a deeper level. These frames include essential information about **SSID**, **BSSIDs**, and **authentication methods**. They allow you to see how devices are associating with your network and whether they're being dropped or unable to reconnect. By looking at these frames, you can troubleshoot issues related to **network access**, **SSID broadcasting**, or **security configuration**. Wireshark's deep dive into these frames gives you a complete picture of how your devices are connecting to your network.

In conclusion, **Wireshark is an invaluable tool for troubleshooting wireless networks**. It helps you capture, analyze, and visualize everything that's happening in the airwaves—from interference and congestion to security issues and poor performance. Whether you're optimizing a small home network or managing a large-scale enterprise Wi-Fi setup, Wireshark equips you with the insights needed to make informed decisions and improve performance. So next time your Wi-Fi starts to falter, grab Wireshark, fire up those filters, and start hunting down the problem—your wireless network will thank you! Happy analyzing!

As you dive deeper into the **Wireshark analysis of wireless networks**, you'll come to appreciate the intricacies that make wireless troubleshooting both a challenge and a reward. Unlike wired networks, where the path is more predictable, **wireless networks** can be like trying to read a book while it's being tossed around in the wind. There are more variables at play: interference, distance, and even weather can affect the signal strength and performance. But with Wireshark, you have a powerful tool that helps you capture and analyze those invisible signals, giving you a much clearer picture of what's happening under the surface.

One thing to always remember when working with wireless networks is the **importance of channel management**. As we've mentioned earlier, **overlapping channels** in Wi-Fi networks, especially in the crowded 2.4 GHz band, can cause significant performance problems. Wireshark can help you monitor the **channel utilization** by capturing **802.11 frames** and analyzing the **channel usage** in your area. You might discover that your AP is sharing a channel with too many others, causing packet collisions and slower speeds. Switching to a less crowded channel, especially in the **5 GHz band**, can significantly improve performance, and Wireshark makes it easy to identify this issue.

Another tip is to take advantage of **Wireshark's "Decrypted WEP/WPA" feature** if you're working with older, **weaker encryption** protocols like WEP or WPA. Although these encryption methods are insecure by modern standards, there are still networks out there running them, and Wireshark's ability to decrypt traffic can be crucial for security assessments or troubleshooting legacy systems. While it's generally a bad idea to rely on outdated security protocols, **Wireshark's decryption** functionality can help you assess the vulnerabilities in those networks and determine where improvements can be made. It's a powerful tool for anyone still dealing with older Wi-Fi equipment that hasn't been updated to WPA2 or WPA3.

When you're troubleshooting **wireless security**, Wireshark can help identify **misconfigured access points**, **rogue devices**, and **unauthorized traffic**. By analyzing management frames, you can spot issues like **incorrect SSID configurations**, **devices connecting to the wrong AP**, or even **malicious devices masquerading as legitimate access points**. In crowded environments, such as office buildings or apartment complexes, the number of rogue access points can increase, leading to security risks and performance problems. Wireshark allows you to examine the **Beacon frames** and **Probe requests** to ensure that your network is secure and that only authorized devices are accessing it.

A related issue that Wireshark can help diagnose is **SSID spoofing**, where attackers set up fake access points with the same name as a legitimate network. These rogue APs can trick devices into connecting, allowing attackers to intercept traffic or perform **man-in-the-middle (MITM) attacks**. By inspecting **SSID and BSSID** information in Wireshark, you can check for mismatches or **duplicate SSIDs** that might indicate the presence of a rogue AP. If you find one, you can take immediate action to disconnect it and secure your network.

Let's also talk about **high-density environments**. In places like stadiums, offices, or coffee shops, **Wi-Fi congestion** becomes a major problem. Multiple access points can cause **interference** and **co-channel contention**, leading to poor performance for everyone. Wireshark's ability to capture and analyze **Beacon frames** and **Probe requests** allows you to see how many devices are connected to each AP and where congestion might be occurring. You can use this information to strategically adjust AP placements, channel assignments, and even the number of access points deployed to optimize performance for all users.

In **enterprise settings**, **Wi-Fi roaming** becomes critical. As users move throughout the building, they need to seamlessly connect to different access points without dropping calls or experiencing lag. If there are issues with **roaming performance**, Wireshark can help you analyze the **802.11r** (fast roaming) or **802.11k/v** (radio resource management) extensions that help devices roam more efficiently. If devices are failing to roam properly, causing dropped packets or slow handoffs, Wireshark will highlight the issues in the packet exchange process, making it easier to diagnose the root cause.

Another powerful feature of Wireshark is the ability to capture and analyze **Wi-Fi traffic on both the 2.4 GHz and 5 GHz bands**. The 5 GHz band is less crowded and offers faster speeds, but it also has a **shorter range** compared to the 2.4 GHz band. If you're troubleshooting performance, it's important to monitor traffic on both bands and ensure that the network is using the available spectrum efficiently. Wireshark helps you spot **bandwidth utilization**, **signal-to-noise ratios (SNR)**, and **channel congestion**, which allows you to make the right decisions about where to allocate bandwidth or adjust your channel settings.

When it comes to **wireless troubleshooting**, one of the most frustrating issues is **intermittent connectivity**. A device may work fine one moment and then drop the connection the next, only to reconnect minutes later. Intermittent issues can be caused by **signal interference**, **weak coverage areas**, or even **incorrect power settings** on your access points. Wireshark helps by allowing you to capture traffic over a longer period, so you can see exactly when and where these issues occur. By isolating the times of day, location, or specific APs where the drops occur, you can diagnose whether the issue is related to external interference, poor signal strength, or faulty network equipment.

Sometimes, the root cause of **wireless performance issues** is **excessive noise** on the network. Wi-Fi networks are highly susceptible to interference from other wireless devices, like **microwaves**, **Bluetooth**, and **cordless phones**, all of which operate on the same or nearby frequencies. Wireshark's ability to analyze **802.11 frames** allows you to capture and analyze **signal strength and interference** from competing devices. By visually analyzing the network performance and checking for excessive noise or traffic spikes, you can determine if the problem is environmental or related to a specific device.

Another challenge in **wireless analysis** is dealing with **Wi-Fi authentication failures**. If devices are unable to authenticate with your access point, they won't be able to connect to the network. This can be caused by misconfigured security settings, expired certificates, or incompatible authentication methods. Wireshark lets you capture the **EAP (Extensible Authentication Protocol)** and **RADIUS** traffic during the authentication process, allowing you to see exactly where the process fails. If you spot failures in the authentication exchange, you can adjust the settings on your AP or authentication server to resolve the issue.

Wi-Fi channels are another critical aspect of **wireless network performance**. When multiple access points are operating on the same or overlapping channels, **interference** can cause slow speeds and dropped connections. Wireshark lets you capture **channel usage** and monitor which channels are being used by nearby APs. If you notice overlapping channels, it may be time to manually adjust the channels on your access points or use **automatic channel selection** to ensure that each AP operates on a unique, non-overlapping channel. This can help reduce interference and improve performance for all connected devices.

In **large environments**, **mesh networks** have become a popular solution for extending Wi-Fi coverage. These networks allow multiple access points to work together to create a seamless coverage area. However, troubleshooting mesh networks can be tricky, as traffic may be routed through multiple nodes before reaching its destination. Wireshark helps you capture and analyze the **traffic flow** between mesh nodes, allowing you to identify issues like **slow handoffs**, **misconfigured backhaul connections**, or **packet loss** between the nodes. By understanding the traffic flow, you can pinpoint the weak links in the network and address them to improve overall performance.

When dealing with **wireless network security**, **Wireshark** can help you monitor for **unauthorized access points** (rogue APs) or **malicious devices** trying to connect to your network. These rogue devices can cause all sorts of issues, from **interfering with legitimate connections** to **spying on your network traffic**. By analyzing **probe requests** and **association requests**, you can identify when devices are trying to connect to your APs. If you spot devices that shouldn't be there, you can take action to remove them from the network or configure stronger **802.1X authentication** to prevent unauthorized access.

Lastly, Wireshark is **great for optimizing your network**. By **analyzing traffic**, **signal strength**, and **interference**, you can gain insights into the areas of your network that need improvement. Whether it's adjusting your **AP placement**, **reconfiguring your channels**, or upgrading your **Wi-Fi standards**, Wireshark provides the data you need to make informed decisions. By regularly monitoring your network's performance, you can ensure that it's running at peak efficiency, providing **fast, reliable**, and **secure Wi-Fi** for all users.

In conclusion, **Wireshark is an essential tool** for anyone troubleshooting or optimizing wireless networks. With its ability to capture and analyze 802.11 traffic, Wireshark allows you to dive deep into the performance of your wireless network, diagnose issues like interference, congestion, and security threats, and optimize your setup for the best possible performance. Whether you're managing a small home network or a large enterprise system, Wireshark gives you the insights you need to keep your wireless network running smoothly. So grab your **Wi-Fi adapter**, fire up **Wireshark**, and start analyzing your wireless network today! Happy troubleshooting!

Chapter 17: Advanced Filtering Techniques

In the world of packet analysis, **filters are your best friend**—they allow you to sift through mountains of data and focus only on the packets that matter. If you've ever looked at a Wireshark capture and thought, "Wow, this is a lot of information," you're not alone. As the traffic piles up, it's easy to get lost in the sea of data, but fear not! **Advanced filtering techniques** are here to save the day. In this chapter, we'll explore how to apply some serious filtering power to your packet captures, so you can navigate the chaos and uncover exactly what you're looking for. Think of it as setting a **treasure map**—you'll know exactly where to dig to find the golden nuggets.

Let's start with the basics of **Wireshark filters**. Filters in Wireshark can be applied to both **capture** and **display**. **Capture filters** are applied while you're capturing traffic and allow you to filter out unwanted packets from being recorded. On the other hand, **display filters** are applied after the capture is complete, letting you hide irrelevant data and focus on what's important. When you're dealing with a large capture file, **display filters** are your go-to tool. They can make or break your analysis, so getting comfortable with them will drastically improve your efficiency.

First, let's talk about **basic filtering**. If you want to see all the traffic between two devices, you can filter by **IP address**. For instance, the display filter `ip.addr == 192.168.1.1` will show all packets involving the device with the IP address `192.168.1.1`. It's the packet equivalent of pulling out a highlighter and circling just the important stuff. Want to zoom in on **HTTP traffic**? The filter `http` will instantly filter out everything except HTTP packets. It's simple, effective, and perfect for when you just need to see the basics. But hold on—things are about to get much more interesting as we explore more advanced filtering techniques.

Now that you've mastered the basics, let's dive into **protocol filtering**. Wireshark is designed to work with **thousands of protocols**, so filtering by a specific protocol is essential for deep packet analysis. For example, if you want to focus on **TCP traffic**, you can filter with `tcp`—this will exclude everything except TCP packets. If you're dealing with **SIP (Session Initiation Protocol)** traffic, a filter like `sip` will help isolate the SIP messages involved in call setups. **Protocol filtering** is a game-changer when you want to focus on specific types of communication and discard everything else. It's like looking at the world through a pair of specialized goggles designed to block out all the noise.

But what if you want to be even more specific? What if you're interested only in **HTTP requests**, for example, and you don't care about HTTP responses? That's where **compound filters** come in handy. You can combine multiple criteria to create complex filters, such as `http.request && ip.addr == 192.168.1.1`. This filter will show you all HTTP request packets that involve the IP address `192.168.1.1`. It's like telling Wireshark, "I want to see HTTP requests **and** I only want to see traffic related to this particular device." You can combine filters using logical operators like `&&` (AND), `||` (OR), and `!` (NOT), which allow you to build almost any filter combination you can imagine.

Time-based filtering is another great technique for narrowing down your packet analysis. If you want to focus on a specific time window, Wireshark allows you to filter packets that are captured within a particular range. For instance, if you're troubleshooting a network event that occurred between 2:00 PM and 2:30 PM, you can use the filter `frame.time >= "2025-04-09 14:00:00" && frame.time <= "2025-04-09 14:30:00"`. This will isolate packets captured during that time period, making it easier to analyze the problem. Time-based filtering is incredibly useful when you need to isolate issues that occur during specific time intervals, such as a sudden spike in traffic or a brief network disruption.

If you're working with **large captures** and need to isolate **specific packet types**—for example, you want to identify **TCP retransmissions**—you can apply **advanced display filters** like `tcp.analysis.retransmission`. This filter will show you only the retransmitted packets in your capture file. Wireshark even allows you to track other packet issues, such as **duplicate ACKs** and **out-of-order packets**, using filters like `tcp.analysis.duplicate_ack` or `tcp.analysis.out_of_order`. These types of advanced filters allow you to focus on specific network anomalies, making it easier to pinpoint and resolve issues.

Wireshark is also smart enough to allow you to filter by **packet contents**. Want to search for a specific string in a packet's payload? You can use `frame contains "example.com"` to search for packets that contain the string "example.com." This is perfect for when you're troubleshooting a web server, and you want to find all the requests that mention a certain domain or URL. Filtering by packet contents helps you track down communication related to specific services, applications, or URLs.

Regular expressions can take filtering to the next level. If you're familiar with **regex**, you'll love how Wireshark lets you use it for advanced pattern matching. For example, you can use a regular expression filter like `http.request.uri matches ".*login.*"` to find HTTP requests that contain the word "login" in their URI. Regex filters allow you to **precisely match patterns** in packet contents, which is incredibly useful when dealing with large datasets and complex traffic. If you're the type of person who loves crafting regex patterns, Wireshark's support for them will feel like a power-up.

Sometimes, you might want to isolate packets based on **packet length**. For instance, you could filter packets with a size greater than a certain number of bytes using the filter `frame.len > 500`. This will show you only packets larger than 500 bytes, which can be helpful when troubleshooting large data transfers or looking for performance bottlenecks. Wireshark allows you to filter packets based on size, which can reveal issues with oversized payloads or identify large chunks of data that are affecting your network performance.

The next level of filtering comes with **advanced field extraction**. Wireshark allows you to filter based on **specific fields within packets**, such as **IP addresses**, **ports**, **protocols**, or even **application-layer data**. For example, if you're analyzing **DNS traffic** and want to focus only on requests to a particular domain, you can filter using `dns.qry.name == "example.com"`. This allows you to zero in on specific packets related to DNS queries, and it's incredibly useful for troubleshooting **DNS resolution** issues or **misconfigurations**.

Filter macros are another great way to simplify your workflow. If you find yourself using the same filters over and over again, Wireshark allows you to save custom filter macros. For example, if you frequently filter for **HTTP GET requests** and **specific IP addresses**, you can create a custom macro and save it for future use. This way, you can apply your complex filters with just a single click, saving time and effort. Filter macros are a fantastic productivity boost, especially when you're analyzing traffic regularly and need to stay organized.

If you're ever in doubt about the syntax of a filter or want to learn more about what's possible, **Wireshark's filter expression help** is your best friend. You can access a list of all available filter fields and syntax by going to the "Expression" button next to the filter bar. This will bring up a list of all the display filter options, with descriptions and examples for each. It's a quick and easy way to **refresh your memory** on available filters or discover new ones that might be useful for your current analysis.

Wireshark's filtering capabilities are also perfect for **grouping traffic**. For example, you can filter by **TCP stream** using the filter `tcp.stream eq 1`. This isolates traffic belonging to a specific **TCP conversation**, which is particularly useful when troubleshooting **long-duration connections** or tracking communication between two devices. By filtering by TCP stream, you can analyze the conversation in isolation, making it easier to identify issues with specific connections, such as delays, packet loss, or retransmissions.

Sometimes you'll need to **combine filters with captures**. For example, if you want to only capture **HTTP traffic** during your capture session, you can use a capture filter like `tcp port 80`. This allows you to focus on HTTP traffic as it's being captured, filtering out everything else from the start. It's an excellent technique for narrowing your focus while reducing the overall capture size, ensuring that you're only recording the relevant packets for your analysis.

Let's not forget about **statistical filters**. Wireshark offers the ability to perform statistical analysis on your captures, such as showing **protocol hierarchies** and **flow graphs**. These tools aggregate data to give you a **big-picture view** of your network's behavior. By applying filters and viewing the statistical breakdowns, you can uncover trends and patterns that might otherwise go unnoticed. If you need to track **protocol usage** or **traffic distribution**, these statistical tools will give you a high-level summary, allowing you to dive deeper into the areas that need attention.

Finally, as with any **advanced tool**, **practice makes perfect**. The more you use Wireshark's filtering features, the more intuitive they will become. Experiment with different filters, combine them in new ways, and see how they affect your captures. The flexibility of Wireshark allows you to adapt your filters to any situation, giving you an incredibly powerful tool for analyzing network traffic at every level.

In conclusion, **advanced filtering** is one of Wireshark's greatest strengths. By mastering display and capture filters, using logical operators, applying regular expressions, and exploring Wireshark's wide range of filtering options, you can transform your network analysis from overwhelming to manageable. Filters allow you to zoom in on exactly what you need and extract the most valuable insights from your captures, whether you're troubleshooting a network issue, conducting security analysis, or monitoring performance. So, start filtering like a pro and unlock the full potential of Wireshark—your network's secrets are waiting to be uncovered!

As you continue to master **Wireshark's advanced filtering techniques**, you'll find that your efficiency in network analysis improves exponentially. Being able to quickly isolate traffic, pinpoint issues, and extract meaningful insights from a packet capture is like having a superpower. **Advanced filtering** is a skill that separates the **casual packet viewer** from the **network sleuth**, and as you get more comfortable with filters, you'll begin to recognize patterns and anomalies much faster. The key is experimenting with different combinations of filters and understanding the specific needs of your analysis.

One powerful feature of Wireshark filters is the ability to **chain filters together**. You can combine multiple conditions to narrow down your analysis even further. For example, if you're looking at traffic between two devices, but you only care about **GET requests** from a specific **IP address**, you can combine filters like `ip.addr == 192.168.1.1 && http.request.method == "GET"`. By chaining filters with **AND** (`&&`) or **OR** (`||`) operators, you can perform incredibly refined searches. This makes **packet sleuthing** far more efficient, allowing you to quickly find the packet you're looking for without wading through irrelevant data.

Wildcard filtering is another advanced technique that allows you to search for patterns within fields, especially when you're looking for packets that contain part of a value but not the entire thing. For example, you can filter for any **HTTP URI** that contains a specific keyword using a display filter like `http.request.uri contains "login"`. This is especially useful when you're analyzing traffic to see if sensitive actions (like logging in) are being done over **HTTP** instead of the more secure **HTTPS**. Wildcard filtering helps you spot potential **security risks** and **protocol violations** that might not be obvious in a sea of packets.

To get the most out of Wireshark's **advanced filtering capabilities**, you also need to understand **field names** and how to apply them to your specific analysis. Field names are identifiers that reference specific attributes in the packet data, such as `ip.src` for the source IP address or `tcp.port` for the TCP port. If you're ever unsure of the field name you want to filter by, Wireshark's **display filter reference** is a great resource. You can right-click on any field in the packet details pane and select "**Apply as filter**" to automatically create a filter for that field. This allows you to quickly filter based on exactly what you're looking for without having to memorize field names.

For **deep packet inspection**, **Wireshark's "Follow" feature** can be a lifesaver. If you're troubleshooting a specific **TCP stream**, you can follow it with the **"Follow TCP Stream"** option, which isolates the conversation between two devices. This removes all extraneous data and lets you focus on the communication between the two parties. You can even export the captured stream for further analysis or share it with colleagues. It's a great way to track the entire conversation, especially when you're troubleshooting issues like **HTTP errors**, **file transfers**, or **VoIP calls**. Wireshark's "Follow" feature is perfect when you need to dive into a single conversation but don't want to get bogged down by the noise of unrelated packets.

Another helpful aspect of Wireshark filtering is **time-based analysis**. **Time-stamped filters** allow you to investigate **network anomalies** based on when they occurred. For example, if a network slowdown happens during a certain period, you can filter packets by timestamp using filters like `frame.time >= "2025-04-09 10:00:00" && frame.time <= "2025-04-09 12:00:00"`. This helps you focus on a specific timeframe to correlate events, whether it's a sudden **network congestion** spike, **packet loss**, or any **latency issues**. Time-based filtering is crucial for troubleshooting intermittent problems that only occur during certain hours or when specific events take place.

Wireshark's **expression-based filtering** is another feature that takes your filtering capabilities to the next level. If you're dealing with **complex conditions** and want to get as specific as possible, **Wireshark's filter expressions** let you write highly customizable filters using logical operators, mathematical comparisons, and even regex. For instance, if you want to identify packets with certain header values within a particular range, you could write `tcp.len > 100 && tcp.len < 500` to focus on TCP packets of medium size. By fine-tuning the filters, you can uncover issues that might be hidden in larger captures, like inefficient connections or rogue traffic patterns that might not be immediately apparent.

When you're troubleshooting **network performance** issues, **Wireshark's I/O Graphs** are a handy visual tool that can complement your filtering. These graphs allow you to plot packet capture data over time, so you can visualize the **traffic volume**, **latency**, or **packet loss**. By combining I/O graphs with **advanced filtering**, you can pinpoint **traffic spikes**, track **bandwidth consumption**, and observe the effects of specific network conditions on performance. It's like having a time-lapse view of your network's activity, helping you see when things go wrong and how the network reacts in real-time.

Filtering for errors is another advanced technique that's indispensable for identifying issues within your network. You can use **Wireshark's error-related filters** to detect things like **checksum errors**, **TCP resets**, **duplicate ACKs**, or **missequenced packets**. Filters like `tcp.analysis.retransmission` or `ip.checksum_bad` will automatically show you packets where something went wrong during transmission. These error filters help you quickly spot where **network issues** are occurring, whether it's due to **hardware failure**, **network misconfigurations**, or **connection timeouts**. By focusing on these errors, you can drill down into the root cause of the problem and correct it before it escalates.

If you're working in a **multi-protocol environment**, **filtering by multiple protocols** can help you understand how different systems are interacting with each other. For instance, if you're analyzing a scenario where **HTTP** traffic is being sent over **VPN**, you can filter for both protocols with a combined filter like `http && ipsec`. This will allow you to see how the two protocols are interleaved and identify any potential conflicts or issues with the tunnel or session. In environments where multiple applications are using the network at once, filtering for different protocols allows you to hone in on specific communications without being overwhelmed by unrelated data.

Wireshark also allows you to filter by **flags** within packets, which can be incredibly useful when diagnosing **TCP connection issues**. TCP flags such as **SYN**, **ACK**, and **FIN** are used to manage the state of the connection. For example, if you're troubleshooting a **three-way handshake**, you can filter for `tcp.flags.syn == 1` to focus on packets where the connection is starting. If you're investigating **connection resets**, you can filter for `tcp.flags.reset == 1`. Flag-based filtering helps you isolate packets that change the state of a connection, which is useful for diagnosing connection establishment or termination problems.

Another useful technique is to **analyze traffic from specific ports**. By filtering based on **source or destination ports**, you can zoom in on specific services and troubleshoot issues related to them. For example, if you suspect an issue with **DNS resolution**, you can filter packets by `udp.port == 53` to show only DNS queries and responses. Port-based filtering is invaluable when you're focusing on particular services like **HTTP**, **FTP**, or **DNS**, allowing you to isolate that traffic and quickly diagnose service-specific issues.

Wireshark's **colorization** is a great complement to filtering, especially when you want to visually distinguish between different types of traffic. By combining **color rules** with your filters, you can quickly identify important packets, such as **retransmissions**, **errors**, or specific protocols. For instance, you might color-code retransmitted packets in red, and successful TCP connections in green. This visual aid makes it easier to identify issues in real-time and speeds up the troubleshooting process. It's like having a visual dashboard that highlights the key data points as you analyze the capture.

For **network security professionals**, Wireshark's **filtering capabilities** are invaluable when identifying **malicious traffic**. Whether it's **Port Scanning**, **DDoS attacks**, or **suspect IP addresses**, filtering helps you quickly spot anomalies. For example, a filter like `ip.src == 192.168.1.100 && tcp.flags.syn == 1` might highlight **SYN scanning** attempts, where an attacker is trying to discover open ports. By filtering out the normal network traffic, you can isolate and investigate suspicious packets and take immediate action to mitigate the threat.

As you get more advanced, you'll find that **filtering by packet attributes** can reveal important insights about how protocols are interacting in your network. By focusing on **specific packet fields**, such as **sequence numbers** in TCP or **DNS query types**, you can uncover details that explain underlying performance or security issues. The more granular your filters, the more detailed your analysis becomes. Wireshark's filtering tools let you cut through the noise and examine the fine details, whether you're tracking down packet loss, latency, or intrusions.

In conclusion, **advanced filtering techniques** in Wireshark allow you to take your packet analysis from "just looking" to **serious investigation**. Whether you're isolating specific traffic, tracking errors, or looking for network anomalies, Wireshark's filters give you the ability to zoom in on exactly what you need. By mastering these advanced techniques, you'll be able to conduct faster, more efficient analysis, and uncover the root causes of network issues with precision. So, go ahead and start experimenting with filters, and before long, you'll be navigating your network traffic like a seasoned packet detective. Happy filtering!

Chapter 18: Wireshark Scripting and Automation

Imagine this: You're staring at an endless stream of packets, your eyes squinting with fatigue as you manually filter through data to isolate the culprit behind network issues. Hours pass, and you're only a fraction of the way through your capture file. Sound familiar? If so, welcome to the world of **Wireshark Scripting and Automation**. In this chapter, we'll dive into how you can automate the tedious parts of packet analysis with **Wireshark's scripting capabilities**. Think of it as giving your Wireshark superpowers—allowing you to speed up your analysis, streamline repetitive tasks, and save countless hours of manual labor.

Let's start with **Wireshark's native scripting capabilities**. Wireshark isn't just a packet analyzer; it also supports scripting to automate tasks using **TShark**, the command-line version of Wireshark. TShark allows you to capture packets, apply filters, and even save your analysis results, all from a terminal. You can use TShark for **batch processing** large capture files or for setting up **automated network monitoring**. With a few simple scripts, you can replace hours of tedious packet hunting with a few clicks. It's like turning Wireshark into your personal packet detective who works tirelessly, 24/7, without ever complaining about too many packets.

To get started with TShark scripting, you'll need to familiarize yourself with **basic command-line syntax**. For example, if you want to capture packets on a specific interface, you can run `tshark -i eth0` to capture traffic on the `eth0` interface. You can also add filters, such as `tshark -i eth0 -f "port 80"`, to capture only **HTTP traffic**. This allows you to create very specific capture sessions with just one command. The power of TShark is that it can filter traffic at the point of capture, saving you from collecting unnecessary data and focusing only on what you need.

Let's say you want to **automate the extraction of specific packet data** from a large capture. Instead of manually combing through thousands of packets, you can use TShark to filter and extract information automatically. With the command `tshark -r capture_file.pcap -Y "http.request" -T fields -e ip.src -e http.host`, you can extract the **source IP address** and **HTTP host** for all HTTP request packets in a capture file. This allows you to quickly compile the relevant information without ever having to manually look at individual packets. You can use this same approach to automate the extraction of almost any field you need.

Want to take it a step further? **Scripting with TShark** can be used to **generate reports automatically**. Imagine having TShark scan through a set of capture files, filtering out specific events like **TCP retransmissions** or **DNS resolution failures**, and then generating a summary report. A simple script like `tshark -r capture_file.pcap -Y "tcp.analysis.retransmission" -T fields -e frame.time` can give you a timeline of all retransmissions. By automating this process, you're saving yourself a huge amount of time that would otherwise be spent clicking through each packet individually.

But wait—there's more. For those of you who are more comfortable with scripting languages like **Python**, **Lua**, or **Perl**, you're in luck. Wireshark and TShark offer extensive support for integrating with external scripts. **Python**, in particular, is a popular choice for automating Wireshark tasks. Using the `pyshark` library, you can **parse capture files** and **filter traffic** programmatically. With a bit of Python code, you can extract data, run advanced analysis, and even trigger alerts if specific conditions are met. Python can help you scale up your packet analysis, turning Wireshark into an integral part of a larger automated system.

For example, let's say you want to **automatically monitor for suspicious behavior**, such as a **sudden spike in SYN packets** indicating a potential DDoS attack. With Python and **pyshark**, you could write a script that continuously analyzes the packet stream for unusual patterns. If the script detects an anomaly, it could trigger a notification or even automatically **block the offending IP address**. You can build a whole **packet monitoring system** that works in the background and alerts you only when something important happens—making your network more secure without requiring constant manual oversight.

Let's get into the specifics of **Wireshark Lua scripting**. If you've ever thought, "I wish I could just add my own custom protocols or dissectors," Lua scripting allows you to do exactly that. **Wireshark's Lua interface** allows you to write custom scripts that can analyze non-standard protocols or modify how existing protocols are displayed. For example, if you're dealing with a proprietary protocol and want to see it in Wireshark, you can write a Lua dissector to decode the packets. This is a great way to **extend Wireshark's functionality** and tailor it to your specific network needs.

If you're dealing with **high-volume traffic**, **Wireshark's automation capabilities** can help you quickly analyze large files. Instead of opening the entire capture file in the Wireshark GUI and getting bogged down by thousands of packets, you can automate the **extraction and filtering process** with TShark. Once the data is processed, you can save the results to a file or a database for further analysis. This is especially useful when you're monitoring traffic over long periods of time and need to extract trends or anomalies from **massive capture files**. This can save both time and resources, allowing you to focus on what's important.

Batch processing is another advantage of Wireshark scripting. For example, if you have hundreds or thousands of capture files that need to be analyzed, writing a script that processes each one automatically will save you a lot of effort. You can run TShark or Python scripts in **batch mode**, where the script processes each capture file one by one, applies your custom filters, and outputs results to a report. This is particularly useful for **long-term network monitoring** or **incident response**, where you need to analyze multiple captures from different time periods or locations.

If you're concerned about **real-time analysis**, Wireshark can also be automated to provide **live packet monitoring**. By integrating **TShark with a Python script**, you can continuously monitor the network for specific packet types. For example, you might create a script that captures packets in real-time, filters for **SIP calls**, and sends an alert if a call fails or if **call setup time** exceeds a certain threshold. Real-time automation can be essential in high-stakes environments where quick responses are necessary, such as **VoIP troubleshooting** or **security monitoring**.

On the **network security side**, Wireshark scripting and automation can help you detect **intrusions** and **network attacks**. For example, you could write a Python script that uses **pyshark** to capture **SYN floods** or **port scanning** activity by watching for an unusual number of connection attempts from a single IP address. Once the script detects suspicious activity, it could trigger an automatic response, like blocking the IP address or notifying an administrator. This allows you to **automate threat detection** and response, reducing the manual effort involved in monitoring your network.

As you get more advanced, you can combine **Wireshark scripts with other network monitoring tools**. For example, you might use **Wireshark** to capture packets, then use **Splunk** or another network monitoring tool to analyze the data further. By combining these tools, you can create a more comprehensive automated network monitoring system. Wireshark captures the data, and then the automation systems can filter, alert, and respond accordingly. This kind of integrated system is highly scalable and can be applied to **large enterprises** or **high-traffic networks**.

Automation can also help you with **scheduled packet captures**. If you know you need to capture packets during specific times, such as during a network performance test or a scheduled downtime, you can set up a script to automatically start the capture process at the designated time. By scripting the start and stop of captures, you eliminate the need for manual intervention, and you ensure that you're always capturing traffic at the right time.

Another way to use automation is by **automating your analysis reports**. Rather than manually creating reports after each analysis, you can use TShark and Python to generate reports automatically from each packet capture. The script can filter out the relevant packets, summarize the data, and even format it into a readable report, complete with timestamps, source and destination addresses, and specific packet details. This is a great time-saver when you need to share results with stakeholders or create documentation for ongoing network monitoring.

One of the most powerful features of **Wireshark scripting** is its ability to create **custom dissectors**. If you're dealing with proprietary protocols or systems that aren't natively supported by Wireshark, you can write custom dissectors in Lua to decode the data in a meaningful way. This adds a whole new level of **customization** to Wireshark, allowing you to work with non-standard protocols and tailor the analysis to your specific needs. This is a game-changer if you're in a specialized industry or dealing with custom-built systems.

In conclusion, **Wireshark scripting and automation** can drastically improve your efficiency and capabilities as a network analyst. Whether you're automating packet captures, generating reports, or detecting security threats, the power of scripting lets you take Wireshark to the next level. By automating the tedious and repetitive tasks, you free up your time to focus on solving the more complex network problems that require your expertise. With TShark, Python, Lua, and a little creativity, the possibilities are endless. So, go ahead—start scripting, automate your workflow, and watch your network analysis reach new heights. Happy automating!

As you dive deeper into **Wireshark scripting and automation**, you'll unlock even more powerful features that can transform how you handle network troubleshooting and analysis. The key takeaway is that automation is not just about saving time—it's about working smarter, enabling you to focus your energy on solving problems rather than spending hours sifting through raw data. Whether it's for **incident response**, **security monitoring**, or **performance testing**, Wireshark's scripting and automation capabilities can bring a level of consistency and efficiency that manual analysis simply can't match.

For example, consider **automating routine network health checks**. With scripting, you can schedule packet captures at specific times or intervals, ensuring that you're always capturing traffic during high-traffic periods or potential trouble spots. Once the capture is complete, you can automate the analysis to check for common issues such as **high latency**, **packet loss**, or **retransmissions**. If an issue is detected, your script can generate a report or send an automated alert to the network team, letting them know exactly what needs attention. This allows you to stay proactive and catch issues before they affect performance or security.

You can also use Wireshark's automation capabilities to create **custom alerts** based on specific packet behaviors. Imagine a scenario where you want to monitor your network for specific **TCP flags**, such as a sudden spike in **SYN packets**, which could indicate a **SYN flood attack**. With **TShark** and a Python script, you could set up a rule to capture and analyze traffic in real-time. If your script detects the threshold for SYN packets, it can automatically trigger an alert and even take action to block the source IP address. This type of real-time automation helps improve your network security by allowing you to respond to threats **instantly**.

Wireshark scripting also opens up the opportunity for **data visualization**. After automating packet capture and filtering, you can write scripts to plot out network performance metrics over time, creating **visual representations** of key data points like throughput, latency, or packet loss. These visual reports can be incredibly useful in identifying trends or recurring issues. Whether it's for presenting to management, tracking performance over long periods, or simply getting a clearer picture of network health, combining Wireshark with data visualization tools takes your automation to the next level.

One of the most efficient ways to implement Wireshark scripting is by integrating it with your existing network monitoring and management systems. Wireshark can be scripted to run alongside other tools like **Nagios**, **Prometheus**, or **Zabbix**. For example, Wireshark can capture packets when a system event is triggered, such as high CPU usage or a drop in performance, then analyze the traffic to pinpoint the source of the issue. By integrating Wireshark with these tools, you create a **more holistic monitoring environment**, where everything is connected and can be managed from a central dashboard.

Another aspect of Wireshark's scripting power is the ability to work with **automated packet processing pipelines**. Instead of analyzing packets manually after they've been captured, you can set up a pipeline where packets are captured, filtered, analyzed, and then processed through a series of automated steps. For instance, you could create a script that captures packets, applies display filters, extracts specific data (like **IP addresses, ports**, or **protocols**), and stores the results in a database. This streamlined workflow eliminates the need to interact with the Wireshark GUI and speeds up the process, especially when you're dealing with large-scale network environments.

Wireshark's scripting flexibility extends to handling **multiple capture files**. If you've got a large number of captures that need to be analyzed, instead of opening each one manually, you can write a script that processes all of them automatically. For instance, you could use TShark to iterate through a directory full of capture files, apply filters to each, and extract the relevant data. By batching the process in this way, you save time and ensure consistency across all captures, making it easy to process hundreds or even thousands of files in a fraction of the time.

Moreover, **Wireshark's scripting capabilities** make it ideal for **complex network tests**. For example, let's say you want to run a test to measure the performance of different network segments under heavy traffic loads. With a combination of TShark for packet capture and Python for scripting, you can automate the creation of large traffic loads, capture those packets, and then run analysis scripts to determine the network's performance. You can then generate automated reports showing how the network responds under stress, pinpointing any weak spots in your infrastructure that need attention.

When you're working with a **distributed network**, **Wireshark automation** can be particularly helpful for **coordinated packet capture and analysis** across multiple locations. By setting up Wireshark to automatically capture and send packets to a central server for analysis, you can monitor and troubleshoot network traffic across the entire network infrastructure from one central location. This kind of setup is especially useful for **multi-site enterprises**, **data centers**, or **cloud networks**, where issues might crop up in different geographic locations, and you need to analyze traffic in real-time across multiple areas simultaneously.

Wireshark scripting can also help with **regression testing** when you need to validate network performance after a change. For instance, after deploying new network equipment or software, you can use TShark to capture packets before and after the deployment. A Python script can automatically compare the captures to detect any degradation in performance, packet loss, or latency changes. This is an excellent way to ensure that network changes don't negatively impact performance or security.

If you're working in a **cloud environment** with **virtual machines** or **containers**, you can use Wireshark's automation features to monitor **network traffic** between virtualized systems. By automating packet capture between VMs or containers, you can ensure that your **microservices architecture** or **virtual networks** is communicating efficiently. The added benefit here is the ability to monitor and troubleshoot traffic in **isolated environments**, where traditional packet capture might not be possible without automation. Wireshark scripting ensures that even **virtualized environments** are under your watchful eye.

Sometimes you need to deal with **periodic packet captures** over long periods of time, especially in **network diagnostics** or **traffic analysis**. With scripting, you can automate **scheduled captures** so that Wireshark runs at specific intervals without needing human intervention. This can be particularly helpful in diagnosing intermittent issues that only occur during certain times of day or when network conditions are changing. For instance, you might set up Wireshark to capture traffic every 30 minutes, then automatically analyze the capture files every day at midnight to check for abnormal patterns or spikes in traffic. It's a perfect way to keep your network monitoring on autopilot.

Wireshark and scripting are especially powerful when it comes to **security monitoring**. By scripting packet captures and running analysis tools that automatically look for suspicious activity, you can set up continuous monitoring for **malware**, **port scans**, or **unauthorized access attempts**. You can configure alerts to notify you immediately when certain patterns or anomalies are detected in the traffic, such as large amounts of traffic from an unfamiliar IP address or an unexpected spike in **SYN packets**. This automation allows you to respond to potential threats **instantly**, without having to wait for a human to notice the problem.

One common use case for Wireshark scripting is **automated reporting**. Rather than manually reviewing packets and creating reports each time, you can automate the process so that reports are generated and sent to the relevant teams. For example, after a packet capture, you could script TShark to generate a detailed report that includes key metrics like packet loss, latency, and error rates. This can be especially helpful when **network performance reports** need to be shared with management or other stakeholders, and you don't want to spend time manually summarizing the data.

For those of you who are involved in **network auditing** or **compliance monitoring**, **Wireshark scripting** can be used to automatically verify that your network is adhering to security protocols and standards. For example, you can create scripts to check if **TLS certificates** are properly used, ensure that **SSL/TLS handshakes** are valid, or verify that **unencrypted HTTP traffic** isn't being used. Automated scripts ensure that your network remains compliant and that any violations are quickly flagged.

Lastly, **Wireshark scripting** can significantly improve your **response time** during security incidents or network breaches. By automating the detection of unusual traffic patterns, such as **DoS attacks**, **ARP spoofing**, or **packet sniffing**, you can immediately receive alerts and begin analyzing the situation. Automated scripts allow you to pinpoint the source of the issue quickly, track suspicious behavior, and take action to contain the threat before it escalates.

In conclusion, **Wireshark scripting and automation** are game-changers for anyone looking to take their network analysis to the next level. By automating repetitive tasks, generating reports, running real-time analysis, and integrating with other network monitoring tools, you can unlock the full potential of Wireshark and streamline your workflow. Whether you're dealing with massive capture files, complex network environments, or ongoing security threats, scripting allows you to focus on solving problems rather than being bogged down by manual tasks. So, start writing those scripts, automate your packet analysis, and watch your productivity skyrocket. Happy scripting!

Chapter 19: Advanced Packet Dissection

Welcome to the **fine art of advanced packet dissection**—where you transform yourself from an ordinary network analyst into a **packet surgeon** with a scalpel. At its core, packet dissection is the process of **breaking down** a packet to understand its components and analyze its purpose, and in Wireshark, it's the skill that lets you peel back the layers of data to see what's truly going on under the surface. If you've ever found yourself staring at a packet, thinking, "What in the world does this mean?"—fear not. By the end of this chapter, you'll be able to dive deep into your packets and understand even the most obscure protocols with ease.

Let's kick things off by discussing the importance of **protocol dissection**. In Wireshark, every packet you capture has a **protocol stack**, with each layer encapsulating data from the layer above it. Think of it as peeling an onion: first, you have the physical layer, then the link layer, followed by the network layer, transport layer, and finally, the application layer. Each layer plays its part in moving data from one place to another, and Wireshark is your magnifying glass for examining how each part functions. As you dissect a packet, you're effectively reverse-engineering the layers to understand the complete communication process.

One of the first things to learn in **advanced packet dissection** is **following the protocol hierarchy**. Wireshark displays this hierarchy in the packet details pane, showing you each protocol and its fields. For example, in an **Ethernet frame**, you'll see the **MAC addresses**, followed by the **IP header** containing source and destination IP addresses. By drilling down into each protocol, you can follow the **data journey** from one layer to the next. This is essential for troubleshooting because it allows you to pinpoint the exact layer where an issue might lie— whether it's a routing problem, a transport issue, or something deeper in the application layer.

Once you've got the basics down, it's time to move on to **decoding complex protocols**. The **TCP/IP protocol suite** is the backbone of most network traffic, and understanding how to dissect it is crucial for network analysis. When you inspect a **TCP packet**, for instance, you can see the **SYN**, **ACK**, and **FIN flags**, which help establish the connection or close it. But you can go deeper: **sequence numbers**, **acknowledgment numbers**, and **window size** all help you understand how data flows and whether the connection is behaving as it should. If you're seeing **out-of-order packets** or **duplicate ACKs**, it's a sign that something isn't quite right, and you can investigate further.

Next, let's talk about **TCP analysis flags**. Wireshark provides a lot of context about **TCP retransmissions**, **duplicate acknowledgments**, and **zero window sizes**—all of which can help you diagnose network problems. If you're analyzing a TCP stream and notice **retransmitted packets**, you know there's packet loss somewhere in the network. If **duplicate ACKs** keep appearing, it could indicate **delayed packets** or **congestion**. And if you see **zero window size**, it means the receiving device can't accept more data, which is often a sign of **buffering issues**. Dissecting these flags helps you piece together the puzzle of why your TCP connections might be sluggish or failing.

Now, let's dig into **protocol-specific dissections**. Wireshark is an expert at decoding a variety of protocols—everything from **HTTP** and **DNS** to **VoIP** and **FTP**. For example, when dissecting **HTTP traffic**, you can break down **GET requests**, **POST requests**, and **response codes**. Want to find a specific website visit or identify a redirect? Wireshark's dissection capabilities allow you to extract **hostnames**, **URLs**, and even **cookies** from the packet payload. **HTTP headers** such as **User-Agent**, **Content-Type**, and **Authorization** reveal a wealth of information about the communication between client and server. The more you dissect, the more you uncover about the traffic between systems.

For deeper dives, consider **VoIP** traffic analysis. VoIP is sensitive to delay and packet loss, and Wireshark can dissect **RTP (Real-time Transport Protocol)** packets, showing you how audio is being transmitted. You can inspect the **sequence numbers** to check for lost packets, **timestamps** to measure jitter, and **payload types** to understand what codec is being used. If the voice quality is bad, Wireshark lets you break down the conversation into manageable components, making it easier to find the root cause of issues like **high jitter**, **low bandwidth**, or **lost packets**.

Let's not forget about **DNS traffic dissection**—after all, every website you visit starts with a DNS request. Wireshark can dissect **DNS queries** to reveal the **domain names**, **query types**, and **response codes**. Whether you're troubleshooting a **slow DNS response** or diagnosing a **DNS poisoning attack**, understanding the DNS protocol inside out is essential. Wireshark helps you uncover details like **TTL values** (Time to Live), which can indicate **cache issues**, or **response errors** like **NXDOMAIN**, which signals that the queried domain does not exist. With this info, you can troubleshoot DNS issues quickly and efficiently.

When you dig into **packet payloads**, you're diving into the **heart of communication**. In protocols like **HTTP**, **FTP**, or **SMTP**, the payload contains the actual data being transmitted. By dissecting the payload, you can extract useful information, such as **text files**, **images**, or **authentication data**. However, if the data is encrypted (as it often is in HTTPS traffic), Wireshark won't be able to show you the contents directly. This is where **decryption** becomes useful, and we'll touch on that later. If the data is unencrypted, though, you can analyze every byte to understand what's being transmitted between systems.

To make things even more interesting, **Wireshark allows you to decode custom protocols**. Sometimes, you may come across proprietary protocols or systems that aren't natively supported by Wireshark. But no worries—**Lua scripting** lets you create custom dissectors for those protocols, decoding them in the same way Wireshark decodes well-known protocols. This is especially useful if you're working in a highly specialized network environment where proprietary protocols need to be analyzed. You can customize the dissection process to match the exact format and structure of your custom data, making Wireshark even more versatile.

One of the more advanced dissection techniques is **multi-layer packet analysis**. Sometimes, packets are **encapsulated** within other packets, such as when **IPsec** or **VPN** protocols are in use. In these cases, Wireshark decodes the outer layer first and then digs into the encapsulated protocol, allowing you to dissect each layer of the communication. This can be particularly useful when analyzing **encrypted traffic**, as it lets you see the **original payload** even if it's wrapped in multiple layers of security. Dissecting multi-layer packets is like peeling back an onion, layer by layer, until you reach the core.

Speaking of **VPNs**, **Wireshark dissection** can help you understand how **VPN tunnels** work. If you're troubleshooting a VPN connection and suspect that traffic isn't being routed properly, Wireshark can show you the **IPsec** headers and **ESP** (Encapsulating Security Payload) data. By analyzing this data, you can see how packets are encapsulated and transmitted through the VPN tunnel, helping you spot issues like **misconfigured encryption**, **fragmentation**, or **tunnel leaks**.

Another powerful feature of Wireshark is the ability to **analyze fragmented packets**. When large packets are sent over a network, they're often **fragmented** into smaller chunks to fit into the maximum transmission unit (MTU). Wireshark can dissect these fragments and reassemble them to give you a complete picture of the original packet. This is crucial for troubleshooting **fragmentation issues** and understanding how data is being transmitted across networks with varying MTU sizes.

Packet decoding and reconstruction also play a role in **reconstructing sessions**. For example, if you're analyzing an **FTP session**, you might need to see the entire session flow, from the **authentication request** to the **file transfer**. Wireshark's "Follow TCP Stream" feature makes this process easier, as it allows you to extract the entire conversation. This can be especially helpful when investigating **data exfiltration** attempts or understanding the sequence of commands that led to an error or malfunction.

Let's talk about **TCP reassembly** in more detail. When analyzing **HTTP**, **FTP**, or **email traffic**, you're often dealing with large amounts of data spread across multiple packets. Wireshark's **TCP reassembly** feature allows it to piece together these fragmented packets into a single, coherent view of the data being transferred. This is essential when trying to understand the **complete data stream** and diagnosing issues like **incomplete downloads** or **corrupted file transfers**.

One of the more specialized areas of advanced dissection is **VoIP call analysis**. VoIP packets are sent over **RTP**, and Wireshark allows you to dissect each RTP packet to see information like **sequence numbers**, **timestamps**, and **payload types**. By analyzing this data, you can measure **jitter**, **latency**, and **packet loss**, which are critical for understanding call quality. If you notice a **high level of jitter** or **loss**, Wireshark can help you pinpoint whether the issue lies with **network congestion** or the **VoIP infrastructure** itself.

Finally, **protocol development** can also benefit from advanced packet dissection. If you're building your own protocol or system, Wireshark allows you to test and debug your protocol by analyzing the **raw packets** it generates. By examining how your protocol interacts with the network, you can identify potential issues and optimize the design for better performance and reliability. With the ability to see **every byte** and **every field** in the packet, Wireshark provides the ultimate feedback mechanism for anyone developing or implementing a custom protocol.

In conclusion, **advanced packet dissection** is a cornerstone of network troubleshooting, security analysis, and performance monitoring. Whether you're dissecting complex protocols, analyzing encrypted traffic, or debugging custom systems, Wireshark equips you with the tools to break down every packet into its core components. Mastering these dissection techniques will elevate your ability to diagnose problems and uncover hidden issues, allowing you to fix network problems with precision and expertise. So, the next time you encounter a complex protocol or an elusive network issue, remember: Wireshark is your trusted scalpel, ready to dissect and reveal all the secrets of your network's communication. Happy dissection!

As you continue mastering **advanced packet dissection**, one of the most satisfying aspects of using Wireshark is its ability to **reveal hidden details** in seemingly complex or encrypted traffic. As you get more familiar with the ins and outs of **protocol layers**, **flags**, and **fields**, you'll become an expert in spotting anomalies and understanding the true nature of network communication. The beauty of packet dissection is that it's not just about finding the immediate cause of a problem—it's about **understanding the deeper story** each packet tells.

Network security professionals will also appreciate how **advanced dissection** can help uncover **security vulnerabilities**. By dissecting traffic, you can identify **suspicious patterns** or **malformed packets** that indicate potential attacks. For example, a **SYN flood attack** might show up as an unusual number of **SYN packets** without their corresponding **ACK packets**. With Wireshark, you can dissect the TCP stream and see exactly how the attack is unfolding, allowing you to stop it before it escalates. The ability to view every packet in detail gives you **precise visibility** into the behavior of malicious actors on your network.

Advanced dissection also helps you **trace network issues** that span across multiple systems. For example, if you're analyzing a **multi-hop routing issue**, Wireshark allows you to break down each hop along the route and examine the **round-trip times**, **TTL values**, and **ICMP error messages**. By following the **path of each packet**, you can isolate where the delay or failure is occurring in the network. This level of dissection is invaluable when troubleshooting complex connectivity problems or when working with **distributed systems**.

Another critical area of dissection is understanding **network flows**. **Wireshark's stream analysis** allows you to follow **TCP streams**, viewing all packets in a conversation between two endpoints. This is especially useful when debugging **application-level protocols** like **HTTP**, **SMTP**, or **FTP**. By examining the entire conversation, you can understand exactly how the client and server are communicating. This can help uncover **protocol misconfigurations**, **timeouts**, or **data corruption** that might otherwise go unnoticed. If a particular communication keeps failing, following the entire stream lets you see each step of the process, revealing exactly where things are going wrong.

To aid in your dissection process, **Wireshark has a rich set of display filters** that let you zero in on exactly the data you want to see. Want to focus only on **TCP segments** that contain a particular string or keyword in the payload? No problem. By using Wireshark's filter syntax, you can create a filter that isolates the **fields** that matter to your analysis. Whether it's filtering by **protocol**, **source IP**, **destination port**, or even **specific content**, the display filter allows you to zoom in on what's important without getting distracted by irrelevant data. This is like having a magnifying glass that helps you focus on the packet of interest, making it easy to uncover patterns and trends.

For those who work with **encrypted traffic**, **Wireshark's decryption capabilities** come into play during advanced dissection. For instance, if you are troubleshooting **HTTPS traffic**, Wireshark can decrypt SSL/TLS packets as long as you have the necessary **private key** or session secrets. With this, you can break down the encrypted data and see the actual **HTTP requests** and **responses**, just as if they were in plain text. This feature is a lifesaver when trying to understand issues like **certificate mismatches**, **SSL/TLS handshake failures**, or **encrypted**

data leakage. It's like turning a locked treasure chest into an open one, where you can see exactly what's inside.

Now, let's talk about **Wireshark's ability to analyze fragmented packets**. Fragmentation is a common technique used when large packets need to be sent across a network where the **maximum transmission unit (MTU)** is smaller than the packet size. This is often seen in **IP** networks, where large data packets are broken into smaller fragments and reassembled at the destination. Wireshark makes this process straightforward by reassembling fragmented packets in real-time. When analyzing **fragmented packets**, Wireshark lets you view both the **individual fragments** and the reassembled data, giving you the full picture. If there are issues with **packet loss** or **reassembly failures**, you'll be able to pinpoint the fragments that aren't being received and troubleshoot the root cause.

Another advanced feature in Wireshark's packet dissection toolkit is the ability to **decode proprietary protocols**. If you are working with a system that uses a custom or proprietary protocol, Wireshark's built-in dissectors might not be able to decode it properly. But with **Lua scripting**, you can create a **custom dissector** for your proprietary protocol. This allows Wireshark to understand how your custom data is structured and display it in a human-readable format. Whether you're working with a new IoT device, proprietary application, or a **vendor-specific protocol**, creating a custom dissector will allow Wireshark to break down the data into meaningful information.

Protocol tunneling is another area where Wireshark's advanced dissection features shine. Tunneling occurs when one protocol is encapsulated within another, such as when **HTTP** traffic is tunneled through **SSL** or when **VPN** traffic is encapsulated inside **IPsec**. Wireshark allows you to dissect the outer and inner layers, showing you exactly how the data is being carried over the network. You can see both the **original packet payload** and how it's being encapsulated, helping you understand how traffic flows through the tunnel. This is especially useful for troubleshooting **VPN performance** or diagnosing issues related to **encapsulated protocols**.

Another advanced dissection feature is **reconstructing full sessions** from packet captures. For example, if you're troubleshooting **file transfers** over FTP, Wireshark can piece together the **entire file transfer session** by following the **TCP stream**. This allows you to see the files being transferred in their entirety, including any errors that occurred during the process. Whether it's **HTTP downloads**, **FTP uploads**, or **email exchanges**, session reconstruction helps you see the full flow of data between endpoints, giving you insight into how well your network is performing or where it might be failing.

Wireshark's ability to capture and dissect encrypted traffic is particularly useful for security professionals. **SSL/TLS decryption** is a critical feature when you need to understand what's happening inside **secure communication channels**. If you have access to the **private key** or the **session key** (in the case of modern protocols like **TLS 1.3**), Wireshark can decrypt the traffic in real-time and present the data in a human-readable form. This enables you to identify **man-in-the-middle attacks**, **certificate issues**, or simply understand why a secure connection is failing. Decrypting this traffic gives you the **insight you need** to understand the actual content of encrypted communications, helping you troubleshoot and secure the network.

If you're dealing with **VoIP calls** and need to dissect **RTP streams**, Wireshark's advanced dissection tools can break down each packet in the conversation. It can identify **sequence numbers**, **timestamps**, and even measure **jitter** and **latency**. This level of analysis is invaluable when troubleshooting **voice quality issues** or identifying issues like **packet loss** or **delay** in the stream. You can even listen to the reconstructed audio directly in Wireshark, which makes it easier to understand exactly what's happening in a VoIP call.

Wireshark can also help you with **advanced filtering** during dissection. Let's say you want to isolate only the **packets with errors** or **certain flag settings**. With advanced display filters, you can isolate packets that meet specific criteria, such as `tcp.analysis.retransmission` to focus on retransmitted packets, or `dns.flags.response == 0` to look at DNS queries. Filtering lets you zoom in on the problematic packets and analyze them in depth without being overwhelmed by irrelevant data. It's like having a **laser pointer** that helps you focus on exactly what needs your attention.

To finish up, **advanced packet dissection** isn't just about **decoding packets**—it's about unlocking the **full story** behind network communications. With Wireshark, you're not just looking at numbers or raw data; you're understanding how each packet fits into the larger puzzle of network behavior. Whether you're dealing with **performance issues**, **security threats**, or **custom protocols**, Wireshark's advanced dissection features provide the tools you need to diagnose, analyze, and resolve issues with precision. So, next time you're faced with a packet that seems impenetrable, don't worry—just dissect it with confidence, and you'll uncover the secrets it holds. Happy dissection!

Chapter 20: Wireshark Plugins and Extensions

Wireshark is like a Swiss Army knife for network analysis—it does a lot, but what if you want it to do **even more**? Enter **Wireshark plugins and extensions**—the extra tools that turn Wireshark into an unstoppable force of network analysis. Whether you're dealing with proprietary protocols, need a custom dissector, or want to automate tasks in new ways, plugins and extensions open up an entire world of possibilities. In this chapter, we'll explore how to extend Wireshark's functionality to meet your exact needs, making it more powerful and tailored to your network analysis needs. Let's jump in and see how you can add some **extra firepower** to your Wireshark arsenal.

Let's start with **what plugins are**. Wireshark plugins are additional pieces of software that you can load into Wireshark to **extend its capabilities**. These plugins come in many forms: from **protocol dissectors** that allow Wireshark to understand custom or non-standard protocols, to **capture file parsers** that enable Wireshark to work with unique file formats. You can even write your own plugins in **Lua**, **C**, or other programming languages to **tailor Wireshark** to your needs. Think of them as little helpers that **expand Wireshark's functionality** in ways you might not have imagined.

One of the most common uses of plugins in Wireshark is for **custom dissectors**. Sometimes, you need Wireshark to understand **non-standard or proprietary protocols** that aren't supported by default. This is especially useful if you're working in a **specialized industry** or analyzing

homegrown applications. Wireshark allows you to write your own dissectors, which are small pieces of code that interpret the specific structure of your protocol. The good news is that you don't have to be a **programming wizard** to get started. With a bit of **Lua** scripting, you can easily write a dissector for your custom protocol, allowing Wireshark to **decode and display the data** exactly as you need.

If you're not familiar with Lua, don't worry—**Wireshark has extensive documentation** on how to write dissectors and load them as plugins. Lua is a **lightweight scripting language** that's embedded into Wireshark, making it easy to create custom dissectors and automate various tasks. Wireshark even has built-in support for **Lua scripting** via the **Wireshark Lua API**, which makes it incredibly easy to interact with packets and manipulate them in real-time. By writing your own Lua plugin, you can unlock the ability to decode everything from custom **TCP protocols** to obscure application-specific data.

But Wireshark plugins aren't just about creating custom dissectors. **You can also write plugins to automate tasks** or extend Wireshark's functionality in other ways. For instance, you might want a plugin that automatically highlights **specific packets**, such as **DNS queries** to a suspicious domain, or **HTTP requests** with specific user agents. Writing these **automation plugins** in Lua allows you to streamline your workflow by eliminating repetitive tasks and making your packet analysis more efficient. Automation plugins can make Wireshark smarter, allowing it to do some of the heavy lifting for you, so you can focus on solving the problem.

Another popular category of Wireshark plugins is **statistics and reporting tools**. Wireshark already provides a host of statistics (like protocol hierarchies, I/O graphs, and expert information), but what if you need something more specialized? Perhaps you want to track **packet loss** across specific connections over time or generate reports that summarize **network performance metrics**. Writing a custom plugin allows you to gather this specific information and format it into a report that suits your needs. This is particularly useful when you need **automated network health checks** or want to regularly generate performance **benchmark reports** without manually pulling the data each time.

Wireshark plugin repositories are a goldmine when it comes to finding **ready-made solutions**. Many developers and network professionals share their custom plugins with the community. You can find repositories of **Wireshark plugins** that include everything from **custom protocol dissectors** to **advanced filtering tools**. These community-driven plugins can save you time and effort, as they've already been tested and fine-tuned by others. Simply download and install the plugin, and you're ready to start using it in your analysis. It's like **borrowing someone else's Swiss Army knife**—a tool that already has all the bells and whistles you need.

To get started with installing plugins, **Wireshark makes it easy**. Plugins can be downloaded directly from the official Wireshark website, and the installation process is typically as simple as **drag-and-drop**. Once you've downloaded your plugin, just move it to the **plugin directory** in Wireshark's installation folder, restart Wireshark, and the plugin is ready to use. If you're using TShark (the command-line version of Wireshark), the plugin is also available for use from the terminal, giving you even more flexibility for automation and batch processing. Installing plugins is straightforward, but make sure to check compatibility to ensure the plugin works with your version of Wireshark.

You can also use **Wireshark extensions** to add entirely new functionality. Extensions are slightly different from plugins in that they often integrate **external tools** or libraries into Wireshark to **extend its analysis capabilities**. For example, you can integrate **external machine learning models** to analyze network traffic patterns or use **external databases** to correlate packet-level information with other network data. Extensions add another layer of customization and integration, making Wireshark not just a tool for packet analysis, but a part of a broader network management or monitoring solution.

If you need to work with **specific capture file formats**, there are **capture file parsers** that can be added as plugins. Wireshark supports many capture file formats, but sometimes you'll need to work with **non-standard formats**—perhaps a proprietary file format used by your company or by a specialized piece of equipment. By creating or installing a **capture file parser plugin**, you can tell Wireshark how to handle these files and analyze them just like any other packet capture. This is especially useful if you're working in a **niche field** where custom capture file formats are common, such as **industrial control systems** or **embedded network devices**.

Another great feature is **external analysis tools**. Some Wireshark plugins allow you to interface with external analysis tools, such as **Wireshark's integration with external Python scripts**. For example, you might use Python to perform statistical analysis or run machine learning algorithms on packet data. These external tools can pull packet data from Wireshark, process it in real-time, and return analysis results to Wireshark. This makes Wireshark a part of a much larger toolkit that leverages both **real-time packet analysis** and advanced **post-processing**.

For **packet injection and manipulation**, you can also use **Wireshark extensions** that allow you to create or modify network packets. This is particularly useful for **penetration testing** or **network diagnostics**, where you need to simulate **network conditions** like **latency**, **packet loss**, or **congestion**. These extensions let you inject specially crafted packets into the network to observe how devices react to various conditions. By combining packet capture with injection capabilities, Wireshark becomes not just a tool for analysis but also a tool for **active testing**.

You may also want to look into **custom GUI extensions** for Wireshark. While the default Wireshark interface is pretty intuitive, certain use cases might require **tailored interfaces**. Custom GUI extensions let you add buttons, menus, or even entirely new panes to Wireshark's interface, allowing you to create a **bespoke workflow** for specific tasks. For example, if you're frequently analyzing **DNS traffic**, you could create a custom GUI that gives you quick access to the most relevant filters and statistics for DNS analysis. These extensions make it easier to interact with Wireshark, saving time and improving efficiency.

For **real-time packet processing**, you can develop plugins that automate the analysis as packets arrive. This is ideal for **live network monitoring** or **incident detection**. By building a plugin that processes packets on-the-fly, you can set up **real-time alerts**, extract key metrics, and even trigger actions when certain patterns are detected. Imagine capturing and analyzing **VoIP traffic** in real-time to monitor for issues like jitter, packet loss, or call quality degradation—these are the kinds of scenarios where real-time plugin functionality is a game-changer.

Let's not forget about **cross-platform compatibility**. Many Wireshark plugins are designed to work on multiple operating systems, including **Windows**, **Linux**, and **macOS**. This is incredibly important for teams that work in heterogeneous environments, where different OS platforms are used. Whether you're running Wireshark on a laptop, a server, or a cloud instance, you'll be able to install and use the same plugins across all systems. This cross-platform support ensures that no matter where your Wireshark instance is running, you have the full power of plugins at your disposal.

One of the **most exciting parts of Wireshark plugins** is that they are often developed and maintained by a **community of network professionals**. This means that, as new needs arise, **innovative solutions** are constantly being developed. As part of the Wireshark community, you have access to this ever-growing library of tools. If you can't find the plugin you need, you can **develop it yourself** or ask others for help. This collaborative environment makes Wireshark not just a tool, but a **thriving ecosystem** where your input and contributions can have a lasting impact.

In conclusion, **Wireshark plugins and extensions** turn Wireshark into more than just a packet analyzer—they transform it into a **highly customizable tool** that fits your specific needs. Whether you're creating custom dissectors, automating tasks, analyzing encrypted traffic, or extending Wireshark's interface, plugins and extensions allow you to unlock **untapped potential**. By embracing the world of plugins, you'll find that Wireshark is not just versatile— it's **limitless**. So, start exploring the world of plugins, experiment with new functionalities, and enjoy the **extended power** of Wireshark. Happy extending!

To wrap up, the world of **Wireshark plugins and extensions** is a dynamic and exciting realm that allows you to expand your network analysis toolkit far beyond the basics. Whether you're a **network administrator**, **security professional**, or a **developer**, **customizing Wireshark** with plugins and extensions opens up an entirely new dimension of capability. You can build tools that enhance your workflow, automate your analysis, and create a more tailored experience that aligns with your specific needs.

The power of Wireshark's plugin ecosystem lies not just in its **customizability** but in its **flexibility**. By using plugins and extensions, you can integrate Wireshark with other tools, enhance its built-in capabilities, and even create **entirely new functionalities** that wouldn't have been possible otherwise. You can work with **custom protocols**, generate **automatic reports**, monitor **real-time data**, or even manipulate packets in ways that would make a traditional network tool blush. The real potential lies in your creativity, the problems you're trying to solve, and how you can bend Wireshark's capabilities to meet those challenges.

You don't need to be an expert developer to get started with plugins. With a little **scripting knowledge**, particularly in **Lua**, you can start writing your own plugins to suit your needs. Lua is relatively easy to pick up, and because it's embedded in Wireshark, you can start experimenting right away. You can begin by creating simple **custom dissectors** or **automated filters**, and as you grow more comfortable, you can start building more complex plugins. The **Wireshark developer community** is supportive, with resources, forums, and documentation available to help you along the way.

For those who aren't interested in coding, don't worry. **The Wireshark community** is full of **pre-built plugins** that are available for download. These plugins cover a wide range of use cases, from **custom dissectors** to **report generators** to **packet analysis tools**. Many of these plugins are open-source, and you can modify them to fit your specific needs. This makes it easy to extend Wireshark without having to dive into programming, while still getting the full benefit of powerful, community-developed solutions.

Another advantage of plugins is that they allow you to **stay ahead of emerging technologies**. As new networking protocols, technologies, and security methods are developed, the Wireshark community continues to push out plugins and extensions that allow you to dissect and analyze them. Whether it's **5G network analysis**, **IoT devices**, or **emerging application-layer protocols**, there's a plugin or extension that will keep Wireshark up to date with the latest developments. This ensures that Wireshark remains a **cutting-edge tool** for all your packet analysis needs.

One of the best ways to get started with **Wireshark extensions** is to explore **Wireshark's plugin repository**. It's full of gems waiting to be discovered. From **detailed traffic analyzers** to **real-time alerting systems**, you can find a plugin that suits your specific use case. Many of these plugins are actively maintained by **Wireshark developers** and the community, which ensures that they are reliable and up-to-date. Browsing through the repository can be both a great learning experience and an excellent way to find tools that you didn't even know you needed.

If you're working in a **high-volume environment** where **real-time packet capture** and analysis is essential, plugins for **real-time monitoring** are an absolute must. These plugins allow you to **filter**, **monitor**, and **alert** based on specific conditions as packets arrive, without having to sift through capture files after the fact. Real-time packet dissection can help you spot problems **before they escalate**—whether it's **traffic congestion**, **security threats**, or **protocol failures**. With plugins, Wireshark evolves into a live monitoring tool that alerts you to potential issues, providing you with actionable insights when you need them most.

Let's not forget about **network security analysis**. With the rise of **cyber threats** and **network intrusions**, plugins are indispensable for **automating threat detection**. You can use plugins to look for **signature-based attacks**, **anomalous traffic patterns**, or even specific types of **malware communications**. There are **security-specific plugins** that will automatically analyze packets for **common attack signatures**, like **DDoS**, **SQL injections**, or **port scanning activities**. This allows you to instantly recognize malicious activity and respond swiftly.

For those working with **cloud networks** or **virtualized environments**, extensions allow Wireshark to adapt to the unique challenges of monitoring virtual networks. Plugins can help you **capture and analyze traffic** in virtual machines or containers, which is crucial for maintaining security and performance in cloud environments. Understanding how these virtualized systems communicate is critical, and with the right plugin, you can integrate **Wireshark into your cloud monitoring workflow**, making it easier to manage and troubleshoot these environments.

Wireshark also supports **integration with external tools** via plugins, allowing you to **augment its capabilities** with external data or analysis. For instance, you can integrate Wireshark with tools like **Splunk** or **Elasticsearch** to combine packet-level data with higher-level network monitoring or logging data. This allows you to correlate events across different tools and get a more comprehensive picture of network behavior. By using Wireshark with **external tools**, you can build a **powerful, automated monitoring and reporting pipeline** that keeps you informed and prepared.

While the Wireshark community offers many powerful plugins, **creating your own plugin** gives you the ultimate flexibility. Whether you're looking to create a **custom dissector** for a protocol unique to your company, automate specific analysis workflows, or build entirely new features, the **plugin system** empowers you to tailor Wireshark to your exact needs. **Lua scripting** makes this process accessible to everyone, even those without deep programming expertise. Custom plugins let you transform Wireshark into a tool that's perfectly suited for your unique challenges, whether you're working in network performance, security, or development.

But what about integrating **Wireshark into larger systems**? With the right plugin, Wireshark doesn't have to be an isolated tool. You can integrate it into your existing **network management systems**, **security infrastructure**, or **data collection pipelines**. By writing a plugin that interfaces with your systems, you can ensure that Wireshark is working in tandem with other network tools. This kind of integration allows for **end-to-end network management**, where Wireshark captures and analyzes traffic, then feeds that data into a larger ecosystem for decision-making or automation.

Lastly, there's no need to worry about **compatibility issues**—Wireshark plugins are regularly updated to ensure that they work with the latest versions of Wireshark. If a plugin breaks or falls out of date, the **Wireshark community** is quick to patch and update it. Plus, as a Wireshark user, you have access to an extensive knowledge base and **support forums** where you can find answers, ask questions, and even contribute to the development of new plugins.

In conclusion, **Wireshark plugins and extensions** are the secret sauce that turns an already powerful tool into a **highly customizable solution**. From adding support for custom protocols to automating packet analysis to integrating Wireshark with larger systems, plugins allow you to tailor Wireshark to your specific needs. The **Wireshark plugin ecosystem** is an invaluable resource, whether you're looking for pre-built solutions or want to develop your own custom tools. With plugins, you can push Wireshark beyond its base functionality and adapt it to meet the demands of **your unique network environments**. So, start exploring plugins, create your own extensions, and discover just how much more Wireshark can do. Happy extending!

Chapter 21: Working with Capture Files

Welcome to the world of **Wireshark capture files**, where the packets are the stars of the show, and you, the analyst, are the detective. When it comes to **network troubleshooting**, **security analysis**, or **performance monitoring**, capturing packets is just the first step in understanding what's happening on your network. But let's face it: as much as capturing data is important, you'll spend most of your time **working with capture files**—examining them, analyzing them, and, yes, filtering through endless streams of packets to uncover the nuggets of information that matter. In this chapter, we're going to dive deep into the art of **working with capture files** in Wireshark, teaching you how to handle, analyze, and extract meaningful insights from those raw packet captures.

Let's start with the basics: **what is a capture file**? Simply put, a **capture file** is a file containing a record of network packets that Wireshark has captured during a specific period of time. It's essentially a **snapshot** of all the network activity occurring during the capture session. These files can contain a vast amount of data, sometimes over **millions of packets**, which is why it's so important to know how to **manage** and **analyze** these files efficiently. You don't want to get lost in a haystack when you're searching for the proverbial needle.

The first thing to know about **capture files** is that they come in different formats, but **PCAP** (Packet Capture) and **PCAPNG** (PCAP Next Generation) are the most common. **PCAP** files are the classic format and are widely supported by network analysis tools, while **PCAPNG** is a newer format that provides more features, like support for **multiple interfaces** and **packet annotations**. Wireshark can handle both formats seamlessly, but understanding which format works best for your needs is important, especially when you need to share or export your capture files to others or to different analysis tools. It's like choosing between **MP4** and **AVI**—both can hold video, but sometimes you need the right format for the right task.

Capturing packets in Wireshark is straightforward, but what do you do when the **capture file** gets large? Capture files can grow to **gigabytes** in size, depending on the amount of traffic being captured and the length of the session. If you're working on a large capture file, you'll want to make sure your system is equipped to handle the data efficiently. Don't worry, Wireshark has **built-in tools** to manage large capture files, including the ability to **split** them into smaller files, so you're not overwhelmed with one massive file that's tough to handle. You can also **set capture limits** in Wireshark to avoid creating unmanageable files in the first place. Always be mindful of your system's storage capacity when working with long capture sessions.

Once you've captured a file, you'll likely want to **filter** the data to zero in on what matters. Wireshark has a powerful set of **display filters** that let you focus on specific types of traffic, such as **TCP connections**, **HTTP requests**, or **DNS queries**. You can also apply **time-based filters** to zoom in on specific time periods in your capture. The beauty of Wireshark's filtering system is that it gives you the flexibility to **slice and dice** your data, enabling you to analyze **precise packets** without having to sift through the entire capture. It's like having a search engine for network traffic—find exactly what you need, and leave the rest behind.

If you're dealing with **large capture files** and need to narrow down your analysis even further, **Wireshark's "Follow" feature** is a great tool. This feature allows you to isolate specific **TCP streams** or **UDP conversations**, so you can analyze the full conversation between two devices without getting distracted by other traffic. You can **follow TCP streams** for web traffic, **VoIP calls**, or any other protocol, giving you a complete view of the data flow between two endpoints. This tool is incredibly helpful when you need to troubleshoot **long-duration connections**, track **file transfers**, or just understand how devices are communicating with each other over the network.

When working with **multiple capture files**, it's common to need a way to **merge** them into one. Luckily, Wireshark makes this process easy. The **mergecap** tool, a command-line utility that comes with Wireshark, allows you to combine **separate PCAP files** into a single file for easier analysis. This is especially useful when you've captured data on different interfaces or at different times and need to consolidate everything into one comprehensive file. With **mergecap**, you can maintain the integrity of the original capture files while bringing everything together in a cohesive way. It's like organizing your notes from multiple meetings into one neat file—you can see the whole picture without missing any details.

Exporting data from a capture file is another essential skill for Wireshark users. Once you've filtered and analyzed your data, you may want to export key information to share with colleagues or use in reports. Wireshark lets you **export packet data** in various formats, including **CSV**, **JSON**, and **XML**. This gives you the flexibility to use the exported data in other tools, such as spreadsheets, databases, or data visualization software. Whether you're creating a report for management or sharing findings with a colleague, Wireshark makes it easy to **export the data** in a format that works best for your workflow.

One particularly useful feature in Wireshark is **the ability to search within capture files**. You can search for specific fields, strings, or even **packet contents** within a capture. This is invaluable when you need to locate **particular packets** in a large file or **track down specific events**. Searching for a specific **IP address** or **protocol** helps you pinpoint issues without manually scrolling through thousands of packets. This search functionality can save you tons of time and effort—especially when you're dealing with **massive capture files**. Use the search tool, and you'll find exactly what you need with ease.

Wireshark's **file compression** capabilities also come in handy when dealing with large captures. If you're working with a particularly **large capture file** and need to save space or share it more easily, you can compress the file using **gzip** or **zip**. Wireshark will handle the decompression when you open the file again, so you don't have to worry about losing any data. Compressing capture files allows you to keep a more **organized archive**, saving you valuable disk space without sacrificing the integrity of your packet data. Just be careful not to lose any critical details during compression.

Capture file security is a serious consideration when sharing packet data, especially if the file contains sensitive information. Wireshark allows you to **password-protect capture files** to prevent unauthorized access. You can also redact or **filter out sensitive data** before sharing the file, such as **IP addresses**, **authentication details**, or **session tokens**. This is an important practice for ensuring **privacy and compliance** with security protocols. Remember, while packet captures are incredibly useful for troubleshooting, they can also contain **private or confidential information**, so always take care when sharing or exporting data.

Sometimes, **packet loss** or **capturing traffic intermittently** can result in **gaps** in your capture files. Fortunately, Wireshark can help you identify these gaps by analyzing **sequence numbers** and **timestamps**. If you notice that the sequence of packets isn't continuous, you might have dropped packets, which can lead to incomplete analysis. Identifying packet loss or gaps allows you to **adjust your capture settings** or **retry the capture** to get a more accurate picture of the network's behavior.

When dealing with **encrypted traffic**, **Wireshark's decryption capabilities** come into play when analyzing capture files. If you're capturing **HTTPS**, **IPsec**, or **Wi-Fi** traffic, you might need to provide the necessary **keys** or **certificates** to decrypt the data. Once decrypted, Wireshark can show you the **HTTP payload**, **FTP file transfers**, or other application-layer data that was previously hidden by encryption. Decrypting traffic in capture files is vital when investigating network issues or conducting a security analysis. However, always remember to handle **decryption keys** responsibly and ensure they're stored securely.

Another useful feature for working with capture files is **packet reassembly**. In some cases, packets are too large to fit in a single frame and are broken into smaller fragments. Wireshark automatically reassembles these fragments during the dissection process, but you can manually control **fragmentation behavior** using Wireshark's settings. This feature is especially useful when analyzing protocols like **IP**, **RTP**, or **FTP** where fragmentation might occur. By reassembling fragmented packets, you get a **full picture** of the original data being transmitted, which is crucial for accurate analysis.

Finally, let's talk about **best practices for managing capture files**. One of the most important practices is **organizing your captures**. As you accumulate packet captures, make sure you're labeling them with **descriptive filenames**, including **timestamps**, **network interfaces**, and any relevant metadata (like the purpose of the capture). This organization will save you time later when you need to retrieve specific files or identify the right capture for troubleshooting. Also, consider **archiving old captures** to keep your system tidy. With proper organization and archiving, you'll be able to quickly find the **capture file** you need and dive into the analysis without hesitation.

In conclusion, working with **capture files** is an essential skill for network professionals. Whether you're dealing with large files, need to filter out specific packets, or want to collaborate with teammates, Wireshark gives you the tools to handle **capture files** effectively. From managing file size and security to performing deep packet analysis, Wireshark ensures that you can make sense of even the most complex network traffic. So next time you're faced with a massive capture file, remember: it's just another puzzle waiting to be solved. Happy capturing!

As you continue your journey with **Wireshark capture files**, the possibilities for network analysis seem endless. From dissecting specific protocols and analyzing complex interactions between devices to troubleshooting performance and security issues, **working with capture files** is a vital skill that will serve you well in a wide variety of scenarios. The more you work with **capture files**, the more comfortable you will become in managing large datasets, navigating through them efficiently, and leveraging the full power of Wireshark's **analysis tools** to draw actionable insights.

One of the most important aspects of **working with capture files** is **keeping your analysis organized**. As your captures grow in size and number, it becomes increasingly important to keep a structured approach to storing and labeling files. Using **descriptive names**, clear **tags**, and even **metadata** like **time ranges**, **interface information**, or the **capture's purpose** can save you a ton of time when you need to revisit or share these captures down the road. This is especially critical in **incident response scenarios** where capturing detailed, well-organized files is vital to understanding the timeline of an event or attack. Proper organization and clear documentation allow you to **retrace steps** in your analysis process quickly.

Another useful feature in **Wireshark** is **capture file splitting**, which allows you to break a large capture file into smaller, more manageable pieces. This is particularly helpful when you're dealing with high-traffic environments or **long-term captures** that generate **huge files**. With **Wireshark's capture options**, you can set size limits for capture files, automatically splitting them when they exceed a certain size. This keeps your analysis manageable and ensures that you don't end up with one giant file that's impossible to open or navigate. With the ability to split files efficiently, you can focus on one chunk at a time and analyze data without worrying about file bloat.

When **filtering through capture files**, remember that **time-based filters** are your best friend. If you're dealing with **long-duration captures**, you don't have to analyze the entire file at once. By focusing on specific time windows where you suspect issues might have occurred—whether it's a **performance dip**, **security event**, or **service failure**—you can streamline your analysis. Time-based filters let you zoom in on the period of interest and save you from sifting through hours or days of data. You can even combine these filters with other conditions, like filtering for **DNS traffic** during a certain timeframe, to narrow down the data even further.

If you're dealing with encrypted traffic in a capture file, **Wireshark's decryption tools** are indispensable. Many modern protocols, like **HTTPS** and **IPsec**, encrypt their payloads, making them unreadable at first glance. However, if you have access to the necessary **keys** or **session information**, Wireshark can decrypt the data in real-time, allowing you to analyze the traffic as if it were unencrypted. For example, you can decrypt **HTTPS traffic** using **SSL/TLS session keys**, **private keys**, or **pre-shared secrets**. Once decrypted, Wireshark reveals the **HTTP headers**, **payload**, and **application data** that were hidden within the encrypted packets. This is an invaluable tool when you need to see what's going on inside **secure communications**.

If your capture files include **multi-hop traffic**, where packets traverse multiple network devices, **Wireshark's flow analysis tools** will help you visualize the packet's journey. Understanding the **end-to-end flow** of a packet across different segments of the network allows you to identify **latency**, **bottlenecks**, or **routing issues**. By following packets through their journey, you can see exactly where they go wrong—whether it's stuck in a routing loop or encountering a slow device in the middle of the network. **Flow analysis** helps you not only identify **network problems** but also understand **how data traverses your network** from source to destination.

One of the more overlooked features of **Wireshark** is **exporting captured data**. Sometimes, the best analysis is done not inside Wireshark, but in **other tools**. You may want to export the data into formats like **CSV**, **JSON**, or **XML** for use in **spreadsheets**, **databases**, or **other analysis platforms**. This is especially useful when you need to share data with others or aggregate results from multiple captures. Wireshark makes it incredibly easy to export specific fields or entire packets into these formats. It's like having the flexibility of **data wrangling** in a traditional **network analysis tool**.

Packet loss can be one of the more challenging issues to track in **capture files**. While Wireshark does its best to **reassemble fragmented packets**, sometimes packets can be dropped or arrive out of sequence. By analyzing **TCP sequence numbers**, **ACKs**, and **timestamps**, Wireshark can help you identify where packets are being lost and how the network is compensating for those losses. For instance, if you notice **retransmissions** or **duplicate ACKs**, it's a strong indicator that packet loss is occurring. **Identifying packet loss** within the capture helps you not only understand where the issue is happening but also provides insight into **network reliability** and performance.

For **complex protocols** or **application-layer data**, **Wireshark's expert analysis features** provide high-level insights into what's going on in your capture. Whether you're troubleshooting **VoIP call quality**, **file transfers**, or **database queries**, Wireshark's expert analysis tools automatically highlight potential issues in the packets. These expert messages give you warnings or suggestions, such as **TCP retransmissions**, **SYN floods**, or **DNS resolution failures**, saving you time by flagging problematic packets immediately. By leveraging **expert analysis**, you can quickly pinpoint the most critical issues in your capture and dive into deeper investigation with less effort.

Let's talk about **reassembling TCP streams**. Often, when you're analyzing **TCP-based applications** like **HTTP**, **FTP**, or **SMTP**, the data is spread across multiple packets. Wireshark's **"Follow TCP Stream"** feature helps by reassembling the packets in order to view the complete conversation between two endpoints. This allows you to see the entire **request-response cycle** for HTTP traffic, or follow an **FTP file transfer** from start to finish. This feature is extremely helpful when trying to troubleshoot **multi-step protocols** where the packet order is crucial to understanding the full communication. With this feature, it's as if you're reading a **complete transcript** of the interaction.

If you find that a capture file is **too large to work with**, **Wireshark's capture filters** let you avoid the pain of dealing with unnecessary data. For instance, you can set **capture filters** to only capture **specific traffic types**, such as **HTTP**, **DNS**, or **FTP**. This reduces the size of the file right from the start, eliminating the need for massive file parsing later. Capture filters allow you to get straight to the **data you care about** without worrying about irrelevant traffic bogging you down. For smaller or more specific captures, this proactive filtering strategy helps keep everything neat and easy to work with.

Let's not forget about **handling errors in capture files**. Sometimes, network issues like **packet corruption** or **checksum errors** can appear in capture files, and Wireshark does an excellent job of flagging these problems. By examining the **error messages** and **flags** in the capture file, you can determine the severity of the issue and its potential impact on network communication. **Wireshark's expert information** also helps here by highlighting potential errors, such as **bad checksums**, **misaligned packets**, or **protocol violations**. This makes it easy to spot trouble spots and take action accordingly.

Wireshark also allows you to reanalyze previous captures with the latest features and enhancements. If you're working on an older capture file and Wireshark has released new protocol decoders or bug fixes, you can **reopen and reanalyze** the file with the updated version of Wireshark. This means that even if you've missed something during the initial analysis, you can go back and take advantage of **newly released features** to uncover more insights. Reanalyzing old data ensures that you're always working with the best version of the tool, and that you're not missing anything due to outdated decoders or analyses.

To wrap it up, **working with capture files** in Wireshark is a key skill for any network analyst or security professional. Whether you're filtering for specific traffic, merging multiple files, exporting data for analysis, or reassembling fragmented packets, Wireshark gives you all the tools you need to work efficiently with capture data. By staying organized, using the right filters, leveraging expert analysis tools, and knowing how to handle large files, you can tackle any network analysis task with confidence. So, next time you find yourself working with a capture file, just remember: you've got a wealth of tools at your fingertips to help you make sense of the data. Happy capturing and analyzing!

Chapter 22: Network Performance Monitoring with Wireshark

In the world of network analysis, **Wireshark** is like the Swiss Army knife you never knew you needed. It's the go-to tool when you want to break down packets, troubleshoot connectivity issues, or dive into the **nitty-gritty** of network performance. However, there's a hidden gem in Wireshark that's often overlooked: **network performance monitoring**. If you want to take your network diagnostics to the next level, Wireshark's performance monitoring capabilities will let you do everything from identifying **latency issues** to spotting **bandwidth bottlenecks**. In this chapter, we'll explore how Wireshark can be used as your trusty sidekick for monitoring network performance and keeping your systems running smoothly.

First, let's define **network performance**. At its core, network performance refers to how well your network performs in terms of **speed**, **reliability**, and **efficiency**. Performance problems can manifest in various ways: **high latency**, **packet loss**, **jitter**, or **slow throughput**. These issues can wreak havoc on real-time applications like **VoIP**, **video conferencing**, and **online gaming**. With Wireshark, you can dig into the **root causes** of these issues by monitoring and analyzing packet-level data. Think of Wireshark as the ultimate performance **diagnostic tool** that lets you peek behind the curtain to see what's really going on.

When it comes to **monitoring latency**, Wireshark gives you the ability to track **round-trip times** between devices. Latency is essentially the time it takes for a packet to travel from the source to the destination and back. High latency can be caused by issues like **network congestion**, **routing inefficiencies**, or even **slow hardware**. Wireshark allows you to monitor **TCP handshakes**, **ICMP requests**, and **timestamps** to measure round-trip times accurately. This helps you pinpoint where delays are occurring and identify whether the issue lies with your network or something else in the communication chain. Monitoring latency is crucial for **real-time applications** that are sensitive to delays, and Wireshark makes it easy to get the data you need to diagnose those issues.

Next up is **packet loss**, another critical factor in network performance. Packet loss occurs when one or more packets fail to reach their destination, leading to degraded application performance, especially in **VoIP calls** and **video streaming**. Wireshark helps you **detect packet loss** by analyzing **sequence numbers** in **TCP streams**. If the sequence numbers aren't continuous, it's a red flag that packets have been lost in transit. You can also use **expert information** in Wireshark, which will highlight instances of packet loss and retransmissions. By spotting packet loss early, you can take steps to mitigate it before it becomes a major issue for your network users.

Another key element of network performance is **jitter**, which refers to the variability in packet delay. Jitter is particularly problematic for **real-time communications** like **voice** and **video calls**, where consistent timing is crucial for maintaining quality. Wireshark allows you to measure jitter by analyzing **RTP (Real-time Transport Protocol)** packets. By looking at the **timestamps** of RTP packets, you can determine the **variance** in arrival times. If jitter is too high, it can result in distorted audio or video, causing a poor user experience. Wireshark's **RTP analysis tools** provide you with a **visualization** of jitter and help you figure out if network congestion or routing issues are to blame.

But what about **bandwidth usage**? Wireshark has tools for tracking **network throughput**, which tells you how much data is being transferred across the network over time. You can use **Wireshark's I/O graphs** to visualize throughput and see how much bandwidth is being consumed at different times. This helps you identify **traffic spikes** or periods of **high utilization** that could be causing slowdowns. By analyzing the graph, you can see whether your network is overloaded or if certain applications are hogging all the bandwidth. You can also track **TCP window sizes** and **flow control** to understand how much data is being sent without overloading the network. If you notice that bandwidth is consistently maxed out, it may be time to optimize the network or implement **quality of service (QoS)** to prioritize critical traffic.

One of Wireshark's most powerful features for network performance monitoring is its ability to track **TCP flow control**. TCP flow control is responsible for ensuring that the receiving device isn't overwhelmed with too much data at once. If the **TCP window size** is too small, data will be sent more slowly, which can lead to bottlenecks and poor performance. Wireshark can show you the **window size** and whether it's dynamically adjusting during the session. If you're dealing with a slow connection, looking at the **TCP flow control** and **window scaling** can provide important clues about the underlying issue.

For **large-scale networks**, Wireshark's ability to capture traffic from **multiple interfaces** is essential for performance monitoring. In a complex network, you might need to analyze traffic from different segments or devices to understand how the entire network is performing. With Wireshark, you can capture traffic from multiple interfaces and **combine the data** into a single analysis. This helps you identify where the network is slowing down—whether it's on the **local network**, the **internet gateway**, or between different **subnets**. You can filter and drill down into the data from each interface to understand where the bottlenecks are and address them accordingly.

Now, let's talk about **network congestion**. Wireshark can help you spot congestion by analyzing **TCP retransmissions** and **duplicate ACKs**. When a network is congested, packets can get delayed or dropped, leading to retransmissions and a buildup of traffic. By looking for **high retransmission rates**, Wireshark can give you an early warning that something is wrong with your network. High **duplicate ACKs** indicate that the receiver is missing packets and is requesting them again. If you're seeing a lot of retransmissions, it's a clear sign that your network might be suffering from congestion, and it's time to investigate further.

For those of you in charge of **enterprise networks** or **data centers**, **Wireshark's statistics tools** are invaluable for ongoing performance monitoring. Wireshark can generate detailed **protocol hierarchies**, **flow graphs**, and **I/O graphs** that give you a clear picture of how different protocols and devices are performing. These statistics help you spot performance issues early and understand **network behavior** at a high level. By using Wireshark's statistical tools, you can quickly get a sense of whether your network is performing optimally or if something's causing delays or packet loss. It's like having a **real-time dashboard** for your entire network.

One great tool for monitoring network performance is **Wireshark's expert information** feature, which provides warnings and alerts about potential issues in your capture file. For example, it will highlight **TCP retransmissions**, **duplicate ACKs**, and **packet loss** in real-time. This is incredibly useful when you need to quickly spot performance issues without manually going through every packet. Expert information gives you a heads-up about what's going wrong in your network and allows you to focus on fixing the problem rather than hunting for it. It's like having a **network watchdog** that alerts you whenever something goes off track.

Wireshark also helps you analyze **VoIP performance** through its **RTP stream analysis** tools. If you're troubleshooting a **VoIP system**, looking at the RTP stream is key to identifying performance issues like **jitter**, **latency**, and **packet loss**. Wireshark's RTP analysis tool can show you the **jitter buffer**, **sequence numbers**, and **timestamps** for each RTP stream, allowing you to evaluate call quality in real time. If you're dealing with poor call quality, the **RTP analysis** feature will help you figure out if the problem is related to network congestion, jitter, or packet loss.

If you're working with **wireless networks**, **Wireshark** has a few tricks up its sleeve for monitoring **Wi-Fi performance** as well. By capturing **802.11 frames**, you can analyze wireless network performance and troubleshoot issues like **signal strength**, **interference**, and **channel congestion**. Wireshark provides a detailed breakdown of **signal strength** (RSSI), which can help you determine if poor wireless performance is due to distance from the access point or interference from nearby devices. **Channel overlap** is another common issue Wireshark can help you identify, allowing you to switch to a less congested channel and improve performance.

Finally, let's talk about **best practices** for network performance monitoring with Wireshark. The key is to stay proactive and use Wireshark's tools regularly. Set up **alerts for high retransmission rates**, **monitor network bandwidth usage**, and **track round-trip times** over the course of the day or week. Wireshark's **real-time monitoring features** make it easy to keep an eye on performance while you're troubleshooting other network issues. If you stay ahead of performance problems, you can resolve them before they affect your users.

In conclusion, **Wireshark is an incredibly powerful tool for network performance monitoring**, whether you're dealing with latency, jitter, packet loss, congestion, or throughput issues. With its robust set of analysis tools, you can dive deep into **packet-level performance data** and uncover the root causes of network slowdowns or failures. From **real-time monitoring** to **historical analysis**, Wireshark gives you the visibility you need to keep your network running smoothly. So, start monitoring your network's performance with Wireshark, and you'll be well on your way to ensuring optimal performance for all your users. Happy monitoring!

As we wrap up this chapter on **network performance monitoring with Wireshark**, let's revisit the main takeaways. **Wireshark** is not just a tool for analyzing network traffic; it's a powerhouse for actively monitoring and troubleshooting network performance in real time. By utilizing Wireshark's **latency measurements**, **packet loss detection**, **jitter analysis**, and **throughput**

tracking, you can stay on top of your network's health and quickly identify performance bottlenecks before they disrupt operations.

Latency is one of the first indicators of performance degradation, and with Wireshark, you can pinpoint where delays are occurring—whether it's a slow router, a congested link, or a network misconfiguration. By measuring round-trip times and tracking **TCP handshakes** and **ICMP pings**, you can pinpoint areas that need optimization. Once you spot high latency, you can investigate the **route** the packets are taking, check for network congestion, and even look at **hardware issues** that might be introducing delays.

Packet loss detection is another essential aspect of network performance, especially when you're dealing with **real-time applications** like VoIP or streaming. Using **sequence numbers** and **duplicate ACKs** in Wireshark, you can easily spot dropped packets. Identifying packet loss early allows you to take corrective actions, such as adjusting your **TCP settings** or even tweaking the **MTU** size, to ensure that your applications continue to run smoothly without interruptions.

For those working with **real-time communications**, **Wireshark's jitter analysis** tools are indispensable. Real-time apps like **video calls** and **VoIP** are highly sensitive to jitter, which is the variation in delay between packets. Wireshark's ability to measure and visualize jitter helps you understand whether poor call quality or video distortion is due to **network fluctuations** or issues with the **RTP stream**. By analyzing jitter trends over time, you can proactively optimize your network to ensure smooth communications.

When it comes to **bandwidth monitoring**, Wireshark's **I/O graphs** are an incredibly useful tool. By visualizing the traffic flow in real-time, you can see which devices or applications are consuming the most bandwidth. This can help you identify whether bandwidth hogs are saturating your network, whether it's due to a single user or a specific application. With this information, you can decide whether to adjust **QoS settings**, add more bandwidth, or reconfigure devices to ensure optimal network performance.

Wireshark's flow analysis tools also give you an inside look into how packets are being transferred across multiple devices in your network. This allows you to understand **flow control**, track data **transfer times**, and analyze **end-to-end communication**. Whether it's an issue of congestion or a misconfigured network device, these tools make it easier to track down problems by showing you exactly how data moves through your network. By evaluating **TCP window sizes** and **flow control messages**, you can make adjustments to improve performance and ensure smooth traffic flows.

When monitoring **wireless networks**, Wireshark's ability to analyze **802.11 traffic** adds another layer of insight. With Wireshark, you can monitor the strength of **Wi-Fi signals**, see whether channels are overloaded, and identify potential interference from nearby devices. By monitoring **RSSI (signal strength)** and **noise levels**, you can adjust the placement of access points or switch to less crowded channels to improve wireless network performance. **Wi-Fi performance** is highly susceptible to interference, and Wireshark gives you the tools to optimize and troubleshoot your network setup.

One of the most powerful features of Wireshark in network performance monitoring is its ability to **track individual TCP streams**. This allows you to see how traffic is flowing between specific endpoints, which is especially helpful when troubleshooting **slow connections** or **retransmissions**. You can follow a **TCP stream** from start to finish and observe how the network behaves over the course of the communication. This provides a complete picture of the interaction and highlights **performance issues** that may be hidden in a massive packet capture.

For those of you working in **enterprise environments**, **Wireshark's scalability** ensures that it can handle large networks and complex setups. By capturing and analyzing traffic across multiple interfaces, Wireshark provides an all-encompassing view of the network's performance. You can monitor **subnet-level** activity, examine **cross-network traffic**, and ensure that your network infrastructure is working as expected. In larger environments, this level of monitoring is crucial for maintaining smooth operations and ensuring that no performance bottleneck goes unnoticed.

If your network has a history of **performance issues**, **Wireshark's ability to analyze historical captures** is a lifesaver. You can analyze past packet captures to identify recurring problems, such as **persistent retransmissions**, **periods of high latency**, or **bandwidth spikes**. By understanding past network behavior, you can take proactive steps to fix issues before they escalate again. This retrospective analysis also helps in **performance tuning**, ensuring that the network operates optimally moving forward.

For those focused on **network security**, Wireshark can also assist in monitoring **performance degradation due to attacks**. In a network under attack, you might see a **significant spike in traffic**, causing congestion or delays. With **Wireshark's traffic analysis tools**, you can spot **DoS (Denial of Service)** or **DDoS (Distributed Denial of Service)** attacks as they occur, allowing you to quickly respond to the threat. Analyzing **suspicious traffic patterns** in Wireshark can help you separate **attack traffic** from legitimate traffic and adjust your network accordingly.

Let's not forget about **quality of service (QoS)** and how Wireshark can help you evaluate and optimize it. In many networks, certain types of traffic—like **VoIP** or **video conferencing**—are given higher priority over **general internet browsing**. Wireshark's ability to analyze **DSCP (Differentiated Services Code Point)** values in packets allows you to ensure that critical traffic is properly prioritized. If you notice that certain applications are not being treated with the appropriate priority, Wireshark helps you fine-tune your QoS settings for better network performance.

Wireshark also gives you the ability to **generate reports** based on your network's performance data. This is especially useful when you need to document network performance over a specific period of time or during an incident. You can export data into a **CSV**, **JSON**, or **XML** file format for easy analysis and report generation. Whether you're preparing a **performance report** for management or an incident report for network troubleshooting, Wireshark makes it simple to create meaningful, actionable reports.

Another important aspect of performance monitoring is the ability to **compare network traffic over time**. Wireshark's **I/O graphs** allow you to track performance metrics and visualize traffic patterns across multiple time intervals. This helps you spot **long-term trends** in your network's behavior and identify potential areas of improvement. You can compare graphs over different times of day or days of the week to find patterns of peak traffic and adjust your resources accordingly. Analyzing **traffic trends** over time can reveal issues that wouldn't be apparent from a single snapshot of your network.

When it comes to **real-time monitoring**, Wireshark can work hand-in-hand with other network management tools. By exporting captured data to a **centralized dashboard** or integrating with other **performance monitoring systems**, Wireshark can provide ongoing, real-time insights into your network's health. You can use **real-time packet capture** in conjunction with tools like **SNMP** or **netflow** to gain a holistic view of your network's performance. This kind of integration helps you monitor the network continuously and take action before performance problems impact end users.

Lastly, **Wireshark's filtering capabilities** are essential when it comes to **targeted network performance monitoring**. By applying filters to isolate **specific protocols**, **IP addresses**, or **TCP streams**, you can zoom in on the performance of particular services or devices on your network. If you're troubleshooting a slow web server or trying to track down a **network bottleneck**, applying the right filters helps you focus on the packets that matter. You can filter based on any number of criteria—whether it's **high-latency TCP packets** or **DNS request anomalies**—to identify exactly where the performance issue lies.

In conclusion, **Wireshark** is an invaluable tool for **network performance monitoring**. From identifying latency and jitter issues to tracking throughput and packet loss, Wireshark allows you to understand your network's behavior in real time and take corrective action when needed. Its robust analysis tools, real-time monitoring features, and ability to drill down into **packet-level details** make it a powerful ally in ensuring optimal network performance. So, the next time you're tasked with **network performance monitoring**, grab Wireshark, dive into the data, and uncover the issues that could be affecting your users. Happy monitoring!

Chapter 23: Integrating Wireshark with Other Tools

If you think of **Wireshark** as the **Swiss Army knife** of network analysis, then integrating it with other tools is like building a **custom toolbox** to tackle any network challenge. Wireshark on its own is an incredibly powerful tool for capturing and analyzing packets, but sometimes you need to **level up** your network analysis game by combining Wireshark with other tools. Whether it's for real-time monitoring, enhanced reporting, or integration into a larger **network management system**, Wireshark can work hand-in-hand with various tools to provide you with a holistic view of your network. In this chapter, we'll explore how to integrate **Wireshark with other tools**, making your network analysis even more powerful and efficient.

Let's start with the **basics of integration**. Wireshark doesn't exist in a vacuum. It's a **network analysis tool** that can provide you with detailed insights into **traffic flows**, **latency**, **packet loss**, and much more. But for many tasks, you'll want to integrate Wireshark with other software that complements its capabilities. For example, you might use **Wireshark alongside SNMP tools** like **PRTG** or **Nagios** for monitoring network devices or gather data from multiple network sources. The beauty of this integration is that it allows you to combine **real-time traffic data** with **historical device information**, giving you a fuller picture of your network's health.

One of the most popular tools to integrate Wireshark with is **Splunk**—a **data aggregation platform** that allows you to collect, index, and analyze large volumes of machine-generated data. By exporting your **Wireshark capture files** into **Splunk**, you can run powerful **queries** and **visualizations** on your network traffic data. This integration helps bridge the gap between packet-level analysis and broader network performance monitoring. For example, you can combine **Wireshark packet captures** with **Splunk's indexing** to generate actionable insights about network performance, security incidents, or traffic trends over time. Splunk makes it easier to track **real-time events** and integrate data from **multiple sources**—think of it as a **command center** for your network.

Another integration with Wireshark that can be incredibly useful is with **Grafana**, a popular **data visualization** tool. With Wireshark's ability to export capture files in formats like **CSV** or **JSON**, you can import that data into Grafana to create stunning, interactive dashboards. These dashboards can display **traffic patterns**, **packet loss**, **latency** statistics, and much more in an easy-to-understand format. By visualizing network traffic in Grafana, you can identify trends and bottlenecks at a glance, making it easier to communicate findings with stakeholders. If you're into **network monitoring**, using Wireshark with Grafana is like having your **network's heartbeat** on display in real time.

If you're working in a more **enterprise-focused environment**, integrating Wireshark with a **SIEM (Security Information and Event Management)** tool like **Splunk**, **ELK Stack**, or **Graylog** can be an absolute game-changer. SIEM tools aggregate logs and security events, and by combining them with **packet-level analysis** from Wireshark, you gain a much broader view of network performance and security. For example, you can use Wireshark to capture traffic and export that data to a SIEM tool for **security monitoring**. When an unusual network event occurs, such as a **DDoS attack** or **unauthorized access**, the SIEM tool can correlate the **packet capture data** with other network logs, giving you a comprehensive view of the situation. This is where **Wireshark** and **SIEM integration** becomes invaluable for detecting and mitigating security incidents.

Wireshark also integrates seamlessly with **Nagios**, an open-source **monitoring system** that helps you track the availability and performance of network devices. By combining **Nagios** with **Wireshark**, you can create an integrated **monitoring solution** where Nagios provides **alerts** and **thresholds** for device performance, while Wireshark dives deep into the **packet-level data** when an issue arises. For example, if Nagios detects that a **router's CPU usage** is spiking, Wireshark can help you investigate the **traffic patterns** that might be contributing to the load. This integration creates a powerful feedback loop that helps you proactively manage your network.

In the world of **security analysis**, **Wireshark** works perfectly in conjunction with **Suricata** or **Snort**, which are open-source **intrusion detection systems (IDS)**. Suricata and Snort monitor network traffic for signs of **malicious activity** like **malware infections**, **denial-of-service (DoS) attacks**, or **network reconnaissance**. By capturing traffic with **Wireshark** and feeding that data into Suricata or Snort, you can gain **real-time insights** into potential threats. If the IDS detects suspicious activity, Wireshark can help you analyze the raw packets and determine the **source** and **nature** of the attack. This integration helps you not only detect security issues but also **drill down** to the packet-level details to see exactly what's happening.

When it comes to **automating network monitoring**, integrating Wireshark with **Python** can provide a whole new level of functionality. With **pyshark**, a Python library that wraps Wireshark's capabilities, you can automate the capture and analysis of network traffic. Python allows you to **parse PCAP files**, **apply display filters**, and even **generate reports** based on specific traffic patterns or events. This integration is perfect for those who want to automate the process of **packet capture analysis** and **incident reporting**. With Wireshark and Python, you can set up a system that continuously monitors traffic, runs scheduled analysis, and generates reports with minimal manual intervention. It's like setting up a **network monitoring robot**.

For **cloud-based network monitoring**, integrating **Wireshark** with cloud-native tools like **Amazon Web Services (AWS)** or **Azure Monitor** can provide a unique edge. Cloud environments often rely on **distributed systems** with complex communication patterns. By capturing network traffic within these cloud environments with **Wireshark**, and then feeding that data into cloud-based monitoring tools, you can track **application performance** and **network health** across multiple regions and data centers. These integrations allow you to spot network issues that might be specific to the cloud infrastructure, like **inter-region latency** or **cloud firewall misconfigurations**. Wireshark and cloud integration is essential for maintaining optimal network performance in the cloud.

Wireshark is also great when paired with **ElasticSearch**, a real-time distributed search engine. ElasticSearch allows you to index and query massive amounts of data, and Wireshark can export **packet-level information** into **ElasticSearch** for fast querying and analysis. With this setup, you can build **complex queries** to search for specific packet patterns across months of data. This is especially useful when you need to perform **historical network analysis**, like identifying recurring performance issues or spotting slow network components over time. Combining Wireshark's deep packet inspection with **ElasticSearch's querying power** results in a system that can quickly pinpoint performance bottlenecks across vast amounts of network data.

Wireshark can also work hand-in-hand with **Docker** and **Kubernetes** for **containerized environments**. When monitoring **microservices architectures**, you often need to analyze traffic between containers, services, and hosts. By capturing traffic between containers using Wireshark, you can perform detailed **flow analysis** between different parts of your system. Integrating Wireshark with tools like **Cilium** (which focuses on **network security for containers**) can help you better understand **how traffic flows** and where performance issues may arise in your containerized environments. Wireshark's ability to capture traffic at the packet level ensures that you can debug issues at a granular level.

For **large-scale networks** that require **ongoing monitoring**, integrating **Wireshark with Zabbix** or **PRTG Network Monitor** offers an effective solution. These tools provide **real-time monitoring** and **alerting** for network devices and infrastructure, while Wireshark gives you the ability to dive deep into packet-level data when something goes wrong. If a **bandwidth threshold** is exceeded or a device shows signs of **degraded performance**, these monitoring systems can trigger an alert, and Wireshark can be used to capture the traffic that caused the issue. Together, these tools provide a **complete view** of network health, allowing you to quickly respond to problems before they affect users.

Let's not forget about **remote packet capture** with **Wireshark**. In situations where you need to capture packets from a device that's far away (whether it's a **remote server**, a device in a different country, or a satellite office), integrating **Wireshark with SSH or VPNs** allows you to **remotely capture** traffic. By using **Wireshark's remote capture feature**, you can start a capture session remotely and then pull the data back for analysis. This integration allows you to monitor network traffic in locations where you wouldn't be able to physically connect to the network, providing real-time access to network performance no matter where you are.

When working with **web traffic analysis**, integrating **Wireshark with Burp Suite**—a **web vulnerability scanner**—can give you a clearer picture of how traffic behaves between **clients** and **servers**. By capturing the traffic with Wireshark and sending it to Burp Suite, you can analyze web traffic for issues like **HTTP vulnerabilities**, **cross-site scripting (XSS)**, or **SQL injections**. This combination helps you gain visibility into **client-server interactions**, and it's perfect for security professionals who need to perform **penetration testing** on websites and web applications.

Finally, don't overlook the power of **Wireshark and **log management** tools like **Logstash** and **Fluentd**. These tools help you aggregate and analyze **logs** from various sources—servers, routers, firewalls, and applications. By forwarding packet-level data from **Wireshark** to a **log aggregation platform**, you can correlate network performance data with logs from network devices or **applications**. This allows you to build a more holistic view of your network's performance and security, ensuring you have all the necessary information to make informed decisions.

In conclusion, **Wireshark's integration with other tools** opens up a whole new world of possibilities for network analysis, monitoring, and security. Whether you're feeding Wireshark's packet-level data into **SIEM systems**, using **Grafana** for **real-time dashboards**, or combining it with **cloud-based monitoring tools**, the integration power of Wireshark makes it a vital part of your network management toolkit. So, start building your **integrated network monitoring system** today, and let Wireshark work in harmony with other tools to keep your network healthy, secure, and efficient. Happy integrating!

To wrap up, the ability to **integrate Wireshark with other tools** truly transforms it from a great network analysis tool into a **central hub** for holistic network monitoring and troubleshooting. Whether you're using it alongside **SIEM systems** for security, **Splunk** for data aggregation, **Grafana** for visualization, or **ElasticSearch** for powerful querying, Wireshark's integrations ensure you can tailor it to fit into your existing infrastructure seamlessly. This **multi-tool approach** provides a more comprehensive view of network health, security, and performance, helping you solve problems faster and more efficiently.

Wireshark's versatility in integration extends far beyond the capture of raw packet data. The ability to work hand-in-hand with **network monitoring tools** like **Nagios**, **Zabbix**, or **PRTG** ensures that you have **continuous monitoring** in place and can dive deep into packet-level analysis when specific events or thresholds are triggered. With the integration of **Python scripts** via the **pyshark** library, Wireshark becomes a powerhouse of **automation**, enabling routine analysis tasks to be automated and run without manual intervention.

Working in **cloud environments** or **containerized systems**? Wireshark's integration with **Docker**, **Kubernetes**, and cloud-based tools like **AWS CloudWatch** and **Azure Monitor** means you can track and troubleshoot traffic across distributed systems. Understanding traffic flow between **microservices** or across **cloud regions** is crucial in modern-day network performance, and Wireshark enables you to capture and analyze that traffic with ease, no matter where it resides.

Even in a **large-scale network** environment, where **hundreds of devices** are constantly sending and receiving traffic, Wireshark's integration with **centralized log management systems** like **Logstash** or **Fluentd** allows you to correlate **packet-level data** with logs from routers, servers, and firewalls. This level of integration is critical when identifying **patterns** or troubleshooting issues that span across multiple devices, applications, or locations. By correlating network traffic with other logs, you gain **valuable context** that helps speed up problem identification and resolution.

Don't underestimate the value of **remote packet capture** when it comes to integration. Wireshark's **remote capture capabilities** allow you to capture packets from remote locations or devices without being physically connected to the network. Whether you're troubleshooting issues at a **satellite office**, **data center**, or **client site**, you can use Wireshark's **SSH or VPN integration** to start a capture remotely and bring the data back for analysis. This gives you the **flexibility** to troubleshoot from anywhere while still having access to the in-depth packet analysis you need.

The ability to **export Wireshark's captured data** to external platforms for further analysis is a critical component of its integration capabilities. Whether you're exporting to **Splunk** for long-term storage and advanced query analysis, **Grafana** for visual reports, or **ElasticSearch** for fast data searchability, Wireshark's **export options** provide a bridge to external tools that enhance your overall network analysis. These exported data files can be shared across departments or teams for better collaboration or can be **archived** for later use, allowing you to store critical network data for future investigations.

Let's not forget **Wireshark's connection to third-party security tools**. Integrating Wireshark with **IDS/IPS tools** like **Suricata** or **Snort** creates a **highly effective security monitoring** system. By capturing and analyzing **network traffic** with Wireshark and then integrating it with **intrusion detection systems** (IDS), you get **real-time alerts** when suspicious behavior is detected, and you can immediately dive into the packets to investigate. This integration allows you to connect **network behavior** with **security incidents** and respond faster to emerging threats.

For **VoIP troubleshooting**, Wireshark integrates seamlessly with **VoIP monitoring tools**. If you're experiencing **quality issues** with voice traffic, **RTP analysis** in Wireshark can be enhanced by integrating it with tools like **RTPEngine** for **packet loss detection** or **jitter analysis**. When a VoIP issue arises, you can rely on Wireshark to trace the **source of the issue**, whether it's **network-related**, **codec problems**, or **server performance**, while the integration with specialized tools provides added layers of analysis.

Another powerful feature of Wireshark is its ability to integrate with **cloud-based networks**. In a **cloud-first environment**, traffic between cloud services, on-premise data centers, and **hybrid architectures** can be complex to track. Wireshark's integration with **cloud-native tools** like **AWS VPC Traffic Mirroring** or **Azure Network Watcher** gives you the ability to capture, inspect, and analyze traffic between cloud-based instances, ensuring that network performance is optimized, and **security is tight**. This integration also enables you to troubleshoot issues that span both **on-premise and cloud environments**, which is essential for modern IT infrastructure.

On the **performance monitoring side**, Wireshark integrates well with **network performance monitoring tools** like **Ixia**, **Auvik**, and **Wireshark's own I/O graphs**. By using these integrations, you can track metrics such as **packet loss**, **latency**, and **throughput** in real time. If a performance issue arises, you can quickly pinpoint the **bottleneck** or **failure** in the network using Wireshark's in-depth packet analysis combined with the broader performance data collected by these monitoring tools. This gives you **end-to-end visibility** of your network's health, and helps prevent **unresolved issues** from impacting users.

For **advanced troubleshooting** in **network services** like DNS, DHCP, or HTTP, you can integrate Wireshark with **service monitoring tools** to track issues that might not be visible in the network traffic alone. By combining Wireshark with **DNS monitoring services** or **HTTP request tracking tools**, you can identify why certain requests are failing or why services are slow to respond. These integrations allow you to bridge the gap between **network traffic data** and **application-level behavior**, which is essential when troubleshooting complex network issues that involve both infrastructure and services.

Wireshark's integration with configuration management tools, like **Ansible** or **Puppet**, makes it an excellent choice for automating network diagnostics in large environments. By creating scripts that automatically trigger Wireshark captures in response to specific network events or thresholds, you can maintain consistent performance monitoring and troubleshooting without manual intervention. This can be especially useful in large **data center environments** where network issues need to be automatically detected and escalated.

For those who work with **IoT devices, Wireshark's ability to analyze low-level traffic** is key. By integrating Wireshark with **IoT management platforms**, you can analyze communication between IoT devices in the network. Whether it's **zigbee**, **Z-wave**, or **BLE traffic**, Wireshark's packet capture capabilities allow you to inspect the communication between these devices and identify any issues related to **latency**, **signal strength**, or **protocol mismatches**. This is vital for IoT deployments, where network performance directly affects device functionality.

To sum it all up, **integrating Wireshark with other tools** gives you the ultimate network analysis toolkit. Whether you're working with **security monitoring tools**, **cloud services**, **real-time performance monitoring**, or **IoT systems**, Wireshark's ability to integrate with other software allows you to take **network monitoring** and **troubleshooting** to the next level. These integrations provide you with a **comprehensive view** of your network's health, help you diagnose complex issues faster, and give you the ability to automate processes that would normally require manual intervention. With Wireshark, you can not only **capture** and **analyze** packets but also **integrate** those packets into your broader network management and monitoring systems to maintain optimal performance and security. So, start integrating, start automating, and watch your network analysis reach new heights. Happy integrating!

Chapter 24: Wireshark for Troubleshooting Internet Connectivity

Ah, the joys of **internet connectivity issues**. There's nothing more frustrating than when your **Wi-Fi** stops working, your computer's **Ethernet cable** is mysteriously disconnected, or your **VPN** drops right when you need it most. In moments like these, Wireshark becomes your **trusted sidekick**—ready to dive into the digital depths to uncover the root cause of your network woes. Whether you're troubleshooting a slow connection, a dropped packet, or mysterious DNS failures, Wireshark is the detective that always gets to the bottom of the problem. In this chapter, we'll explore how Wireshark can be used to diagnose and solve your internet connectivity problems with precision, wit, and some much-needed expertise.

Let's start with the classic: **is there a physical issue with the connection?** Before diving into complex packet analysis, Wireshark can help you confirm whether the problem lies with the **physical layer**. If you're connected via Ethernet, check if there are any **local issues** with cables or switches. Wireshark's **packet capture interface** will let you see if your device is even trying to send or receive data at all. If there's no activity, it could be that your **router**, **cable**, or **NIC (Network Interface Card)** is the culprit. Wireshark won't magically fix your cable, but it will certainly help you rule out physical problems and move on to more **advanced troubleshooting**.

Now, assuming you've confirmed that everything looks physically sound, let's talk about **IP address issues**. **DHCP** (Dynamic Host Configuration Protocol) is responsible for assigning an IP address to your device when it connects to the network. If there's a problem with **DHCP lease assignment**, you might not be able to connect to the internet, even though your device thinks it's connected. Wireshark's **filtering capabilities** can help you look for **DHCP packets** in the network capture. If you don't see any **DHCP Discover** or **DHCP Offer** packets, there could be an issue with your router's DHCP service, or it might be a problem on the ISP's end. With Wireshark, you can track down this issue faster than you can say "Please reboot your router."

Once your device has an IP address, it's time to move on to **network routing**. Wireshark's packet capture capabilities can help you identify if there's a problem with **local routing** or **gateway communication**. If your computer can't connect to websites, one of the first things you should check is whether packets are successfully reaching your **default gateway** (usually your router). By filtering for **ICMP packets**, you can quickly perform a **ping test** to check if your device can reach the gateway. If the packets aren't making it, there might be a routing issue on the local network or even in the wider internet path. Wireshark will show you exactly where the packets stop, and you can follow the trail to track down the issue.

If your **DNS** is failing, Wireshark becomes an invaluable tool for sniffing out **domain resolution problems**. The **Domain Name System (DNS)** is responsible for translating human-readable URLs (like "www.example.com") into IP addresses. If your device is able to connect to the internet but can't access websites, DNS failure is likely the issue. Wireshark's **DNS packet filtering** will allow you to see if DNS queries are being made, and if so, whether the responses are coming back with the correct IP address. A common problem occurs when the **DNS server** returns an error or the wrong IP address, and Wireshark lets you track these issues down by providing you with **query and response details**.

Speaking of **DNS**, let's dive a little deeper into **DNS lookups**. There's a vast difference between **successful DNS lookups** and those that result in **timeouts** or **NXDOMAIN errors**. By filtering for **UDP port 53** (the DNS port), you can see the **DNS queries** sent from your device. If you don't see any queries or the responses are timing out, it's clear that DNS is where the breakdown is happening. If you do see responses, but they're pointing to the wrong address, the issue could be with the **DNS server's configuration** or even **cache poisoning**. Wireshark helps you follow the trail of DNS requests and responses to get a clear view of what's going wrong.

Now, what if your device can **connect to the internet** but is **sluggish**? You're able to load a website, but it takes longer than it should. It's not a total connection failure, but there's definitely **something off**. This is where **latency** and **packet loss** come into play. Wireshark can help you identify delays and dropped packets by analyzing **TCP handshakes** and **round-trip times**. If you see **retransmissions**, **duplicate ACKs**, or **high round-trip times**, you can be fairly certain that your issue is related to **congestion** or **latency** in your network. By analyzing these packet delays and losses, Wireshark provides the insights needed to identify where the bottleneck is occurring, whether it's your local network, your ISP, or somewhere in between.

On the topic of **slow websites**, Wireshark can also help you analyze **HTTP requests** to see if **server-side delays** are causing the slowdown. When you visit a website, Wireshark captures all the **HTTP GET requests** and **responses** between your browser and the server. If the server is slow to respond, you might see large delays between **request** and **response**. By filtering for **HTTP traffic**, Wireshark lets you zoom in on these delays and analyze whether they're caused by slow server processing, poor network conditions, or maybe even **too many redirects**. Pinpointing where the delays are happening—whether it's **client-side**, **network-side**, or **server-side**—helps you take the necessary actions to **fix the issue**.

A key performance metric in **internet connectivity** is **throughput**. Wireshark can measure **TCP throughput** by looking at **data transfer rates** between devices. If you're noticing slow transfers but have no idea where the bottleneck lies, Wireshark's **TCP stream analysis** and **I/O graphing** capabilities can help. By analyzing **TCP window size**, **segment size**, and the **time between ACKs**, Wireshark reveals whether the throughput is being limited by the local network, the ISP, or even a misconfigured server. If you're seeing lower than expected throughput, it might be time to optimize your **TCP settings**, adjust **MTU sizes**, or check your network equipment for **packet drops**.

What happens when you can't reach **external websites**, but everything inside your network works fine? This could be a **routing issue** beyond your local network, possibly within your **ISP's network**. Wireshark's **traceroute feature** is perfect for this scenario. By sending **ICMP Echo Requests**, Wireshark helps you trace the path your packets take to reach their destination. Each hop along the way is displayed with its respective **latency**, so you can see where the bottleneck or failure occurs. If you notice that packets start getting delayed or lost at a particular hop, it's likely that the issue lies with an **intermediate router** or within your ISP's infrastructure.

If you're working with a **VPN** connection, Wireshark becomes essential for troubleshooting **VPN performance issues**. Whether you're using **OpenVPN**, **IPsec**, or another VPN protocol, Wireshark helps you analyze the **encrypted traffic** and detect any issues with the **tunnel's setup** or **data transfer**. You can look for signs of **VPN connection drops**, **latency spikes**, or even **traffic leaks**. Wireshark's **protocol dissectors** allow you to inspect the inner workings of VPN traffic to see if there are any misconfigurations causing slow speeds or packet loss. This helps ensure that your **secure connection** is as efficient as it is private.

Let's talk about the **ever-present issue** of **Wi-Fi connectivity**. Wi-Fi is notorious for its unpredictability—poor signal strength, interference, or channel congestion can all lead to dropped connections. While Wireshark doesn't exactly **tune your antenna** or tell you to reboot your router, it can give you deep insights into **802.11 frames**. By capturing **Wi-Fi traffic**, you can analyze **signal strength** (RSSI), identify **channel interference**, and pinpoint **transmission retries** that indicate a poor connection. Using Wireshark to monitor **Wi-Fi performance** can help you troubleshoot whether the issue lies with the **router** configuration or the **device** itself.

If you're dealing with **slow web page loads**, **Wireshark's SSL/TLS analysis** comes to the rescue. **SSL handshakes** and **certificate issues** often cause delays when establishing a secure connection to a website. By inspecting **SSL/TLS traffic**, Wireshark lets you see the handshake process and identify delays in certificate validation, session negotiation, or even **mismatched ciphers**. With this information, you can determine whether the issue is at the **application layer**, related to **encryption**, or if it's something deeper in the network stack. Wireshark's ability to dive into **SSL/TLS protocols** is indispensable for diagnosing **security-related performance problems**.

Speaking of **SSL/TLS**, what happens if your website suddenly becomes unreachable because of a **certificate error**? Wireshark can help by capturing the **SSL handshake** and showing you whether the certificate is being validated correctly. If there's a certificate error, Wireshark's dissection of the **SSL handshake** will show you exactly where the process breaks down— whether it's a **certificate mismatch**, **expired certificate**, or **untrusted authority**. This detailed analysis lets you fix **certificate problems** fast, ensuring users can connect to your site securely.

Lastly, **packet capture for troubleshooting** isn't just about figuring out what's wrong—it's also about understanding how your network **behaves under stress**. By capturing traffic during **peak usage periods** or **network congestion**, you can analyze how the network **reacts to high traffic loads**. You can see where the **bottlenecks** are, whether it's a particular **server**, **switch**, or **router**. Wireshark's **flow graphs** and **IO graphs** let you visualize how the network handles stress, making it easier to pinpoint where improvements can be made.

In conclusion, Wireshark is your best friend when troubleshooting **internet connectivity** issues. Whether it's an **IP configuration issue**, **DNS failure**, **packet loss**, or **VPN connection problem**, Wireshark's deep packet analysis can help you find the culprit quickly and efficiently. With its ability to capture, dissect, and analyze traffic from the ground up, you can ensure your network runs smoothly and your internet connectivity issues become a thing of the past. So the next time your **internet connection falters**, grab Wireshark, dive deep into those packets, and let the troubleshooting begin! Happy analyzing!

To wrap up, Wireshark's ability to **troubleshoot internet connectivity** issues is nothing short of magical—well, almost. From **physical connection issues** to more complex problems like **DNS failures**, **routing misconfigurations**, or **Wi-Fi signal problems**, Wireshark gives you the tools to dig deep and discover exactly where the problem lies. The key is understanding how to leverage Wireshark's **powerful filtering and analysis tools** to inspect the packet flow at every layer, from the physical network all the way up to application-level traffic.

When it comes to **packet loss**, Wireshark is the **detective** you need on your team, helping you follow **TCP streams** and identifying where packets are getting dropped. It's especially useful in environments where **high performance** is crucial, like **VoIP**, **video streaming**, or any other **real-time** application. Being able to track down packet loss at the **TCP level** lets you understand whether the issue is **congestion-related**, **device failure**, or something else entirely. Without Wireshark, you'd be left wondering where those missing packets went—and that's a mystery no one wants to solve on their own.

Then there's **jitter**, that pesky issue that makes **real-time communications** sound like a broken record. **Jitter** can ruin the quality of your **voice calls**, **video conferences**, or even **online gaming**. With Wireshark's **RTP analysis**, you can see the **variance in packet arrival times** and take action to reduce the jitter by optimizing network routes or improving device performance. By analyzing jitter and **round-trip times**, Wireshark helps you identify if the issue lies with **network latency**, **router performance**, or even **Wi-Fi interference**. This is where Wireshark shines, giving you the insight needed to **restore smooth communication**.

If you're dealing with a **VPN issue**, Wireshark has the **tools to troubleshoot** everything from **connection drops** to slow performance. By inspecting the **VPN traffic** and **SSL/TLS handshakes**, you can see if there's a problem with your **encryption** or if the **tunnel** isn't configured properly. You'll also be able to track **latency** across the VPN connection and determine if the issue is related to **traffic congestion** or something deeper in the VPN's configuration. This kind of **granular analysis** can help you optimize **VPN performance** and ensure your secure connections remain fast and stable.

For issues involving **Wi-Fi connectivity**, Wireshark takes the guesswork out of the equation. With its ability to capture **802.11 frames**, you can analyze **signal strength**, **channel interference**, and **transmission retries** that are often the root cause of slow or dropped connections. Wireshark helps you visualize the entire **wireless spectrum**, showing you where **interference** from other devices might be slowing down your network. Whether you're dealing with an **overcrowded channel** or **poor signal quality**, Wireshark's **Wi-Fi analysis tools** provide you with the necessary data to make changes that will improve performance.

When analyzing **slow website loads**, Wireshark comes in handy for diagnosing whether the problem is related to **network congestion**, **server performance**, or **application-level issues**. By inspecting **HTTP requests** and **responses**, you can see exactly where delays occur in the web traffic cycle. If the problem isn't in the network but at the **server side**, Wireshark can help you analyze how the **web server** is responding to requests, allowing you to pinpoint issues like **database queries**, **server-side processing delays**, or **slow file transfers**. With Wireshark in your toolkit, **slow web pages** become much easier to diagnose.

Wireshark also helps you track down **latency issues in multi-hop environments**, especially when you're trying to pinpoint where packets are getting delayed across different **network segments**. By using Wireshark's **traceroute features**, you can trace the **path packets take** from your device to the destination and measure the latency at each hop along the way. If one of the hops introduces significant delay, you know exactly where to investigate. Whether the issue is on your **local network**, with the **ISP**, or somewhere deeper in the **internet backbone**, Wireshark's traceroute feature helps you narrow down the culprit.

In addition to **latency** and **packet loss**, Wireshark also excels at **troubleshooting throughput problems**. If your internet connection is sluggish but not entirely down, you might have **bandwidth congestion** or **misconfigured devices**. By analyzing the **TCP window size**, **segment sizes**, and **throughput rates**, Wireshark helps you track down the cause of the slowdown. If you're noticing **TCP retransmissions** or **duplicate ACKs**, Wireshark tells you whether your devices are sending too much data too quickly, or if there's an issue with **flow control**. This analysis allows you to tweak your network configuration to boost throughput and eliminate unnecessary delays.

Wireshark's expert information is another valuable feature for troubleshooting internet connectivity. It automatically flags potential issues like **TCP retransmissions**, **duplicate packets**, or **high round-trip times** that might be affecting your internet connection. If you're staring at a **capture file** with hundreds or thousands of packets, Wireshark's **expert system** makes it easy to spot the anomalies quickly. The expert information view gives you a list of **warnings** and **suggestions** on what might be wrong with the traffic, and helps guide you to the exact packets that need further investigation.

On the topic of **VPN troubleshooting**, **Wireshark's integration with SSL/TLS** traffic analysis is priceless. If your **VPN** suddenly slows down or drops, inspecting the **SSL/TLS handshake** with Wireshark will show you if the issue is related to **encryption negotiation**, **certificate mismatches**, or even **weak ciphers**. By analyzing these issues in real time, you can pinpoint whether the VPN tunnel is taking longer to establish, or if there's a performance bottleneck once the tunnel is established. This can be a **real lifesaver** in environments that rely on secure communications for sensitive data.

If your issue involves **outgoing traffic**, Wireshark can help track the packets from your device to their destination and reveal whether the problem lies with **your router** or **your ISP**. For example, if your packets are not being routed properly, you might notice **high latency** or even **packet loss** after they leave your local network. Wireshark's ability to **track packets in transit** allows you to observe where the packets get delayed or dropped, helping you identify issues within your **ISP's network** or other external network segments.

For **secure internet connections**, Wireshark can assist in troubleshooting issues with **SSL/TLS certificates**. If you're trying to connect to a website or a service that requires **SSL/TLS encryption**, Wireshark can help you inspect the **handshakes** and confirm whether the connection is being established properly. If the connection fails, Wireshark shows you **error codes** and flags issues such as **expired certificates**, **untrusted certificate authorities**, or even **protocol mismatches**. Wireshark's ability to dive deep into **SSL/TLS traffic** makes it indispensable for diagnosing **secure connection failures**.

When you're dealing with a situation where **web traffic** is being blocked or slowed down, Wireshark can help you see if the problem is due to **network congestion** or something like a **firewall** blocking access. By inspecting **HTTP headers** and **requests**, Wireshark lets you see the entire web transaction and whether the request is **timing out** or if the server is simply **not responding**. Sometimes, the issue isn't with your connection, but rather with a **misconfigured firewall** that's blocking outgoing traffic. By analyzing this traffic with Wireshark, you can pinpoint where the traffic is being **blocked** and fix the issue quickly.

In conclusion, Wireshark is an invaluable tool for troubleshooting **internet connectivity** issues. Whether you're dealing with **slow connections**, **DNS failures**, **VPN disconnects**, or **Wi-Fi interference**, Wireshark has the tools to dive deep into the packet-level details and help you diagnose the problem. By analyzing **latency**, **packet loss**, **throughput**, **DNS queries**, and **SSL handshakes**, Wireshark gives you the insight you need to fix your connection woes and get back online. So, the next time the internet decides to act up, grab Wireshark, and let it lead the way to a speedy resolution. Happy troubleshooting!

Chapter 25: Taking Wireshark to the Next Level

By now, you're probably comfortable with the basics of **Wireshark**. You've learned how to capture packets, filter through them, and identify common network problems. But guess what? **Wireshark** isn't just a tool for simple traffic inspection—it's a **powerhouse** of network analysis that can be taken to the next level. Whether you're a **network engineer**, a **security professional**, or a **curious tech enthusiast**, there are endless possibilities to explore in Wireshark. In this chapter, we're going to dive deeper into some of the more **advanced techniques** that can help you unlock the true power of this tool. So, let's roll up our sleeves and get ready to push Wireshark to the next level!

First things first—let's talk about **Wireshark's Lua scripting** capabilities. While Wireshark provides an intuitive GUI for packet analysis, **Lua** scripting opens up a whole new realm of customization. With Lua, you can write custom **dissectors** for non-standard protocols, automate repetitive tasks, and even create custom **analysis tools**. This scripting language is embedded directly into Wireshark, so it's easy to get started without needing a separate development environment. Need to decode a **proprietary protocol**? Lua's got your back. Want to create a custom filter that only shows packets with a specific payload? Lua can handle that too. Wireshark's Lua support allows you to **extend its capabilities** far beyond what's available in the default installation.

Next, let's explore the world of **packet capture automation**. In a large, dynamic network environment, manually triggering packet captures whenever an issue arises can be time-consuming and inefficient. But don't worry—Wireshark is a **master of automation**. By integrating Wireshark with tools like **Python**, **Bash scripts**, or **Ansible**, you can schedule and automate packet captures based on specific triggers or time intervals. Imagine setting up a script to capture traffic only during peak usage hours or when a particular error occurs. This is especially useful for troubleshooting intermittent problems that only happen at certain times of the day. By automating the capture process, Wireshark helps you save time and ensures that you don't miss key events.

On the topic of **large-scale packet analysis**, Wireshark excels in environments where **voluminous traffic** is the norm. But sometimes, sifting through **millions of packets** can feel like searching for a needle in a haystack. Here's where **Wireshark's display filters** become your best friend. If you haven't already mastered the art of filtering, now's the time. With Wireshark's advanced **filtering syntax**, you can narrow down large capture files to show you exactly what you need. Want to see only **HTTP traffic** from a specific IP address? Done. Interested in **DNS queries** for a specific domain? Easy. Filters allow you to focus on specific packets, making it possible to analyze even the largest datasets with ease.

To really **take Wireshark to the next level**, you've got to master **Wireshark's statistics tools**. In addition to simple packet analysis, Wireshark offers a variety of statistics that can give you insight into the overall health and performance of your network. Tools like **I/O graphs**, **protocol hierarchies**, and **conversations analysis** allow you to visualize network activity in real time. For example, **I/O graphs** show you **packet rate** and **throughput** over time, making it easy to spot spikes or drops in network activity. **Protocol hierarchy statistics** provide an overview of the distribution of different protocols in the capture file, giving you a high-level view of what's happening on your network. These statistics are key to identifying network **bottlenecks**, **high-traffic protocols**, and overall **performance trends**.

If you're troubleshooting **network latency**, Wireshark can help you go beyond simple packet capture to **analyze timing and sequencing**. By using **round-trip time analysis** or **TCP flow graphs**, you can measure the **latency** between different network devices and identify which devices are contributing to slow performance. With **TCP stream graphs**, Wireshark lets you visualize the flow of packets between devices, helping you pinpoint where delays occur in the network. By examining the **time between packets** and **round-trip times**, you can uncover areas of the network that need optimization or additional resources.

A common pitfall for advanced users is diving into Wireshark's deep analysis without considering the **context of the data**. **Network traffic analysis** is only useful if you have the right context around it. Wireshark's **Expert Information** tool is there to provide that context. The Expert Information panel automatically flags **issues** in the capture, such as **TCP retransmissions**, **duplicate ACKs**, or **protocol errors**. While the data itself is valuable, understanding **why packets behave the way they do** is crucial to solving performance issues. By leveraging **Wireshark's expert information**, you can quickly identify **problematic packets** and start fixing issues faster.

Now, let's dive into the world of **multi-layer packet dissection**. In complex networks, you'll often encounter **packet encapsulation**, where one protocol is wrapped inside another. This is especially true with technologies like **VPNs**, **IPsec**, or **SSL/TLS**. Wireshark excels at dissecting these multi-layered packets, providing you with a **layer-by-layer view** of the data as it travels through the network. By applying **display filters** and using Wireshark's built-in dissectors, you can peel back the layers and see the **inner details** of each protocol. Whether it's **SSL handshakes** or **IPsec tunnels**, Wireshark helps you uncover the details of encapsulated data, making it easier to troubleshoot complex network issues.

If you're a **security professional**, you'll want to take Wireshark to the next level by integrating it with **intrusion detection systems** (IDS) or **security incident and event management** (SIEM) tools. Combining Wireshark with tools like **Suricata**, **Snort**, or **Splunk** can enhance your ability to detect malicious network activity. For example, Suricata can flag potential **DDoS attacks** or **port scans**, and Wireshark can be used to analyze the packet-level details. By integrating these tools, you can correlate **real-time attack indicators** with **historical network data**, allowing for faster detection and response. Wireshark's ability to provide a **packet-level view** of security incidents makes it an essential tool for **network defense**.

Another advanced technique for taking Wireshark to the next level is **automating reporting**. If you're regularly analyzing packet captures for specific issues—like **DNS failures**, **latency spikes**, or **protocol violations**—you can automate the **report generation** process. Wireshark has several features that allow you to export data to formats like **CSV**, **JSON**, or **XML**. By using these exports, combined with scripting languages like **Python**, you can create customized reports that show trends in network behavior or highlight potential areas of concern. Automating this process reduces the time you spend analyzing data manually and allows you to focus on fixing problems.

Wireshark's **remote capture capabilities** are a game-changer for network analysis in large or distributed environments. If you're trying to capture traffic from a device in a remote location or from multiple devices across different sites, Wireshark's ability to perform **remote captures** using **SSH** or **TShark** makes it easy. This feature is invaluable when troubleshooting issues that span across multiple geographic locations or involve remote devices. By remotely capturing and analyzing packets in real time, you can gather the data you need without needing to be physically present on-site.

Let's talk about **Wireshark and the cloud**. With more businesses migrating to the cloud, **analyzing cloud traffic** has become an essential skill for network professionals. Wireshark can be used to capture **cloud traffic** in platforms like **AWS**, **Google Cloud**, or **Azure**. By setting up packet captures in cloud environments, you can troubleshoot issues related to **cloud-to-on-premise connectivity**, **virtual network performance**, or **cloud service interaction**. Integrating Wireshark with cloud-based monitoring tools also gives you a comprehensive view of how data flows in and out of the cloud, making it easier to identify problems related to **latency**, **bandwidth**, or **cloud security**.

Packet capture filters are a powerful tool, and mastering them is crucial for taking your Wireshark skills to the next level. Wireshark allows you to filter packets based on a wide range of criteria, from **IP addresses** and **ports** to **specific data patterns** within packets. The ability to create **custom capture filters** means you can limit the data Wireshark captures to the **most relevant traffic**, ensuring that you don't get overwhelmed by unnecessary information. Custom filters also let you focus your analysis on particular protocols or events, such as **HTTP errors** or **TCP retransmissions**, allowing for more focused and effective troubleshooting.

When working with **large datasets**, Wireshark can sometimes feel like trying to find a needle in a haystack. That's where **Wireshark's TShark** (the command-line version) becomes invaluable. TShark allows you to automate packet capture and analysis, and you can combine it with **shell scripting** or **Python** to process large capture files. By using TShark in combination with **log aggregation** tools like **ELK Stack** or **Splunk**, you can analyze packets at scale and correlate data across multiple sources. TShark and **command-line processing** take Wireshark's capabilities and apply them in **automated workflows** for even greater efficiency.

If you're dealing with **encrypted traffic**, Wireshark's ability to decrypt protocols like **SSL/TLS** is a critical feature. Once you have the **private keys** or **session secrets**, Wireshark can help you decrypt the traffic and view the data in its **original form**. This is incredibly useful when troubleshooting issues with secure traffic, such as **SSL certificate errors** or **handshake failures**. Being able to decrypt traffic and inspect its contents in detail allows you to uncover problems that would otherwise be hidden behind encryption.

Finally, don't forget about the **Wireshark community**. As you advance your Wireshark skills, you'll discover an **active community** of network professionals, developers, and security experts who contribute custom dissectors, filters, and **best practices**. Joining the Wireshark community on platforms like **GitHub**, **Wireshark forums**, or **Reddit** can provide valuable insights, scripts, and plugins that help you tackle even the most challenging network issues. The **Wireshark community** is an invaluable resource for sharing knowledge, discovering new features, and staying updated on the latest developments in network analysis.

In conclusion, **taking Wireshark to the next level** means going beyond basic packet analysis and leveraging its full potential. Whether you're scripting custom dissectors, automating analysis, working with cloud networks, or integrating Wireshark with other tools, there's a wealth of possibilities for **advanced network troubleshooting** and **performance optimization**. The more you explore, the more you'll realize just how powerful Wireshark can be. So, take these skills and start using Wireshark not just as a tool for packet capture, but as a **comprehensive network analysis** and **troubleshooting platform**. Happy advanced Wiresharking!

To wrap up this chapter, **taking Wireshark to the next level** means pushing beyond the basics and delving into more advanced techniques that will make you a true network analysis expert. Whether you're **scripting** custom dissectors, **automating captures**, or integrating Wireshark with other advanced tools, the sky's the limit when it comes to what you can accomplish. It's about evolving your skillset, refining your workflows, and making Wireshark an even more powerful tool in your troubleshooting toolkit.

By leveraging **Lua scripting**, you can tailor Wireshark to handle **non-standard protocols** or create your own analysis tools. This level of customization allows you to go from basic packet inspection to writing **advanced dissectors** and **automation routines** that fit your specific needs. This isn't just about capturing traffic; it's about capturing exactly what you need, when you need it, and processing that data with precision. Lua scripting opens the door to countless possibilities in packet analysis, so don't be afraid to dive in and create the tools you wish Wireshark had out of the box.

Mastering **display filters** and **capture filters** is another essential step in taking Wireshark to the next level. Filters are the secret weapon of every experienced network analyst. They allow you to focus on the most critical traffic, filter out the noise, and make large datasets manageable. The ability to craft complex filters that zero in on specific protocols, packets, or even data patterns means you can quickly isolate issues, saving time and effort in the process. So, if you're still using the default filters, it's time to start building your own and elevating your analysis workflow.

Don't forget about the power of **statistics tools** in Wireshark. These tools can help you visualize network behavior, spot **anomalies**, and identify performance bottlenecks. From **I/O graphs** to **protocol hierarchies** to **flow graphs**, Wireshark's statistics tools give you a high-level view of your network's health. They also allow you to dive deeper into specific performance metrics and visualize network data trends over time. These insights are invaluable when analyzing network performance, especially in large or complex networks where manual inspection would be impossible.

Another advanced technique is using **TShark** for automated packet analysis. As the **command-line counterpart** to Wireshark, TShark allows you to script packet capture and analysis tasks, making it easy to automate routine network diagnostics. Whether you need to analyze captures over extended periods or run continuous monitoring, TShark is your ticket to **automated network troubleshooting**. Combine TShark with **Python** or other scripting languages, and you have a full-fledged **network monitoring automation system** that works on your terms.

In the world of **network security**, Wireshark's ability to work with **IDS/IPS systems** and **SIEM tools** is another advanced feature that can take your analysis to new heights. By integrating Wireshark with systems like **Snort**, **Suricata**, or **Splunk**, you gain the ability to analyze network traffic in real-time, correlating suspicious packets with security events and logs. This makes Wireshark a valuable tool not just for **network performance monitoring**, but also for **security incident response**, giving you a more comprehensive view of potential threats.

Don't overlook the power of **Wireshark's remote capture capabilities**. In large networks or **distributed environments**, Wireshark allows you to capture traffic from remote locations using **SSH** or **TShark**. This means you can capture traffic from servers, devices, or network segments that are geographically distant, giving you the ability to diagnose problems on the fly. Whether you're managing a **multi-location network** or analyzing traffic from a **remote data center**, Wireshark's remote capture capabilities ensure that distance is never an obstacle to effective analysis.

If you work in cloud environments, **Wireshark's integration with cloud-native tools** makes it an invaluable asset for troubleshooting **cloud networks**. Whether it's analyzing **AWS VPC** traffic, **Azure network performance**, or **Google Cloud traffic**, Wireshark allows you to capture and inspect traffic in cloud environments, ensuring that your cloud-based services are running smoothly. It also helps you spot network misconfigurations or **performance bottlenecks** in cloud-to-on-premise communication. The cloud is full of complexities, and Wireshark's ability to capture and analyze cloud traffic is a must-have for modern network analysis.

Another advanced technique is to leverage **Wireshark with external monitoring tools**. Whether it's integrating with **Grafana** for visualizing traffic trends or **Splunk** for advanced data aggregation and search, Wireshark's ability to export data in multiple formats means it can be a **central hub** for all your network analysis. Integrating Wireshark with these tools lets you build a **comprehensive network monitoring system** that takes your packet-level insights and elevates them into real-time dashboards or detailed reports.

The use of **Wireshark's expert information** is essential for more advanced users. While novice users might overlook the **expert info panel**, seasoned professionals know that it's a **goldmine** for catching subtle issues. Expert information flags **retransmissions**, **duplicate ACKs**, **protocol violations**, and **other network anomalies** in real-time. When you're analyzing large packet captures, the expert information panel allows you to quickly focus on the most important warnings, helping you detect issues faster and fix them more efficiently.

For those who deal with **multi-layer protocols** like **VPNs** or **SSL/TLS**, Wireshark provides the ability to dissect **encapsulated packets** in great detail. Whether you're troubleshooting **IPsec VPN tunnels** or investigating **SSL/TLS handshake issues**, Wireshark's ability to break down these layers helps you pinpoint the exact step where the issue occurs. This allows you to troubleshoot complex network configurations more effectively, ensuring that encrypted or tunneled traffic doesn't stand in your way.

If you're working with **IoT networks**, Wireshark is the perfect tool for analyzing low-level traffic between IoT devices. With **Wireshark's ability to capture protocols like Zigbee**, **Z-Wave**, and **BLE**, you can dive deep into the communication between these devices. Whether it's diagnosing **latency issues**, analyzing **traffic congestion**, or troubleshooting **protocol incompatibilities**, Wireshark provides you with the tools to understand how IoT devices communicate and how to optimize their performance.

Another powerful feature of Wireshark is its **ability to visualize network traffic** through **flow graphs**. These visualizations show how packets flow through your network, helping you spot delays, congestion, or irregularities in communication. Wireshark's flow graphs allow you to trace the **path of data** between two devices and measure **latency**, making it easier to troubleshoot issues with complex network interactions.

When working with **large packet captures**, **Wireshark's ability to split and merge captures** becomes invaluable. If you're dealing with **gigabytes of data**, splitting the capture into smaller, more manageable files makes analysis much easier. You can split captures based on size or time, ensuring that you can always access the data you need without dealing with **overwhelming files**. If you need to **combine captures** from different network segments or interfaces, Wireshark's merge functionality allows you to create a cohesive analysis from multiple sources.

Finally, don't forget about **Wireshark's community-driven dissectors** and **plugins**. By leveraging the contributions of the community, you can unlock **custom protocol support** and **advanced features** that aren't available in the default installation. Whether it's a new protocol, a tool for analyzing a specific type of network traffic, or a **custom plugin**, Wireshark's thriving community offers endless opportunities to extend its capabilities.

In conclusion, **taking Wireshark to the next level** is about mastering the advanced features, integrating it with other tools, and applying it to a wider variety of network troubleshooting tasks. Whether you're automating captures, diving into complex protocols, or visualizing network traffic, the more you learn about Wireshark's capabilities, the more you'll realize just how powerful it can be. So, take these advanced techniques, dive deep into the data, and continue to refine your skills—Wireshark has a world of possibilities waiting for you. Happy analyzing!